PERSIAN FOOD

PERSIAN FOOD

from

THE NON-PERSIAN BRIDE

AND OTHER KOSHER SEPHARDIC
RECIPES YOU WILL LOVE!

by Reyna Simnegar

FELDHEIM
JERUSALEM · NEW YORK

PERSIAN FOOD FROM THE NON-PERSIAN BRIDE
AND OTHER KOSHER SEPHARDIC RECIPES YOU WILL LOVE!
By Reyna Simnegar

Editing Felice Eisner
Proofreading Marcy Gilbert
Photography Marina Karassellos at http://marinakarassellos.carbonmade.com/
Food and Prop Styling Reyna Simnegar
Art Director and Book Designer Amanda Nugent at http://amandanugent.carbonmade.com/
Farsi Calligraphy Shahla Simnegar
Arabic Calligraphy Meryem Ouhirra
Web Designer MegaPleaxus Coorporation at http://www.megaplexus.com/
Blog Designer Maya Escobar and Loren Wells at http://mayaandloren.com/
Video Production MVM Post at http://www.mvmpost.com/
Represented by: Phi Lan M. Tinsley at http://www.klgates.com

Feldheim Publishers
POB 43163 / Jerusalem, Israel

208 Airport Executive Park
Nanuet, NY 10954

www.feldheim.com
www.kosherpersianfood.com

Printed in Israel.

Library of Congress Cataloging-in-Publication Data

Simnegar, Reyna.
Persian food from the non-Persian bride : and other kosher sephardic
recipes you will love! / Reyna Simnegar.
p. cm.
Includes bibliographical references and index.
ISBN 978-1-58330-325-2
1. Cooking, Iranian. 2. Sephardic cooking. 3. Cookbooks. I. Title.
TX725.I7S565 2011
641.5955--dc22
2010036122

As a sign of my gratefulness to Hashem, all my personal proceeds from this book will go to charity.

To my dear husband Sammy Simnegar,
you are the source of all my inspiration.

For my children,
Ariel, Eliav, Yosef, David, and Daniel, with all my love.

❧

PERSIAN FOOD

from

THE NON-PERSIAN BRIDE

AND OTHER KOSHER SEPHARDIC
RECIPES YOU WILL LOVE!

❧ INTRODUCTION ❧

I was still staring at the beautiful diamond engagement ring my dear Persian husband-to-be had just placed on my finger when he politely suggested it was time for me to pay a visit to his mother's kitchen to learn the art of Persian cooking. That was fine with me; the truth is that since the moment we started dating I knew how important it was to him to have Persian food be part of his everyday life…okay, why am I being so polite? I knew there would be no wedding if I didn't learn how to make *Chelo kebab*! I knew what I was getting myself into and, if you are a non-Persian bride or simply marrying into a different culture, I hope you know it as well! The good news is that you are in for the most amazing culinary experience of your life, and, since no one expects you to know anything about Persian food, you are going to be put up on a pedestal just for making the attempt to "cook Persian"!

Persians love their food. Persians love their music. Persians love everything Persian (even Persian cats!). They are by far the people who are the proudest of their culture I have ever encountered. In fact, every time my in-laws invite us to eat out for dinner we end up at—you guessed it—a Persian restaurant…even though we just had Persian food for lunch! My husband says it is called Persian Pride…and he is right. So, if you are coming into this culture (or any Sephardic tradition) with a strong culture of your own (as I did), be ready to compromise—a lot. The journey can be difficult, but take advantage of the opportunity to learn and indulge in an exotic, fascinating culture without ever putting a foot in Iran!

When I started dating my dear husband I became enamored with Persian culture. I loved all the Middle Eastern flavors, the smell, the music, the color. I really wanted to learn to cook Persian food to make him happy (fine, to make ME happy!!). Fortunately, my gracious mother-in-law welcomed me into her kitchen and taught me almost everything in this book. Have you ever tried to get a recipe from your mom or grandma? Are you familiar with directions like, "Add a bit of salt, but not too much," or "Add enough water, until it cooks," and totally random instructions like those? Well, that is exactly what I encountered. I needed to break the code and figure out exactly how many tablespoons of salt and how much lime were right. As a result, this book was born!

I wrote this book with many people in mind. As soon as I started having children and realized G-d was blessing me with boy after boy, I came to terms with the fact that my future daughters-in-law would need guidance on how to make their husbands happy. So, this book is for them! Also, as many of my friends constantly requested my Persian recipes, I realized that many non-Persians love Persian food too. So, this book is for them! And last, I became aware that many young Persian brides could tell there was *Chorosh Sabsi* being made at their home because of the delicious smell they detected, but they had no idea how to make it themselves. I realized that, due to the demands of life in America, many Persian mothers were not teaching their own daughters the art of Persian cuisine, but rather were allowing them to be married without handing down the precious knowledge of Persian delights and intricate traditions. So, this book is also for them!

My first exposure to Persian culture was through my husband. I had no idea that this people with such a vibrant culture existed. I didn't know Persians are not considered Arabs or that they speak Farsi. I had no idea there were Jews today in Iran. In sum, I was totally clueless. Marrying a Persian Jew gave me the greatest appreciation for an unbroken lineage that dates back to the times of Queen Esther and King Achashverosh! Therefore, I genuinely felt it was natural that my in-laws wanted a Persian girl for their son. Actually, my in-laws specifically wanted a Shirazi girl from a good family, preferably one who lived down the street from their home back in Iran! So, even though at times it was hard for me to understand their obsession, today I can see where it came from. The good news is that presently we all appreciate and love each other very much and dwell on the funny instances where I have been culturally "off"! I think I could write another whole book on funny episodes of life living among Persians!

Therefore, having been around these amazing people for over 12 years, I felt it was my duty to document all the foods and customs particular to the Jews of Iran when it comes to religious observance. As a religious Jew myself, I find the task to be a privilege and honor. Finally, it is my heartfelt wish that this book will find its home in many kitchens, where the aromas of Persian food and beautiful traditions will forever linger.

Nooshejan! Hearty Appetite! *Biteh avon*! *Buen provecho*!

Reyna Simnegar

Disclaimer
Throughout this book I relate many funny episodes and nuances I have experienced during the many years I have had the honor to be exposed to Persian Jews. Many of these episodes exemplify stereotypes and, throughout the book, I may seem to be mocking various behaviors and expressions. Often, I am making fun of myself and the people I love. Please take my words and memories as what they are: simply funny in the context they were expressed. I treasure my Venezuelan heritage, and I treasure my adopted Persian heritage with all my heart. Let us all laugh together at life!

ACKNOWLEDGMENTS

This book started as a nice little guide I was going to present to my future daughters-in-law after their weddings. After all, I had to learn all these recipes "the hard way," and I wanted them to be able to make their husbands' favorite foods without any hardship. The more I talked about it with my friends, the more they wanted a copy of the recipes. And then, just like a sign, G-d began showering me with amazing, talented people that made this little guide into a beautiful work of art that is greater than I ever imagined.

I owe tremendous gratitude to my friends Alina Koyfman and Larissa Zaretsky for believing in me from the very beginning of this journey and literally holding my hand as I took the first steps in creating this book. I am forever grateful to Marina Karassellos for sharing with me her amazing talent and beautiful soul. Marina's pictures are the very essence of this book. This work of art would not have been possible if Amanda Nugent had not put her heart and time into making it as Persian as a book written by a non-Persian bride could get! Joseph Yashar came to my rescue and designed, with much love, the beautiful website for this book. Maya Escobar made this book reach everyone on earth by designing the amazing blog I get to update myself, along with so much more support, instruction, and great suggestions. Many thanks to Macaela VanderMost and her team at MVM productions for the incredibly professional cooking videos you created for this book.

I am forever grateful to Miriam Schreiber and her daughter Estie Israel for helping me find Feldheim Publishers. This book would not be a reality without the tireless help and expert advice of Eli Hollander and the Feldheim family. There are no words that could acknowledge how much I thank Felice Eisner for editing my every word and thought. Her grace, love, and care went above and beyond the scope of this book. I am indebted to my friend Marcy Gilbert for proofreading every single page of this book with so much dedication. It is thanks to my cousin Channah Barkhordari that I was able to learn so much about the history of Persian Jews. May her research and findings for this book serve as a *zechut* to the memory of her saintly grandfather Lalezar Kohandarvish.

I have no words to thank Rabbi Paysach Krohn, Mrs. Miriam Krohn, and their daughter Genendal Krohn for helping me and guiding me in various areas of this book. I am forever thankful to Rabbi Ba'alhanes and Mrs. Ba'alhanes, Rabbi Louie and Tzippy Louie, and Rabbi Nissim Davidi for all the guidance in terms of Persian Jewish customs and *kashrut* of Persian products. Thank you, Mr. David Fakheri, for sharing with me your cherished memories from Iran. Without every single one of you there would be nothing to pass on to my children. Together, we will rescue and inspire the next generation of Persian Jews. Thank you for keeping the beautiful Jewish Persian customs alive!

I was very fortunate to get expert legal advice from Amiel Weinstock and Ari Behar. I am especially deeply grateful to Phi Lan Tinsley for all her grace and generosity and for making sure all the legal mumbo-jumbo made sense! This cookbook would not exist without the expertise of so many amazing women who shared their recipes with me. Many of them did not want to be mentioned, but I made sure they all get credit for their recipes! I owe a giant thank you to my friend Davida Zimble for letting me borrow her absolutely exquisite collection of dishes for the pictures in this book. I am also indebted to the Israel Book Shop for lending me many of the silver pieces you see in the pages that follow.

I am grateful to my cousin Meryem Ouhirra and my cousin Hila (Tanaz) Zarosim for the Arabic and Hebrew calligraphy in this book. I would not have survived the long photo shoots without Liora Youshaei helping me make the most beautiful Persian food. How can I ever thank my friends Cheryl Sanders and Valerie Levine for being my listening ears and great supporters? Many friends and family came together to be part of this effort. Countless recipe testers came to the task, and some of them made Persian food for the first time in their life! There is no room in these pages to mention each one of you; however, there is plenty of room in my heart to think of and love each one of you. I am so grateful to have you all in my life.

There is one person who worked as hard - if not harder - than I did on making this book: Corina Lemus. Corina is the best personal assistant anyone could wish for. Thank you so much for all your help and genuine efforts to make this book a reality. I am eternally grateful to my parents, Beatriz de Perez and Carlos Perez; my sisters Beatriz Perez and Karla Schallies and my brother-in-law Sven Schallies, along with my sweet nephews Seth and Kyle for supporting me throughout the making of this book. G-d willing, the next book will be *Latin Food from the Latin Bride*! I am forever indebted to my dear in-laws, Shahla Simnegar, Ezzy Simnegar, and Sandra Simnegar, for making me part of their beautiful family and teaching me the beauty of Jewish Persian traditions. Momom, I can't thank you enough for putting so much work into this book and for sharing with me all your wisdom and love. Thank you also for sharing your beautiful calligraphy! A special thanks to Mrs. Sultanat Rabbizadeh (Momonbosergue) for all the love and support you have always given me, *duset daram*!

I have no words to thank my precious children, Ariel, Eliav, Yosef, David, and Daniel, for the countless times you tested my recipes and loved my food. Thank you so much for being so great at taking pictures and for all your love and support.

There would be no "non-Persian bride" without the most important person in my life, my dear husband Sammy. The support, love, understanding, wisdom, and complete selfless devotion you have showered me with all our years of marriage are the greatest gift Hashem has given me. You have been by my side since the first day, and you always believed in me. I love you more than anything in my life, and I am grateful to Hashem for giving me the honor of being your wife. Thank you for being the pillar of my life, our family, and our community. May we continue sharing *nachat* from our precious children for many years to come. *Ben Porat Yosef*!

And finally, how can I possibly start thanking Hashem for giving me all of the above? How can I thank the Creator for giving me such an amazing ride in life with so much potential and fulfillment? I can only hope to be able to live up to His will and to follow His *mitzvot* as closely as I am able. As a sign of my gratitude, all my share of the proceeds of this book will go to charity. Thank you, Hashem, for showing me your Torah and for allowing me to get closer to You and Your people. Thank you, Hashem, for every heartbeat, for every breath, for everything....

❧ THE JEWS OF IRAN ❧

I am embarrassed to admit it, but when I met my husband I had no idea there were ever any Jews in Iran. I really thought he was joking. I really thought that even if there had been Jews in Iran, they would be gone, just like the Persian Empire was gone. I thought that just like Persepolis lay in ruins, any trace of the descendants of Queen Esther and her people were laid in ruins. However, now I know that what would seem a logical course of history for other nations is simply not applicable to Jews. The chosen nation is inextinguishable. Unbreakable. Eternal.

The Jews of Iran have an incredibly long history that begins over 2,700 years ago and continues through today. They first arrived in the region during the Achaemenid period after King Nebuchadnezzar captured Jerusalem and Judea, exiling tens of thousands of their Jewish inhabitants, who were expelled to lands all across the east, including today's Iran. In 539 B.C.E., Cyrus of Anshan invaded, liberating Babylon and causing many Jewish leaders to hail him as the figure described in *Isaiah* (45:1-6) who would redeem them and provide them with the hope of returning to Judea. Indeed, when he became ruler, Cyrus sent a group of Jews to Jerusalem to rebuild the Holy Temple; but while some returned, many more remained in Iran.

Famous figures in the Jewish Bible are cited as living in or traversing the areas of Iran, and its populations are described in numerous books of the Tanach. The prophet Daniel, for example, who is more widely known for his interactions with Nebuchadnezzar, was born and lived in Shushan (Susa). Chabakuk, another biblical *navi*, was a descendant of Jews exiled from Babylonia who traveled to Iran. Shushan was also home to Esther, the most celebrated Persian heroine of the Jewish tradition, and the site of the story of Purim. As it is written in *Megillat* Esther, Esther and Mordechai saved the Jews of the 127 provinces under King Achashverosh's rule from a decree for their total annihilation issued by a royal vizier, Haman.

By the time of the story of Purim, the *megilla* relates that in every province there existed a Jewish presence. But the Purim victory didn't solidify universal tolerance for Jews by any means, and they still had many threatening enemies. After the miraculous salvation of the population under King Achashverosh, Jews were able to continue to live in their respective communities in Persia, but their numbers have alternately increased and decreased over the years.

Since the times of Queen Esther, however, Jews have maintained a strong presence in Iran. At the beginning of the Common Era, there were many converts to Judaism in the Middle East, and Jews are said to have made up over 20% of the Empire's inhabitants. By the time of the fall of Jerusalem with the destruction of the Second Temple in 70 C.E., Christianity had become the most rapidly thriving faith, and Jews were among the first to convert (Dangoor 2001).

Less than a millennium later, in 693 C.E., through wars, invasions, and conquests, the Jewish presence in Iran was still extant, and Shiraz was established as the capital of the Fars province. Though it would not grow to shelter as many Jews as other cities (such as Teheran, Iran's capital), over the centuries Shiraz flourished into a religious, cultural, and socioeconomic center for Persian Jewry, even amidst enduring harsh anti-Semitism and persecution. The Islamic conquest of Persia, which would span 600 years, shook the sociopolitical and cultural dynamics of the entire region and made conditions exceedingly difficult for Jews and others practicing non-Islamic faiths. By the 12th century, near the end of the conquest, Shiraz alone is said to have been home to 10,000 Jews, a majority of whom were manufacturing wine for Europeans.

The pattern of relative calm followed by intense anti-Semitism continued for hundreds of years. Intolerance always resurfaced, and under Shah Abbas of the Safavid era in the late-16th century and beyond, Jews were actively forced to wear identifying garments and eventually required to convert to Shiism. In *Ketab-e anusi*, *The Book of a Forced Convert*, 17th-century author Babai ben Lotf discusses the circumstances of Jews in Iran at the time, and writes of his experience as one of the many *anusim*, outward converts who kept Judaism in secret. At the rise of Shah Abbas' grandson, Shah Safi I, a few decades later, Jews were free to readopt their faith; but not long afterward, under Shah Abbas II, they were once again persecuted by those who disagreed with the removal of the ban.

Intolerance resurfaced in every dynasty throughout Iran's history, and by the 18th and early 19th centuries the Jewish population had been reduced significantly. The approximately 3,000 Jews living in Shiraz by 1830 had shrunk to a mere 500 over the next twenty years, and historians have concluded that around 2,500 of them converted to Islam to escape persecution (*Jewish Encyclopedia*, "Shiraz"). Nonetheless, the victimized communities, however small, maintained a presence in Iran—even when their leaders were imprisoned or tortured.

The Challenges of Spiritual Leadership

The viziers of Iran would arrest Jews such as Mullah Elijah, then chief rabbi of Shiraz, and require them to pay an exorbitant fee or convert to Islam. At first, Elijah said he would convert and become a Muslim, but he would need time to prepare for the transformation. However, when his time was up he refused to convert, so he was locked in a dungeon and brutally whipped. Unsurprisingly, missionaries who visited Shiraz at the time found that many of Shiraz's outward converts were both socioeconomically and religiously miserable, held an inward contempt for Islam, and maintained the appearance of being identical to their Muslim neighbors while they continued to practice Judaism within their own homes.

Rab Yusef, also known as Ohr Shraga, was an Iranian mystic and Jewish leader for the community in Yazd during the late 18th century. A direct descendant of King David, he is known for performing many miracles, and his tomb in Yazd is considered a religious holy site for Jews and Muslims alike even today (Lalezar 2006). His counterparts were Mullah Mosheh Halevi of Kashan, a kabbalist, rabbi, and author of books on Jewish mysticism, and later Mullah Rabbi Isaac of Tehran, one of the first rabbis to contact the Alliance Israelite Universelle in search of protection for the Jews of Iran from persecution by Shiite government officials.

Preserved marriage contracts show that intermarriage was also common among Persian Jews, even in ancient times. Ezra and Nechemia, two of the later Jewish figures of the Tanach, publicly banned intermarriage and issued punishments to those who married outside the faith (Price 1996). In the century and a half that followed the construction of the Second Temple, the final codification of Jewish law—with its clear rule against intermarriage—was one of the prominent factors ensuring the continuation of the Jewish people in the Middle East, and Iran in particular. While it has not always been adhered to, the law, combined with a nearly constant threat of persecution, has been integral to the continued survival of Iranian Jewry (Bard 2010). The mass emigration of Jews from Iran in the mid- to late-twentieth century has proven the most trying to its preservation of faith and custom; hence, the more isolated communities that opted not to emigrate, such as the Jews of Mahshad, have seen lower rates of intermarriage than others.

Etymology

Last names in Iran were not customarily used until the early 20th century, when Reza Shah, in an effort to modernize the country, decreed that everyone should take on last names. Family names of Persian descent usually end in suffixes that connote something of their relation to others, or contain the names of the cities from which their ancestors presumably hail. Suffixes such as "-i", meaning "of," would be added to a city name, such as Shiraz, to form "Shirazi," a common Persian last name. Those indicating family ties are "-zadeh," born of; "-pour," son of; or "-nejad," from the race of. These suffixes would be added to the former first names of ancestral antiquity. Some have the suffixes "-ian" or "-stan," traditionally indicating that the family is from Iran. Still others are more difficult to place, possibly indicating some quality or feature that may have distinguished an ancestor, or used as a marker of unknown symbolic significance. Last names such as Ghermezi, for instance, translates to mean "of red." In the case of our family, the name *Simnegar* means *silversmith*, indicating the trade for which the family was known. Our other last name is *Rabizadeh*, indicating "born of rabbis," which would mean my husband is a descendant of both working people and rabbis.

Persian Jews Today

In the decades following the Islamic Revolution of 1979, an estimated 85% of the Jews living in Iran (over 60,000) immigrated to Israel and America. Israel now hosts the largest population of Iranian Jews, at more than 47,000, with an additional 87,000 descendants of paternal lineage only, and 65-70,000 of maternal lineage (CBS Statistical Abstract 2008). Kfar Saba is a social center for Persian Jewry, while many also settled in Jerusalem, Netanya, and Tel-Aviv. Immigration to the United States brought entire communities to coastal cities, most prominently Great Neck, New York, and Los Angeles, California, where Jewish traditions have been maintained more potently than were upheld by immigrants of European countries. The estimated number of Persian Jews in America is in the high tens of thousands, but it's not certain the numbers will continue to increase.

Assimilation is rising very rapidly, especially among the younger generation of Iranian Jews. Sadly, many Persian Jews are today losing their heritage and customs that date back thousands of years and for which so many of their ancestors perished. Today, as in my case, many Persian Jews are also marrying non-Persian Jews. In addition, many Persian Jews have also returned to Torah and have become *Ba'alei Teshuva* through various types of outreach programs. However, while this is completely wonderful, many have embraced the more widely known customs of our Ashkenazi brethren. I strongly feel Jewish Persian customs are in jeopardy if we don't educate our children and make them aware of the beauty and riches of the Persian Jewish heritage. The main impetus for writing this cookbook was to help re-ignite and preserve the Iranian Jewish heritage for the youth through food…not to mention that I want to make sure my future daughters-in-law know how to cook authentic *kebab* and *tadig* for my boys. Girls, make sure to put those boys to work as well—at least they should wash the dishes!

Wedding of Ezzy and Shahla Simnegar, signing the Ketuba (wedding contract) with Rabbi Zimozar (Shiraz, 1971)

Iranian Youth holding a Sefer Torah at The Hebrew Discovery Center. Woodland Hills, CA. Picture courtesy of Rabbi Louie and HDC.

Iranian Youth praying at The Hebrew Discovery Center. Woodland Hills, CA. Picture courtesy of Rabbi Louie and HDC.

HOW IS THIS BOOK KOSHER?

You are probably wondering…what makes this book kosher? You might be thinking that, after all, Iran is a Muslim country, and it is probable—very probable—that people there do not eat non-kosher things like, say, pork? Well, if that was in your mind, you are totally right. However, it happens that there is a lot more to kosher than just not eating pork…because keeping kosher is a diet for the soul.

So, what is "kosher"? What does this word mean? Clean? Low-fat and healthy? Blessed by the rabbi? Well, hardly any of the above! The word *kosher* means "fit." Not as in "you look fit," but actually as in "properly prepared." However, the word *Kashrut* actually refers to the rather complex set of norms that make food kosher, or fit for consumption. These set of laws involve Biblical laws and rabbinical extensions to those laws.

You might have heard people say, "Judaism is not a religion, but a way of life," and that statement is very close to the truth. Jews were given the blueprint to live life to its fullest. For Jews, holiness is not confined to specific places or specific times in one's life. It actually pertains to every day and every single move one takes, making living a constant sacred undertaking. Hence, for Jews, a seemingly mundane activity like eating can be elevated to a totally different spiritual level.

Is keeping kosher easy? Well, it all depends. I am a firm believer that everything in life comes down to attitude. So I will say keeping kosher is easy, especially if one lives in the United States. There are countless kosher butchers, numerous kosher restaurants, and endless kosher products to make almost any cuisine in the world. There are almost no limits! They have even invented a kosher shrimp look-alike, which is great for people with shrimp withdrawal. You guessed it, real shrimp is not kosher.

However, the truth is that what makes keeping kosher hard for some people is not really the lack of kosher food (or taste), but the lack of discipline. Judaism completely condemns the absolute negation of bodily needs or pleasures. In fact, Judaism encourages man to live to his potential and enjoy the world that was created for this very purpose. However, Judaism does encourage eating and behaving in the most ethical and dignified way possible. Although one may conclude that these laws are restrictive and almost enslaving, our rabbis teach that a person who controls his impulses and passions has actually freed himself of being a "slave" to his tendencies…hey, we all know how good it feels when you say *no* to that extra brownie! No one ever comes home saying, "Shame on me! I should have overeaten!"

Trying to explain all the laws of *Kashrut* in a few paragraphs is impossible. So I will only provide you with the most basic information for you to understand how this book is kosher. However, on my website, kosherpersianfood.com, you can find many links to all the information about *Kashrut* I can't fit here!

When it comes to non-kosher Persian food, the problems with *Kashurt* arise mostly in the realm of mixing milk and meat, which is a Biblical prohibition. In Persian cuisine, sometimes meat is supposed to be marinated in milk, and it is traditional to have a dairy drink named *dooch* as the quencher of choice when eating *kebab*. Moreover, some of the desserts include dairy products and usually follow a meat meal. Hence, this book addresses all these kosher-related issues, making sure there is no mixing of meat and milk. Also, many of the dessert recipes will require nondairy substitutes, while *dooch* (which is absolutely delicious and refreshing) is reserved for other times besides *kebab* time.

Iranian Jews are known for being zealous about keeping with tradition. In fact, it is common to see even non-religious Persian Jewish women keeping a certain degree of *Kashrut* in their homes. So when and if you ever visit a Jewish Persian household, you will likely not only experience an overabundance of delicious food which you are supposed to eat until you are about to explode, but you will also see much of the Torah being observed with devotion and love! In fact, I have been told by Rabbi Ba'alhanes that back in Iran women were so devoted to the laws of family purity that they would even go to the *mikvah* in the winter, breaking through the layer of ice on the surface and plunging into the icy waters. It is indeed in the merit of women and their special devotion to Torah and Judaism that we will see the ultimate redemption.

❧ ABSOLUTELY NECESSARY THINGS ❧
THE NON-PERSIAN BRIDE MUST HAVE IN HER PERSIAN KITCHEN

I find this list to be incredibly useful. I have gone through all the products and kitchen utensils you might possibly need, as well as possible substitutes if the authentic items are hard to find. Keep in mind that many towns have Middle Eastern groceries. For a list of online resources, access my website and enjoy a video where I take you shopping with me! Get ready for a cultural experience and pay these stores a visit; you might really like what you see. These grocers usually carry gorgeous fruits and vegetables. Also, they carry many great kosher products you might have never known existed. I love going to these stores and being approached by the cute old Persian ladies who want to know if I am married. Most often, they think I am Persian and want to set me up with their grandson—who, by the way, is an internal medicine doctor and drives a Lexus! When they finally realize that not only am I not Persian, but I'm already married, they pat me on the shoulder and blurt out, in the funniest Persian accent, "That's okay, next time, next time!"

I researched the *kashrut* status of these products under the guidance of Orthodox rabbis who are familiar with Persian culture and Middle Eastern products. I also contacted major Orthodox *kashrut* agencies for guidance. However, please take into consideration your background and family customs and contact your local Orthodox rabbi if you have further questions.

Spices and Seeds Used in Persian Cooking

NAME	DESCRIPTION	KOSHER STATUS	WHERE TO FIND IT
Turmeric	This spice makes everything yellow, and a little bit goes a long way. It stains like ink so be careful!	It is preferable to buy it with a kosher certification. But if a spice is 100% pure, it does not need a kosher symbol (*hechsher*).	Middle Eastern markets. Visit kosherpersianfood.com for internet resources.
Saffron	This spice is expensive, but used in small amounts. See page 190 for more info.	It is preferable to buy it with a kosher certification. But if a spice is 100% pure, it does not need a kosher symbol (*hechsher*).	Middle Eastern markets. Visit kosherpersianfood.com for internet resources.
Cardamom	This spice comes ground or in whole pods. It is the third most expensive spice, after saffron and vanilla.	It is preferable to buy it with a kosher certification. But if a spice is 100% pure it does not need a kosher symbol (*hechsher*).	Easily available in regular groceries. (McCormick carries it with a kosher symbol.)
***Sumac* Pronounced "soomak"**	It is a deep purple flake that goes on top of white rice when eating it with *kebab*.	It is preferable to buy it with a kosher certification. But if a spice is 100% pure it does not need a kosher symbol (*hechsher*).	Middle Eastern markets. Visit kosherpersianfood.com for internet resources.
Cumin	It comes ground or as seeds.	It is preferable to buy it with a kosher certification. But if a spice is 100% pure it does not need a kosher symbol (*hechsher*).	Easily available in regular groceries.

Spices and Seeds Used in Persian Cooking

NAME	DESCRIPTION	KOSHER STATUS	WHERE TO FIND IT
Chicken or *kebab* seasoning	All the right spices mixed for your convenience!	Since this spice is a mixture of many spices, it must have a kosher symbol (*hechsher*).	Middle Eastern markets. Visit kosherpersianfood.com for internet resources.
Baharat Spice	Also known as *advieh* (in Farsi), it can be substituted with allspice.	Since this spice is a mixture of many spices, it must have a kosher symbol (*hechsher*).	Allspice is available at any regular grocery, while *baharat* and *advieh* are available at Middle Eastern stores or visit kosherpersianfood.com.
Cinnamon	Also known as *darchin* in Farsi.	It is preferable to buy it with a kosher certification. But if a spice is 100% pure it does not need a kosher symbol (*hechsher*).	Available at regular groceries.
Nutmeg	Always used in small amounts.	It is preferable to buy it with a kosher certification. But if a spice is 100% pure it does not need a kosher symbol (*hechsher*).	Available at regular groceries.
Ginger	I always use it ground, but fresh is delectable. This spice is not regularly used in Persian cuisine.	It is preferable to buy it with a kosher certification. But if a spice is 100% pure it does not need a kosher symbol (*hechsher*).	Available at regular groceries.
Curry	This spice is not regularly used in Persian cuisine, but it is loved by many cooks in the Middle Eastern and Asian world.	Since this spice is a mixture of many spices, it must have a kosher symbol (*hechsher*).	Available at kosher groceries with certification.
Pumpkin Spice	This spice is not regularly used in Persian cuisine, but it is loved by many cooks!	Since this spice is a mixture of many spices, it must have a kosher symbol (*hechsher*).	Available at any regular grocery.
***Ziadune* seeds Also known as nigella seeds**	These little matte black seeds taste like onions. They can be substituted with black sesame seeds for color, not taste.	Does not require kosher certification.	Middle Eastern markets.
Roasted Sesame Seeds	Very convenient when already roasted.	No need for kosher symbol as long as they are not roasted; then you must roast the raw seeds yourself.	Available at any regular grocery; JFC brand comes with a kosher symbol (*hechsher*) and already roasted.
Charoset Spice (Haleg Spice)	Used on Passover to make Persian *Charoset* (*Haleg*). Substitute mixing equal parts of cardamom, ginger, and cinnamon.	Since this spice is a mixture of many spices, it must have a kosher symbol (*hechsher*).	Available at Persian kosher grocers or visit kosherpersianfood.com for internet resources.

Herbs Used in Persian Cooking

NAME	DESCRIPTION	KOSHER STATUS	WHERE TO FIND IT
Dehydrated Greens *Sabsi*	These are very convenient and come in a can ready to use. For the fresh substitute, see page 153.	These greens are Sadaf brand and come with a kosher symbol. They do not require checking for bugs.	Middle Eastern markets. Visit kosherpersianfood.com for internet resources.
Dehydrated Whole Lime (or ground) *Lemon Omani*	Super exotic! These are limes that have been dehydrated and give food a tangy sour taste. Substitution: 1 dried lime = 2 tablespoons lime juice	No need for a kosher symbol, but some brands come with *kashrut* supervision (except these cannot be used on Pesach).	Middle Eastern markets. Visit kosherpersianfood.com for internet resources.
Cilantro and cilantro seeds	Also known as coriander. Seeds are used to give flavor to *tadig*.	No need for a Kosher symbol if fresh, but check for bugs; many kosher groceries also carry this herb in frozen cubes with kosher certification.	Available fresh at regular groceries or frozen from Kosher grocers. Visit kosher-persianfood.com for internet resources.
Fenugreek *Shambelileh*	Often used fresh and added to *Sabsi* stew when available. Very hard to find.	No need for a kosher symbol if fresh, but check for bugs.	Middle Eastern markets and specialty markets.
Parsley (dried, fresh, and frozen)	Used in salad and eaten raw. It has a mild taste compared with cilantro.	No need for a kosher symbol if fresh, but check for bugs; many kosher groceries also carry this herb in frozen cubes with kosher certification.	Available fresh at regular groceries or frozen from Kosher grocers. Visit kosher-persianfood.com for internet resources.
Mint (dried and fresh)	Used in salads, tea, and dairy dishes.	No need for a kosher symbol if fresh, but check for bugs.	Available at regular groceries.
Dill (dried, fresh, and frozen)	Used in salads, dips, and rice. Very convenient when purchased dried or frozen.	No need for a kosher symbol if fresh, but check for bugs; many kosher groceries also carry this herb in frozen cubes with kosher certification.	Available fresh at regular groceries or frozen from Kosher grocers. Visit kosher-persianfood.com for internet resources.
Tarragon	Its flavor is very strong and a little goes a long way.	No need for a kosher symbol if fresh, but check for bugs.	Available at regular groceries.

Most Vegetables and Fruits Used in this Book

Artichoke hearts

Avocados

Beets (fresh and canned)

Butternut Squash

Carrots

Celery

Corn

Cucumbers

Currant raisins

Eggplant (Italian and Chinese)

Fennel

Garlic (fresh and dried)

Green beans

Leeks

Limes, lemons

Mixed greens

Okra (fresh and frozen)

Onion (white and red)

Potatoes (white, Yukon Gold, and sweet)

Quince

Roasted peppers (jarred)

Romaine lettuce

Scallions

Shallots

Spinach

Strawberries

Tomatoes (paste, crushed, whole)

Zucchini

Legumes and Nuts Used in this Book

Legumes, nuts, and seeds don't need a kosher symbol as long as they are not roasted. Make sure to check for insects and wash rice clean. For more information contact your local Orthodox rabbi.

Almonds

American rice

Basmati rice

Black-eyed peas (dried and canned)

Brown lentils

Bulgur

Chickpeas (garbanzos) (dried and canned)

Couscous

Cracked whole wheat

Fava beans (broad beans, frozen)

Kidney beans (dried and canned)

Lima beans (frozen)

Mung beans

Pistachios

Pumpkin seeds

Split peas (yellow and green)

Walnuts (raw, roasted, and candied)

Watermelon seeds

Other Persian and Middle Eastern Ethnic Products

NAME	DESCRIPTION	KOSHER STATUS	WHERE TO FIND IT
Rose Jam and Quince Jam	These are very exotic and give your dishes a nice Middle Eastern flavor.	There are a few kosher brands, that carry exotic jams.	Available in Middle Eastern stores or visit kosherpersianfood.com for internet resources.
Tamarind Concentrate	Absolutely sweet and sour taste.	Needs a kosher symbol (*hechsher*).	Visit kosherpersianfood.com for internet resources and available brands.
Chickpea and Rice Flour	Necessary for many Persian dishes. You can make your own, too!	Does not require a kosher symbol (*hechsher*) if 100% chickpeas or rice are used. Check with your local Orthodox rabbi for more info.	Middle Eastern markets and specialty markets.
Barberries *Zereshk*	Gorgeous crimson, tangy berries.	Does not require a kosher symbol (*hechsher*).	Middle Eastern markets and specialty markets.
Sour grapes (and juice) *Gureh.* Pronounced "gooreh"	Picked before they ripen. They often come frozen.	Does not require a kosher symbol (*hechsher*).	Middle Eastern groceries. Visit kosherpersianfood.com.
Pomegranate Syrup	Gives a delicious tangy and sweet flavor to Persian stews. Now available as juice!	Needs a kosher symbol (*hechsher*).	Available at regular groceries as juice. Visit kosherpersianfood.com for other resources.
Rice Sticks	Used to make Persian ice cream.	There are brands with kosher symbols, but if made of 100% rice it does not need kosher certification.	Available at regular groceries.
Rose Water and Rose Hips	Used in Persian desserts and beverages.	If it is 100% rose water, it does not need a kosher symbol (*hechsher*). Ask your local Orthodox rabbi for more info.	Middle Eastern markets and specialty markets visit kosherpersianfood.com for internet resources and brands.
Tehina	Used in babaganoush or as a dressing and dip.	Needs a kosher symbol (*hechsher*).	Middle Eastern and specialty markets and kosherpersianfood.com.
Balsamic Vinegar	Used in salads and sometimes in meat and poultry.	Needs a kosher symbol (*hechsher*).	Kosher supermarkets.
Sour Cherries in Heavy Syrup	Do not confuse with sour cherry jam. The ones you need come in runny syrup.	Needs a kosher symbol (*hechsher*).	Middle Eastern markets, specialty markets and www.kosherpersianfood.com.
Rock Candy *Nabat*	Crystallized sugar cubes used for medicinal purposes.	Needs a kosher symbol (*hechsher*).	Middle Eastern and specialty markets and kosherpersianfood.com.

Persian and Middle Eastern Gadgets

NAME	DESCRIPTION	WHERE TO FIND IT
Teapot and Kettle *Samovar*	Used to make tea. The teapot rests on top of the kettle to keep the tea essence warm.	Middle Easter, stores or visit www.kosherpersianfood.com for internet resources.
Kebab skewers	Used to make Persian BBQ. You can get them with or without wooden handles. I like using ½-inch-wide skewers.	Visit kosherpersianfood.com for internet resources and available brands.
Electric Rice Cooker	Make *Kateh* the easiest way! It makes *Tadig* automatically! There are several brands: Imperials, Pars, and Royal. My favorite is Pars.	Visit kosherpersianfood.com for internet resources and available brands.
Ghaleb'e Kookoo	This is a tool to shape *kookoos* the same size each time! It is like a falafel maker, but flat.	In Middle Eastern stores or visit kosherpersianfood.com for internet resources.
Ibrik	Long-handled copper jug to make Turkish Coffee. You can use a small saucepan with a handle instead.	In Middle Eastern stores or visit kosherpersianfood.com for internet resources.
Wooden Skewers	Often have to be soaked in water to avoid burning. I like using 5-inch length for individual servings.	Available in regular groceries.
Zucchini and Eggplant Corer	Also known as *ma'vdeh* in Arabic. A melon baller is a fine substitute.	Available at Middle Eastern stores or visit kosherpersianfood.com for internet resources.
Bouquet garni **sachets**	Spice or herb bundled into a small sachet (cloth bag) and dropped into soup or stew; used to infuse liquids with color and flavor allowing for easy removal. You can also use cheesecloth tied at the top with kitchen twine or thread.	Available at Middle Eastern stores or visit kosherpersianfood.com for internet resources.

"IT'S MY KITCHEN AND I'LL MARINATE IF I WANT TO!"

Do you have any cute pictures from when you were a small child dressed as a little bride? Do you remember cradling your baby doll and saying all you wanted to be when you grew up was a mommy? Well, we women have these nice dreams from childhood and many times, thank G-d, these dreams become a reality. However, there is no such a thing as a woman being "just a mommy." There are plenty of demands in life besides the joy of cradling a baby in our arms. Could you relate to the woman in her suit, with her Blackberry in one hand, a bottle in the other, and a toddler pulling on her skirt? How about the woman with the suit, a cup of coffee in one hand, going crazy because she can't find the keys to her car which—by chance—ended up in her husband's jacket hanging at his office? How about the woman who is juggling two carpools, a charity event, and her daughter's piano recital? Whichever of these women you are, the reality is that almost no one has the time and patience today to toil in the kitchen.

Since I am one of those women above, it was crucial for me that all my recipes be as easy to make as possible without sacrificing the taste. You will see that in this book, for the most part, nice little things—like marinating—are only suggestions. It is true that the dish could potentially be tastier if the chicken has been sitting in sauce for two hours. However, I barely have two minutes to put makeup on, let alone two hours to marinate anything! Marinate it overnight? The last thing I want to do with my evening is to be rubbing chicken legs with sauce! Forget it!

I use dry spices and concentrates as much as possible. Who has time to replenish their fridge with fresh limes all the time? Lime and lemon concentrates are wonderful inventions; use them! It is true that anything made with freshly pressed garlic is a gift from heaven…but my sanity is a gift from heaven too! If you don't have fresh garlic, use powdered garlic instead. For the most part, I don't sauté my onions until quite translucent; I just give them about one minute in the heat. Otherwise, I feel it is a waste of my precious time! It really tastes the same–trust me. Also, many brands carry a great selection of frozen herbs—and don't even dare to try to make herb stew from scratch if you have no patience for washing greens! Buy the dehydrated greens and leave the labor to the chefs at restaurants when you eat out.

I have witnessed with horror how much oil can go into Persian food. All my recipes are designed to keep the fat out of your food. I do not fry eggplants (unless absolutely necessary). I use canola and olive oil only, which are the most healthful oils. I do not fry *kebabs* and try very hard not to fry my fish. You do have to understand that there are dishes where oil is absolutely necessary; just be cautious and eat less of those foods.

Last but not least, feel free to experiment. In some recipes, I give you many different options for cooking the same dish. Many of the difficult-to-find products have a fine replacement that is more readily available. You can use almost anything you have in your fridge and still make it taste Persian. Feel free to use my recipes as a starting point and make your own repertoire of recipes that will suit your family's needs. That is exactly what I did when I was learning to cook. This is your opportunity to be creative and exciting! For my Ashkenazi brethren: I am so happy you are able to see there is life beyond kugel! To my Persian friends: Embrace the beautiful, colorful cuisine of your people. And for every single woman: The dollhouse with the kitchen has finally become a reality. It is your kitchen and you can "cook like a goddess" if you want to. Have a blast!

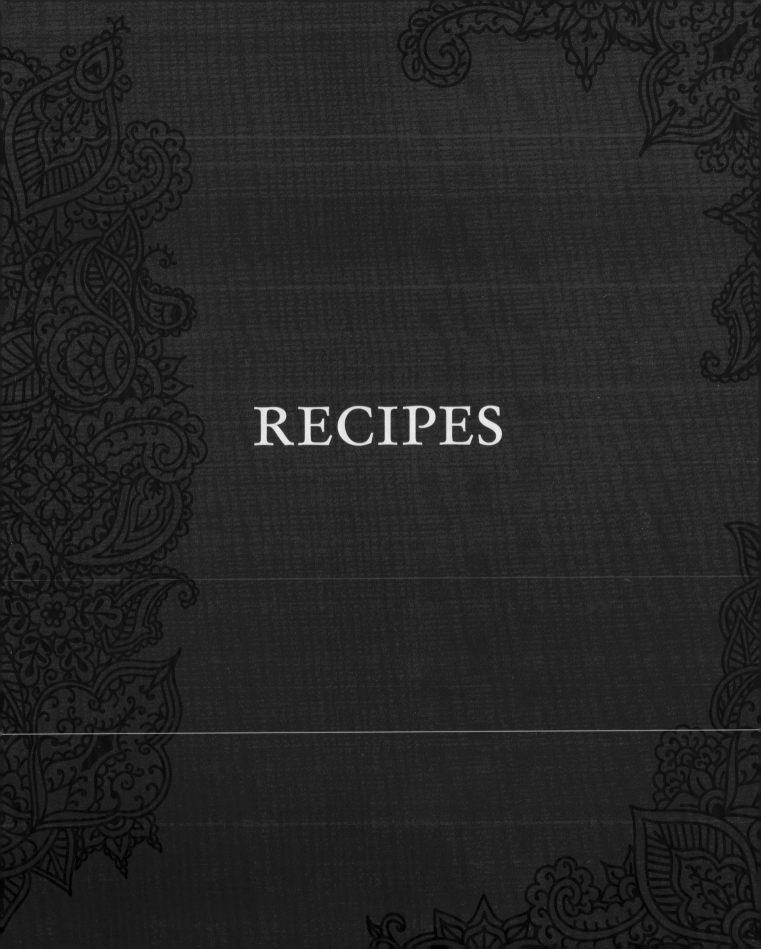

RECIPES

Appetizers and Side Dishes

A backdrop of little Persian delights: The *Sofreh*, 30

❧ APPETIZERS AND SIDE DISHES ❧

Pishkhaza

A BACKDROP OF LITTLE PERSIAN DELIGHTS: THE SOFREH

Picture this: An absolutely gorgeous cover (we call it a tablecloth; Persians call it *sofreh*) with golden embroidery and an intricate design, spread over a Persian carpet. On it are dozens of delightful little dishes, along with all kinds of flat bread, fresh herbs, fruit baskets, fresh flowers, and several kinds of nuts…. I have no doubt this is exactly how Queen Esther embellished the dinners she hosted for King Achashverosh.

Now imagine a lively two-year-old boy running across the middle of the rug, stepping onto the *sofreh*, right foot in the relish, left foot in the nuts—all just to grab an apple from the fruit basket! That is exactly why, in our home, we place the *sofreh* on the table and leave the floor for the crumbs.

These appetizers are perfect for Shabbat dinners and, since they go a long way, they are also favorites for *Seudah Shlishit* (the third Shabbat meal). They are light, great with challah, and everyone will get the impression that you cooked for ages! All of them (except some of the salads) can be made in advance, and all you need are some pretty bowls and a hungry crowd.

Besides the recipes in this chapter, there are many other quick and easy ways to add to your appetizer extravaganza. Traditionally, Persians set a platter of raw vegetables and fresh herbs on the table. Some of the herbs that would be appropriate are fresh parsley, cilantro, mint, tarragon, scallions, radishes, and raw pickling cucumbers (kirbies). I know what you are thinking: you think they are just for decoration! I thought the same way. I figured these veggies looked pretty and were used instead of flowers, but Persians actually eat these vegetables along with their food! At first, I felt like a ruminant chewing all those greens! But pretty quickly I got used to it, and now I love it.

Another idea is a platter of cut-up fresh fruit. Although this is most common as a dessert, for Persians a plate of fruit is always appropriate. In fact, the obsession with fruit goes so far that every time we go to LA for a visit, my mother-in-law meets us at the airport with a huge plastic container filled with all kinds of fruit for the kids to eat in the car on our way to their house. I have to admit I look forward to it myself and snatch a few cherries from my kids.

Another clever and super-easy idea is to set out a few bowls filled with various kinds of roasted nuts. Persians go nuts for nuts. Somehow, they can shell nuts in their mouths so fast that they leave the modern equipment—and parrots—to shame. Persians love walnuts, pistachios, roasted watermelon seeds, roasted pumpkin seeds, raw and dried almonds, raw chickpeas, and more!

Also keep in mind that, if your challah is sweet, you might want to offer another type of bread, since the salty, savory dips go better with either water challah (see Shabbat section for recipe) or other Middle Eastern breads. Persians appreciate the flexibility and taste of breads such as lavash (large and thin, paper-like, very flexible when first baked and crispy when toasted) and barbari (flat but thicker than lavash). Pita is also a favorite. Although recipes for lavash, barbari, and pita can be found on pages 33-37, fortunately, in the interest of saving time and effort, they are also readily available with kosher certification in many supermarkets in the Middle Eastern section and at many Middle Eastern groceries.

Eggplant Quiche with Tomatoes and Zucchini, page 75

ભ BARBARI BREAD ભ

I always had an easy time remembering the name of this bread. That is because, the second I tried it, I said to myself (in my Spanish-speaking brain), "*Que barbaro*!"—which means, "How cool!" Little did I know that Barbaro (which literally means Berber) is exactly the name of the people who created this bread. In any case, this bread is served for breakfast on the Persian table, along with delicious Bulgarian feta cheese, honeydew melon, walnuts, scrambled eggs, and hot sweet *chai* (tea). Barbari bread is shaped into a long rectangle and is about one inch thick. It is best served warm or toasted!

This recipe calls for *ziadune* seeds (nigella seeds), also known as onion seeds or cumin seeds. These are available in many Persian or Indian grocery shops (in Hindu they are called *Kalongi*). They are incredible little sesame-seed-like kernels with a deep black color and a sharp flavor. Not only do *ziadune* seeds give this bread an incredible taste, but they also emit a tantalizing aroma! In fact, these little seeds deserve much more credit than they get. I was flabbergasted to find out even Tutankhamen (the Egyptian Pharaoh) made sure to be buried with some *ziadune* so his slaves could make his favorite dishes in the afterlife! If that is not impressive enough, you should know *ziadune* is also used to cure gastrointestinal and respiratory disorders, such as asthma.

Yeast Mixture

½ cup warm water

1 package active dry yeast

(2¼ teaspoons)

Dough

1 teaspoon baking powder

1 teaspoon salt

1 cup warm water

3¼ cups white flour, divided

canola oil spray

Glaze and Garnish

1 teaspoon flour

1 teaspoon baking soda

⅔ cup water

¼ cup black sesame seeds

or *ziadune* (nigella) seeds

or onion seeds (optional)

1. In a medium bowl, combine the water and yeast. Cover and set aside for 5 minutes to proof the yeast. Line two 17"x12" baking sheets with parchment paper and set aside.

2. In the bowl of a stand mixer fitted with a dough hook, mix baking powder, salt, warm water, and 2 cups of flour until smooth. Add yeast mixture and remaining flour (1¼ cups) and knead for about 5 minutes until the dough is smooth and elastic. If the dough is too sticky, add 1 more tablespoon of flour.

3. Spray the dough with oil, cover with plastic wrap, and set aside in a warm place to rise for 1 hour or until doubled in size.

4. In the meantime, make the glaze: Combine the flour, baking soda, and water in a small saucepan and bring to a boil. Set aside to cool.

5. Preheat the oven to 350°F.

6. Punch down the dough and divide into two equal parts. Shape each half into a large ball and transfer to a baking sheet. Flatten the balls with a rolling pin and shape into a rectangle. Flatten the top of the

rectangle with your fingertips, making several long dents (like trenches) in the dough. Stretch the dough, pulling it from each short end until it becomes a 17"x12"x½" rectangle with grooves along its top.

7. Brush the bread with the glaze and sprinkle with black sesame seeds or *ziadune* (nigella) or onion seeds, if using. Let stand for 5 minutes before placing into preheated oven.

8. Bake for 30 minutes or until golden.

Yield: 2 loaves

✲ LAVASH BREAD ✲

This bread is so delicious! It is perfect for dips and little salads. I love serving it warm and toasty alongside challah (see page 334) on Friday nights. It is so light and crispy! It can also be used as a wrap, and it is often served at the Saturday meal as well.

When making this bread, many recipes call for a baker's peel and a baking stone. A baker's peel is a spatula so large that it looks as if it overdosed on steroids! It is used to transfer dough in and out of the oven. A baking stone is an "organic" baking sheet that absorbs extra moisture, making the bread crispy. Both are really nice tools to have but a bundle to store. So, if you lack them, don't worry… you can also make this bread my way! Unlike the commercially produced kind, this bread has crispy edges and a pliable center. One more thing: Even though this bread is readily available, there is no better feeling of accomplishment than making it yourself. Enjoy!

Yeast Mixture

1 teaspoon active dry yeast

2 tablespoons sugar

½ cup warm water

Dough

6½ to 7 cups white flour, divided

2 teaspoons salt

2 cups warm water

canola oil spray

Glaze

1 tablespoon olive oil

1. Preheat oven to 450 °F.
2. In a medium bowl, combine the yeast, sugar, and water. Cover and set aside for 5 minutes. Line four 17"x12" rimless cookie sheets with parchment paper and set aside.
3. In the bowl of a stand mixer fitted with a dough hook, combine 5 cups flour and the salt. Slowly incorporate the water until well mixed. Add yeast mixture and remaining flour (1½ to 2 cups) until a smooth and pliable dough is formed. Spray with canola oil and cover with plastic wrap. Set aside to rise for 20 minutes.
4. Punch down the dough. Divide into four equal pieces. Form each piece into a ball and place each onto a cookie sheet.

With a rolling pin, flatten each ball into a paper-thin oval as large as the baking sheet permits. Prick the dough all over with a fork. Brush with olive oil and bake for 10 to 15 minutes or until nice and toasted.

Yield: 4 loaves

My obsession with…parchment paper!

I just can't live without it!! It is so versatile! I use it to flatten chicken breasts, to bake bread, and even to wrap presents after my kids have scribbled all over it. But the best usage is, of course, in the oven. Parchment paper is coated with non-sticking agents that make your breads and cookies lift right off without any effort. You can flatten this dough, right on top of a big piece of parchment paper, and then lift it by the sides to transfer to the cookie sheet. Keep in mind that parchment paper is not waxed paper and that, if you keep kosher, it is imperative to get it with kosher certification.

❧ PITA BREAD ❧

My kids go crazy for warm pita straight out of the oven! You will not believe how easy it is to make pita bread. Keep in mind that store-bought pita will look a little different from home-made…but it will not taste better! First of all, commercially produced pita dough is flattened by an industrial press to the thickness of 0.125 inches. Also, the pita is exposed to ovens that can reach temperatures of about 800°F to 900°F for only a few minutes. In almost an instant, any water in the dough turns to steam and that is the reason these are flatter and the inner pocket is more evident. Try duplicating that at home! My version has more of a "cushion" look than the commercially baked. It does produce the "pocket" if you slice it in half. However, it is the taste and smell that will make it worth your while! This bread goes really well with the many dips and salads served at the Shabbat table.

You will have to take *challah* without a *bracha* (blessing) in this recipe. For more information on taking *challah,* please see my blog: kosherpersianfoodblog.com.

Tricks of the trade

You can easily divide this recipe in half or freeze half of the dough for later use. Store pitas in an airtight container or plastic bag.

Yeast Mixture

4 tablespoons active dry yeast

2 teaspoons sugar

½ cup warm water

Dough

8½ cups flour, divided

1 tablespoon salt

3 cups warm water

canola oil spray

1. In a medium bowl, combine yeast, sugar, and water. Cover and set aside for 5 minutes. Layer three 17"x12" baking sheets with parchment paper and set aside.

2. In the bowl of a standing mixer fitted with a dough hook, mix 7 cups of flour and salt. Slowly incorporate the water until well mixed. Add the yeast mixture and 1½ cups flour until a smooth and pliable dough is formed.

3. To take challah, pinch off a piece the size of a lime, but do not say a *bracha* (blessing) on such a small batch of dough.

Then wrap the separated dough in a piece of foil and let it burn in the oven.

4. Spray remaining dough with canola oil and cover with plastic wrap. Set aside in a warm place to rise for 1 hour or until doubled in size.

5. Preheat the oven to 350°F. Punch down the dough. Divide into 16 equal pieces. Add ½ cup flour to a medium bowl. Form each piece of dough into a ball the size of a baseball and dip into the flour. With your hands, flatten each ball into rounds approximately 5 inches by ½-inch. Place on the

baking sheets and prick the dough all over with a fork to eliminate air bubbles.

6. Bake for 30 to 35 minutes or until nice and toasted.

Yield: 16 pitas

❧ EGGPLANT DIP ❧

Babaganoush

You might have a hard time pronouncing this word, but you will have a very easy time eating this food! This is probably the quintessential staple in Sephardic cuisine. Eggplant is to Sephardic Jews what potatoes are to *Ashkenazi* Jews. Just like potatoes, eggplant should be cooked, and salt must be added to bring out the flavor. Yes, you can totally buy *babaganoush* at the grocery store, but once you have made your own (which, by the way, is "easy–shmeezy"), you will never be able to go back to the mass-produced variety! The best smoky results are achieved by roasting the eggplant over an open flame or on a barbecue grill. However, you can also roast the eggplant in the oven. My husband loves this so much that if it were up to him he would use it instead of toothpaste! This dip should be *shmeared* (that sounds better in Yiddish than in Farsi!) on challah or any kind of bread. Choose eggplants that are firm, shiny, and dark. This dish can be stored in an airtight container for up to a week.

3 eggplants, whole

4 garlic cloves, peeled and pureed

¼ cup tahini sauce (or mayonnaise, but tahini is much better)

juice of 3 limes *or* 8 tablespoons bottled lime juice

1 tablespoon salt

½ teaspoon ground cumin

½ teaspoon pepper

1 tablespoon chopped parsley, for garnish

1. You have three options when preparing the eggplant:

a. Roast the eggplants on a grill.

b. Roast them directly over a medium flame on your stove top.

c. Broil them in the oven on high in a 9"x13" aluminum pan, until the skin is blistered and black on all sides.

Make sure to turn the eggplants so that all sides become blistered.

2. Set aside the roasted eggplants for 10 minutes, or until they look heavy and have deflated.

3. In the meantime, combine all the other ingredients in a medium bowl.

4. Peel the eggplants, mash with a fork, and add the pulp to the bowl. Mix until creamy. Garnish with parsley.

Yield: 3 cups

❧ FRIED EGGPLANT ❧

Chatzilim

This is one of my favorite Sephardic appetizers. However, preparing this dish also became a nightmare, because just by looking at all the oil I was using I could feel my arteries clogging! I decided to broil the eggplants instead. The secret is to use oil spray and to cut the eggplants thin enough to produce a crunchy and delicious result. Below I give you both options and you can make the choice! My Moroccan friend Michal Bessler is the genius who taught me this recipe.

Salting the eggplant before frying will extract the excess liquid from the eggplant so that the pieces absorb less oil when fried and expel no liquid when broiled. Salting will also produce a crispier result. Please be careful and keep your children away from the sizzling oil!

2 eggplants, unpeeled, washed, and cut into slices ⅓-inch thick
5 tablespoons kosher salt
canola oil or spray
1 tablespoon chopped parsley, for garnish (optional)

Garnish
¼ cup olive oil
¼ teaspoon paprika
¼ teaspoon cumin
¼ teaspoon salt
¼ teaspoon pepper
3 tablespoons lime juice *or* the juice of 1 lime
4 cloves fresh garlic, pressed

1. Layer the eggplant slices in a large colander, sprinkling generously with kosher salt between layers. Let stand for 30 minutes.

2. Rinse the eggplants in the same colander to wash off the extra salt. Dry with paper towels.

FRYING METHOD

1. Add canola oil to one-quarter of the depth of a very large skillet. Place over medium heat until the oil sizzles when a drop of water is drizzled onto it.

2. While the oil heats, make the garnish sauce by combining all ingredients. Set aside.

3. Fry the eggplant slices in a single layer for 1 minute on each side or until slightly brown on both sides.

4. Drain on paper towels and serve with parsley as garnish, or drizzle garnish on top.

BROILING METHOD

1. Preheat the oven to broil.

2. Spray 2 cookie sheets with oil. Place the eggplant slices on the sheets in a single layer and spray with oil.

3. Broil on rack closest to the flame for 5 to 7 minutes or until the eggplant slices are slightly brown.

4. Carefully remove the cookie sheets from the oven and flip the eggplant slices with a spatula or food tongs. Spray more oil on the eggplants and return to the oven to broil for additional 5 to 7 minutes.

5. Make the garnish by combining all ingredients.

6. Remove eggplants from the oven and serve with the garnish and chopped parsley.

Yield: Serves 4 to 6

Olive Dip

☙ OLIVE DIP ❧

You know that something is good when your guests rave about it. However, when your guests not only rave, but also recognize this dish from eating at other people's tables, then you know it is a winner.... Thanks to Shifra Schwartz at the Chai Center of Brookline for this winner!

2 (10-ounce) jars Spanish olives
stuffed with pimientos
¾ cup low-fat mayonnaise

1. Drain the liquid from the olives. Pour olives into a deep plastic bowl. Add the mayonnaise.

2. Process mayo and olives with an immersion blender until creamy. Serve with bread or challah!

Yield: 16 ounces

☙ SCALLION DIP ❧

This dip is not Persian, but I promise your guests will all be asking for more. It was taught to me by Chana Gray, totally Ashkenazi! This dip is great to use with fresh vegetables, on challah, and over fish.

½ cup chopped fresh parsley
(½-bunch without stems)
½ cup chopped scallions (4 scallions)
1 cup low-fat mayonnaise

2 tablespoons sugar
2 tablespoons lime juice
½ teaspoon mustard

1. Place all ingredients into a small food processor or a deep plastic bowl. Mix until creamy, using a food processor or an immersion blender.

2. Serve in a bowl; garnish with chopped parsley.

Yield: 10 ounces

❧ CHICKPEA DIP ❧

Chummus

When you eat this chummus you will suddenly be fluent in Hebrew! Just joking! My husband says this chummus tastes exactly like the one we had more than 10 years ago under the stars at the shore of Jerusalem Beach in Tel Aviv…. Talk about culinary memories!

You might have to add a few tablespoons of water if the chummus starts thickening in the fridge after a few days, but not draining the chickpeas should do the trick of keeping the chummus creamy.

2 (15.5-oz) cans chickpeas
(do not drain)
juice of 1 lime
½ cup tahini paste
7 garlic cloves

1 tablespoon cumin
2 teaspoons salt
2 tablespoons olive oil, plus more
for drizzling
dash of paprika, for garnish

1. In a food processor fitted with a metal blade, cream all ingredients.
2. Garnish with a drizzle of olive oil and a dash of paprika.

3. Serve with warm challah (page 334), barbari (page 33), or pita (page 37).

Yield: 16 ounces

❧ ROASTED PEPPER DIP ❧

Muhammara

This recipe was given to me by my friend Marcy Gilbert. She might be totally Ashkenazi but she sure has a grip on the Sephardic flavors! This recipe is equally delicious using jarred "fire-roasted" red or yellow peppers. This dip originated in Syria, but Turkish people use it as well, and I can guarantee that no matter where your guests are from, they will love it!

1 cup unflavored breadcrumbs

1 (15-ounce) jar "fire-roasted" peppers (red or yellow), drained

1 cup walnuts *or* almonds

6 garlic cloves

2 tablespoons balsamic vinegar

juice of 1 lime

2 teaspoons cumin

2 tablespoons olive oil

1. Using a food processor fitted with a metal blade, blend all ingredients until smooth.

2. Serve with lavash (page 35), pita (page 37), or challah (page 334).

Yield: 16 ounces

MOROCCAN TOMATO AND ROASTED PEPPER DIP

Matbucha

This dip doesn't last long on the table! Moroccans love it hot, but I actually skip the jalapeño and use hot paprika instead, because it gives flavor but is not as hot as jalapeño. Traditionally *matbucha* is tedious to make, but with the help of modern amenities (i.e., canned stewed tomatoes and roasted peppers), the hard work is cut in half! Thank you, Jennifer Ohana, for this winner!

7 garlic cloves, pressed

¼ cup olive oil

1 (28-ounce) can stewed tomatoes, drained, juice reserved

1 (15-ounce) jar fire-roasted red peppers, drained and diced

2 teaspoons salt

1 teaspoon hot paprika

1 teaspoon sugar

1 green jalapeño pepper, seeded and thinly sliced (optional)

1. In a small saucepan, fry garlic in olive oil over medium heat for 1 minute. Add the drained tomatoes and red peppers. Add one cup reserved tomato liquid. Reduce heat to low; simmer, covered, for 10 minutes.

2. Add salt, hot paprika, sugar, and jalapeño, if using. Cook, uncovered, for 10 minutes over medium/low heat. Stir occasionally to break up any big pieces of tomato; the end result should be chunky, like a salsa.

3. Serve at room temperature with pita (page 37) or challah (page 334).

Yield: approximately 20 ounces

❧ SHIRAZI SALAD ❧

Did you ever hear the rumor that Sephardic men never ever, ever do any housework? Well, I can testify that my father-in-law, Ezzy, has never, ever changed a diaper! However, he is the best fruit-and-vegetable-cutter there is! If you want anything peeled, chopped, or cut—he is the man. So much for stereotypes! When it comes to Shirazi salad, he is my personal chopper. You might think this salad is almost identical to Israeli salad, and you might be right—just don't say it to anyone born in Shiraz! Visit my website to watch a video making this recipe.

Many people use cilantro in this recipe instead of mint. It is fabulous either way.

Salad

2 large tomatoes, washed and diced into ¼-inch squares

½ red onion, peeled and diced into small squares

1 large English seedless cucumber (*or* 1 regular cucumber), diced into small squares

¾ cup chopped mint leaves *or*

¼ cup dried mint leaves

Dressing

¼ cup olive oil

juice of 3 limes (½ cup lime juice)

1 tablespoon salt

½ teaspoon pepper

Garnish

fresh mint *or* cilantro leaves (optional)

1. Mix all vegetables together.
2. Right before serving, pour dressing over and toss salad.

3. Garnish with fresh mint leaves.

Yield: 3 cups

Herb Salad with Lime Dressing

❧ HERB SALAD WITH LIME DRESSING ❧

Sabzi Salad

My father-in-law inspired this salad. He always comes up with great ideas of what to do with leftovers. He realized there were a lot of different kinds of herbs in the fridge ready to go bad (check your fridge, you probably have a bunch of parsley ready to go too!) and designed this salad in the blink of an eye!

Salad

1 bunch fresh cilantro, washed and chopped

1 bunch fresh dill, washed and chopped

1 bunch fresh tarragon, washed and chopped

½ bunch mint, washed and chopped

½ red onion, finely chopped

Dressing

juice of 3 limes (½ cup lime juice)

¼ cup olive oil

½ teaspoon pepper

2 teaspoons salt

1. In a medium bowl, combine all the salad ingredients. Set aside.

2. In a small bowl, combine the dressing ingredients.

3. Toss with the salad when you are ready to serve.

Yield: 3 cups

❧ BEET SALAD ❧

Salad'e Chogondar

An easy salad that can be put together in a blink! I also use this salad for the Persian *Yehi Ratzons* in the Seder for *Rosh Hashana* (see page 337).

2 (14.5-ounce) cans sliced beets

1 bunch scallions, finely sliced

½ cup chopped fresh cilantro

1 teaspoon salt

½ teaspoon pepper

1 teaspoon cumin

1 tablespoon olive oil

Combine all ingredients and toss well.

Yield: Approximately 3 cups, depending on the size of the slices.

❧ PERSIAN POTATO SALAD ❧

سالاد الویه

Salad'e Olivie

You might look at this salad and think, "Hey! That is Russian Potato Salad"—and actually you might be right. But Persians claim, along with many other things, that this salad originates in Iran. Adding grilled chicken breast to this salad is an option that I always skip because I like serving it as an appetizer along with fish. (According to the laws of *Kashrut*, meat and fish are not to be served together.)

Salad

3 large white potatoes, with skin, washed

3 eggs

6 sour pickles, chopped

½ cup green peas (half of a 15-ounce can)

Dressing

6 tablespoons light mayonnaise

2 teaspoons salt

½ teaspoon pepper

Garnish (optional)

cherry tomatoes

olives

pickles

1. Place the potatoes and eggs into a medium saucepan. Cover with water and bring to a boil. Cook, covered, for at least 15 minutes, until the potatoes are fork tender and eggs are hard-boiled.

2. Drain in colander and return to the pot. Refill the pot with cold water to cool the contents. Peel and chop potatoes and eggs into half-inch pieces. Place into a medium bowl and set aside.

3. Add pickles and peas to the bowl.

4. Combine all dressing ingredients. Add to the salad and toss well.

5. Turn salad out onto a platter or into a bowl, using the back of a spoon to smooth the surface and shape it into a dome. Garnish with cut-up pickles, halved cherry tomatoes, and/or olives. Or place a scoop of salad onto endive leaves, making little potato salad "boats."

Yield: 6 cups

❧ TABOULEH SALAD ❧

I always bought this salad already made—until I learned to make it myself! It is a great make-ahead salad that everyone will love. Bulgur requires little cooking, because it is actually whole wheat that has been soaked, steamed, dried, and crushed for your convenience! That is the reason why bulgur, compared to whole wheat, has a nutty flavor and is easier to cook.

Salad

1 cup medium bulgur

2 cups warm water

5 garlic cloves, pressed

3 bunches scallions, including the green parts, sliced (about 21 scallions)

1 cup chopped flat parsley (about 1 bunch, without stems)

½ cup chopped fresh mint (about ½-bunch without stems)

2 large tomatoes, diced

Dressing

¼ cup olive oil

1 tablespoon salt

½ teaspoon hot paprika

½ cup lime juice (*or* the juice of 3 limes)

1 tablespoon cumin (optional)

1. Place bulgur into a medium bowl, cover with warm water, and soak for 15 minutes.
2. In the meantime, wash and chop vegetables and mix together in a large bowl.
3. Drain the bulgur.
4. Combine all dressing ingredients and add to vegetables along with the drained bulgur. Toss well and serve on lettuce or in endive leaves for "endive tabouleh boats."

Yield: 8 cups

Tricks of the trade

This salad is a great make-ahead salad but there is a trick involved. I often serve this salad for Shabbat dinner, but I don't have the *koach* (strength) to make it on Friday… I always try to get all my Shabbat prepping done on Thursday. So, I make the salad on Thursday without soaking the bulgur at all! Overnight, the bulgur absorbs all the juices from the vegetables and lime. By dinnertime on Friday night, the salad is absolutely delicious and the bulgur is perfect!

◦ LIBYAN BUTTERNUT SQUASH SALAD ◦

When I eat this salad, I feel transported to another time, in another country. I can almost hear the tambourine and the rhythmic music just as a scream and a, "He took my piece of *challah*, Mom!" Suddenly I awaken, sitting at my Shabbat table surrounded by family and guests in good old America!

1 onion, finely chopped

8 garlic cloves, pressed

3 tablespoons olive oil

4 cups butternut squash, cut into 1-inch pieces (from 1 medium butternut squash, peeled)

1 teaspoon ground cumin

1 teaspoon paprika

¼ teaspoon ground ginger

1 teaspoon curry powder

½ teaspoon salt

juice of 1 lime

1 (16-ounce) can diced tomatoes, with liquid

chopped cilantro, for garnish (optional)

1. In a medium saucepan, fry onion and garlic in the oil over medium heat until translucent. Add squash, cumin, paprika, ginger, curry, salt, and lime juice. Cover and cook until squash begins to soften, about 15 minutes.

2. Stir in the tomatoes; cook covered over medium heat for about 10 more minutes or until the squash is very tender.

3. Serve cold or at room temperature; garnish with cilantro, if desired.

Yield: 4 cups

❧ FENNEL SALAD ❧

Anise is also known as fennel root. This vegetable has a delicious, sweet licorice flavor and is often served alone. However, I have also accompanied it with chicory lettuce (curly endive) and avocado, making a more substantial salad that plays with the strong licorice taste and the creamy, heavenly avocado. My husband suggests adding some Arak to the dressing, but I decided to keep this book kid-friendly!

1 large fennel root, finely sliced

1 teaspoon salt

½ teaspoon pepper

3 tablespoons olive oil

juice of 3 limes *or* ½ cup bottled lime juice

Mix all ingredients together and enjoy!

Yield: About 3 cups, depending on the size of the fennel

✑ CHICKPEA SALAD ✑

This salad is very easy and quick to prepare. I love canned chickpeas because they come in very handy to dress up any salad or to serve on their own.

2 (15.5-ounce) cans chickpeas, drained

½ red onion, finely chopped

2 tablespoons olive oil

3 garlic cloves, crushed

½ teaspoon salt

¼ teaspoon pepper

½ cup chopped cilantro

1 teaspoon ground dehydrated lime — *lemon omani* (optional)

Mix all ingredients together and serve.

Yield: 4 cups

You are what you eat

Chickpeas are very healthful; they are a great source of dietary fiber and protein. No wonder humans have been eating them for more than 5,000 years!

❧ MOROCCAN SPINACH SALAD ❧

بافولة

My friend Jennifer Ohana is a good Ashkenazi girl married to a very Moroccan man! She is such a great sport, she has embraced the food her husband adores (not that any of us had much choice!). Today she is an incredible Moroccan cook and all of her friends love it. She is the one to share the wisdom of Moroccan salads with me!

3 tablespoons canola oil

1 teaspoon cumin

½ teaspoon paprika

½ teaspoon salt

¼ teaspoon pepper

3 tablespoons lemon juice *or* the juice of 1 lemon

1 (16-ounce) bag frozen chopped spinach, thawed and drained

1. Place a small saucepan over medium heat. Add the oil, cumin, paprika, salt, and pepper. Add the lemon juice. Add the spinach and mix well.

2. Cook, uncovered, over medium/low heat, stirring occasionally, for 8 minutes or until the spinach is uniformly dark green and creamy.

3. Serve at room temperature.

Yield: 2 cups

You are what you eat

Did you know spinach is not as healthful as Popeye made us believe? In the year 1870, Dr. E. Von Wolf calculated the iron content in spinach and made a little mistake with the decimal point, thereby overestimating this number tenfold. This mistake was revealed 67 years later! However, even though spinach might not be the wonder vegetable we thought, it is still healthful and delicious!

❧ MOROCCAN CARROT SALAD ❧

السلادا ديال خيزو

This is a great make-ahead salad. The more time it spends in the fridge, the better it tastes!

10 large carrots, peeled

¼ cup olive oil

2 tablespoons white vinegar

2 teaspoons salt

½ teaspoon pepper

4 garlic cloves, pressed

1 teaspoon cumin

1 teaspoon paprika

1 cup chopped fresh cilantro (one bunch, stems discarded)

1. Place carrots into a medium saucepan and cover with water. Bring to a boil and cook for approximately 12 minutes or until "al dente." Drain and cool.

2. Cut carrots into slices ¼-inch thick and set aside.

3. In a medium bowl, mix oil, vinegar, salt, pepper, garlic, cumin, paprika, and cilantro. Toss in the sliced carrots and mix thoroughly.

4. Garnish with fresh cilantro.

Yield: About 3 cups, depending on the size of the carrots

You are what you eat

Will eating carrots really improve your vision? Sorry to burst your bubble: not really! Carrots are rich in Vitamin A (which is good for healthy eyesight) but it will not improve your vision. While the beta carotene in carrots might reduce the risk of cataracts, you would have to consume a huge quantity to make any difference, and most likely you would end up as orange as a carrot, a condition known as carotenosis!

❧ CUCUMBER SALAD WITH DILL AND SHALLOTS ❧

This salad was an "emergency Pesach salad" that I had to make up in a jiffy. It tasted so good and my in-laws like it so much I decided to share it with you!

Salad

3 English cucumbers, peeled and seeded

1 large shallot, finely sliced (½ red onion is a fine substitute)

1 avocado, chopped

¼ cup fresh dill, chopped

Dressing

¼ cup olive oil

1 tablespoon Dijon mustard

¼ cup mayonnaise

1 teaspoon salt

½ teaspoon pepper

juice of 1 lime or 3 tablespoons bottled lime juice

1. Halve cucumbers lengthwise and use a spoon to remove the seeds. Cut cucumber halves horizontally into slices ½-inch thick. Mix cucumbers, shallots or red onion, avocado, and fresh dill in a large bowl. Cover and set aside. If you are not going to serve immediately, sprinkle with lime juice and stir, to prevent the avocados from darkening.

2. In a small bowl, combine dressing ingredients.

3. Pour dressing on salad just before serving.

Yield: 3 cups

You are what you eat

This recipe calls for shallots. Shallots are little bulbs of pleasure! They are related to onions but are milder in taste, resembling a sweet onion but with a hint of garlic. Shallots are a popular part of Persian cuisine. They are called *mooseer* in Farsi and are often mixed with yogurt (*Must'o Mooseer*; see page 243) or eaten with kebab (see page 118).

SMOKED FISH SALAD
WITH CANDIED WALNUTS AND AVOCADO

This is not a Persian salad at all. But if I told you that even Persians, who totally worship their food, absolutely love this salad, would you believe me? You sure should! In fact, every single person at the table, no matter where they are from, will love it! The secret to this salad is the dressing, so you should be generous when pouring it.

By the way, you can substitute sliced grilled chicken breast for the smoked salmon or seared tuna; simply drape it over the greens. (Just in case you don't remember, "to sear" means to brown meat or fish quickly over very high heat in order to seal the juices inside.)

Salad

1 (7-ounce) bag store-bought greens

4 scallions, finely chopped

½ cup glazed walnuts (store-bought)

¼ cup dried cranberries (Craisins®)

1 (11-ounce) can mandarin oranges, drained

1 avocado, thinly sliced

8 ounces smoked salmon or tuna fillet

2 tablespoons toasted sesame oil (if using tuna fillet)

Dressing

¾ cup canola oil

⅓ cup sugar

½ teaspoon soy sauce

¼ cup seasoned rice wine vinegar

¼ cup toasted sesame oil

1 tablespoon ground ginger

½ teaspoon salt

Optional Garnishes

French-fried onions

narrow chow mein noodles

1 tablespoon toasted sesame seeds

1. If using tuna, sear in a medium skillet in 2 tablespoons very hot toasted sesame oil, 3 minutes on each side; the middle of the fillet should remain pink. Cut into slices ¼-inch thick and set aside.

2. On a large, shallow platter, layer all the ingredients for the salad, starting with the greens and adding, in this order, onions, walnuts, cranberries, and mandarin oranges.

3. Drape the smoked salmon neatly over the top (or fan out the seared tuna slices).

4. Surround the salad with the chopped avocado.

5. Cover with plastic until ready to serve.

6. Before serving, sprinkle fish with French-fried onions or chow mein noodles, if using. Sprinkle with sesame seeds.

7. Combine the ingredients for the dressing; blend together very well to dissolve the sugar. Pour over salad and serve.

Yield: 8 cups

GREEN SALAD WITH SHALLOTS, CELERY, AND AVOCADO

I learned this salad from my friend Celine Sellam. While she is purely *Ashkenazi* and totally French, she ended up marrying a totally Sephardic and incredibly French man with roots in Tunisia and Algeria! As you can imagine, to me her kitchen is a spa for the palate!

I find it hard to make any salad without a beloved ingredient of mine…avocados. When I was a child growing up in Venezuela, I had a backyard with an avocado tree and a dog. It was a dream to have an avocado tree in my backyard—as long as we could get to them before the dog!

Salad

1 bag of prewashed lettuce *or*
2 heads of fresh lettuce, washed and chopped
3 celery stalks, cut up
1 shallot, finely chopped *or*
½ red onion
1 avocado, diced

Dressing

3 tablespoons olive oil
juice of 1 lemon or 3 tablespoons bottled lemon juice
1 teaspoon Dijon mustard
1 tablespoon apple cider vinegar
1 teaspoon salt
½ teaspoon pepper

1. Combine all ingredients for the salad and set aside.

2. Thoroughly combine ingredients for the dressing and add to the salad, tossing well, just before serving.

Yield: 8 cups

You are what you eat

Are avocados fattening? Yes, but they are worth it! Avocados contain good fat. In 1 ounce of avocado you can find 50 calories and 4 grams of fat. However, that little bite contains over 20 vitamins and minerals, which make it an excellent nutritional choice!

✌ EGGPLANT QUICHE WITH TOMATOES AND ZUCCHINI ✌

This dish is not only absolutely delicious, but it is also fabulous-looking! You will definitely get the "Oh my GOSH!" factor going and people will think you have connections with chefs. The truth is that it is very easy!

Whenever I have vegetarians coming for a meal, I make this colorful dish.

Eggplants shrink significantly when cooked, so don't be concerned if all the pieces don't fit into your saucepan at the same time. Keep adding eggplant squares as the others cook down.

Keep in mind that if the dough is too sticky, you might have to add one more tablespoon or so of flour until the right consistency is achieved. This could be a product of cup measurement usage rather than weight. Also, different altitudes can also be a factor when it comes making any kind of dough.

Dough
½ cup water
½ cup olive oil
1 egg
1 teaspoon salt
2½ cups flour

Filling
1 large onion, diced into small squares
3 garlic cloves, pressed
3 tablespoons olive oil
2 large eggplants, peeled and diced into small squares
1 teaspoon salt
½ teaspoon pepper

Garnish
2 zucchinis, sliced
½ cup cherry tomatoes, sliced
¼ cup black or green olives, sliced
dash dried parsley
olive oil spray

1. Preheat oven to 350°F.

TO MAKE THE DOUGH:

2. Combine all dough ingredients in a standing mixer fitted with a dough hook, or in a bread machine. The dough should resemble *challah* dough. Place the dough into a plastic bag and store in the refrigerator until ready to use.

TO MAKE THE FILLING:

3. In a large saucepan, fry onions and garlic in olive oil until translucent. Add eggplant and stir until thoroughly cooked. Add salt and pepper and stir to combine. Set aside to cool.

4. Press the chilled dough into a 9"x13" oven-to-table baking dish that has been sprayed with oil, making sure to cover all sides. Prick the bottom and sides of the dough with a fork.

5. Add the eggplant filling to the dough-lined baking dish and top with a pattern of zucchini, tomato, and olive slices. Sprinkle dried parsley on top and spray with olive oil.

6. Bake, uncovered, for 45 minutes.

Yield: 8-10 servings

Fish and Soups

ماهی و سوپ

When we were first married, my husband and I immediately moved to Boston and left Irangeles (I mean Los Angeles) behind, along with all the Persian glitz. When we arrived in Boston, we moved to a primarily Ashkenazi community. Since all my Jewish background and knowledge had been shaped by Ashkenazi Jews, I was already daydreaming about sweet Yerushalmi kugels and delicious gefilte fish! However, for my husband, this was a catastrophe.

Let me illustrate. The first Shabbat (or should I say Shabbos?) we were invited for a meal, we were offered the choice of gefilte fish or liver as the appetizer. I could see my husband's face transforming into a huge question mark. He politely said, "I'll pass." Now, in my culture there is no such thing as "politely" passing on anyone's food. As we were walking home I gave him such a hard time! All he could say to me was, "Reyna, are you kidding me? Asking a Sephardic man if he wants liver or gefilte fish for an appetizer is like asking him if he wants to be killed with a sword or with a gun!!" So, from that day, he accepts the gefilte fish—and I eat it!!

Marinated Fish with Onions, page 89

My Favorite Baked Salmon

↬ MY FAVORITE BAKED SALMON ↫

All of my guests and friends, Persian or not, simply love this fish. I also love it because it is so easy to make! My mouth waters as I am cooking it. It freezes well, too, but make sure to undercook it before freezing, since it can overcook while reheating. Try it with a drizzle of the Green Relish below…just to die for!

1 skinless salmon fillet (around 1.5 lbs)
cooking oil spray
¼ teaspoon paprika
½ teaspoon seasoned salt

¼ teaspoon salt
¼ teaspoon pepper
½ teaspoon garlic powder *or*
3 cloves fresh garlic, chopped
3 tablespoons olive oil

1. Preheat oven to 350 °F.
2. Coat a 9"x13" disposable aluminum pan or oven-to-table roaster with oil spray.
3. Place fish on the oiled pan.
4. Rub fillet with seasonings and olive oil.

5. Bake for 25 minutes or until a knife easily flakes the fish. Do not overcook; the fish will become very tough. If this dish is to be frozen and reheated before serving, bake only 20 minutes.

Yield: 6 servings, depending on the size of the fillet.

Tricks of the trade

I use Lawry's® seasoned salt in this recipe. It's available in most supermarkets and is a very versatile seasoning.

↬ GREEN RELISH FOR FISH ↫

So simple, yet so incredibly delicious! This relish is heavenly on any fish and on almost anything! I tried it first at the home of one of the best cooks in town: Celine Sellam.

½ onion, chopped
2 garlic cloves, peeled and pressed or finely minced
juice of 4 limes
2 cups chopped cilantro (2 bunches, stems discarded)

1 cup extra-virgin olive oil
½ teaspoon salt
pepper to taste
pine nuts, for garnish (optional)

1. Combine all ingredients.

2. Serve with fish and watch, in astonishment, as it disappears!

Yield: 2½ cups

Tricks of the trade

This relish can easily be made in advance and refrigerated for days (that is, if you manage to have leftovers!). You can substitute fresh dill, parsley, or basil for the cilantro. Just keep it to one green at a time.

❧ SALMON KEBAB ❧

I love the look on people's faces when I bring this appetizer to the table…They love the colors, the fish-on-a-stick idea, and, most of all, the flavor! You can serve it on a bed of lettuce or plain couscous along with a slice of lemon. Make sure not to overcook it. You might be tempted to add lime to this recipe before cooking it…don't do it! The lime will start pickling the fish and it will be tough after you bake it.

1 skinless salmon fillet (around 1.5 lbs), cut into 2"x2" cubes

1 green pepper, washed, seeds removed, cut into 1"x 1"wedges

2 yellow peppers, washed, seeds removed, cut into 1"x 1" wedges

1 red pepper, washed, seeds removed, cut into 1"x 1" wedges

12 miniature onions, peeled *or* 1 regular onion, peeled and cut into 1"x 1" wedges

½ teaspoon paprika

1 teaspoon seasoned salt (optional)

½ teaspoon salt

½ teaspoon pepper

1 teaspoon garlic powder *or* 3 cloves fresh garlic, chopped

¼ teaspoon ground saffron

¼ cup olive oil

5" wooden skewers

canola oil cooking spray

1. Preheat oven to broil.
2. Place fish chunks, peppers, and onions into a large bowl.
3. Add all the seasonings and olive oil. Stir to coat fish and vegetables. Marinate for 1 hour in the refrigerator or simply continue with the recipe.
4. Thread onto the skewers, alternating fish and vegetables.

5. Spray a 9"x13" disposable pan or any oven-safe cooking sheet with canola oil. Place skewers in a single layer onto the pan.
6. Broil closest to the heat for 5 minutes or until nicely browned. Remove from the oven, turn skewers, and return to the oven, closest to the heat, for 5 more minutes. Make sure not to overcook.

Yield: about 12 kebabs

Tricks of the trade

I use Lawry's® seasoned salt in this recipe. It's available in most supermarkets and is a very versatile seasoning.

Many people soak wooden skewers in water before using, but I find that in this recipe, this step is not necessary.

You can marinate the fish and veggies for 1 hour or simply continue with the recipe after adding the spices; after all, who has time to marinate anything nowadays?

❧ FRIED WHITEFISH ❧

This is my mother-in-law's signature dish. I am sorry to tell you—there is no way around it—it must be fried. However, I guess that guarantees that this really tastes good, since I am a firm believer that when it comes to frying you can fry anything, even a Lego piece, and it will always taste good! *Momon* uses trout for this recipe…I like using cod…or even salmon!

3 large white-fleshed fish fillets (approximately 1.5 pounds of tilapia, cod, flounder, or trout)

2 teaspoons salt

½ teaspoon pepper

canola oil, for frying

For dredging

2 eggs

1 teaspoon salt

¼ teaspoon pepper

2 cups flavored breadcrumbs *or* panko breadcrumbs

Garnish (optional)

3 lemons, cut in wedges

1. Cut fish into 3-ounce pieces (about the size of your palm) and place into a large bowl. Season with salt and pepper.

2. Break eggs into a small bowl and beat lightly with a fork. Add salt and pepper and set aside. Place the breadcrumbs onto a shallow plate. Set aside.

3. Pour ½-inch canola oil into a large skillet. Heat oil over medium heat until pan sizzles when tested with a drop of water.

4. While the oil heats, dip each piece of fish into egg mixture and then dredge in the breadcrumbs, coating very well on all sides.

5. Fry fillets for about 5 minutes for thick fillets, less for thinner fish portions, until a nice, crunchy, brown crust forms. Turn over and fry for another 5 minutes on the other side. Transfer to platter.

6. Serve warm or cold, garnished with cut-up lemons, if desired.

Yield: 6 servings

Tricks of the trade

When I make this fish, I always make sure to prepare a platter by draping it with paper towels to absorb the extra oil. Thinking ahead also has saved me from burning this fish many times since I don't have to run around my kitchen looking for a plate when the fish is ready to be taken out of the hot oil. I like to serve this dish with Green Relish (see page 81) or White Dill Sauce (see page 89).

❦ MOROCCAN SALMON ❧

الصومو صعربي

What happens (for the most part) when an Ashkenazi woman marries a Sephardic man? She will have to adopt a lot of the Sephardic cuisine staples that her husband adores.… Suddenly, she will hardly remember the taste of sweet kugel, gefilte fish, and certainly chopped liver.

What happens when a Sephardic woman marries an Ashkenazi man? Her entire new Ashkenazi community starts worshiping her food!! This is what happened when my dear Moroccan friend Michal Bessler married her Ashkenazi *bashert*!

When I asked her for this recipe she just said, "Not a problem—so many people have asked me for this recipe [which she inherited from her dear mother] that I have it all typed and ready in my computer!!"

4 cups water

3 large carrots, cut into ¼-inch rounds or strips

2 cloves garlic, chopped

1 red sweet pepper, sliced

1 green/red hot pepper (optional)

1 tablespoon chicken consommé powder *(parve)*

1 teaspoon salt

2 tablespoons sweet paprika, divided (optional: substitute 1 tablespoon sweet paprika with 1 tablespoon hot paprika)

¼ cup olive oil

2 pounds skinless salmon fillet

1 cup chopped cilantro (1 bunch, stems discarded)

1. In a large deep skillet, bring water, carrots, garlic, and pepper to a boil, covered, over high heat. Uncover and add the consommé powder, salt, and 1 tablespoon paprika. Stir and replace cover. Reduce heat to medium/low and simmer for 20 minutes or until carrots are tender.

2. In the meantime, slice salmon into 5-ounce fillets. Combine olive oil and remaining tablespoon paprika. Let the paprika settle to the bottom of the cup.

3. When the carrots are tender, place the fish in a single layer on the simmering sauce. Drizzle the seasoned oil and paprika onto the fish; sprinkle with cilantro.

4. Return to boil over medium/high heat. Simmer over low heat, covered, for 40 minutes. Baste fish occasionally with sauce.

Yield: 8 servings

Tricks of the trade

Moroccan fish is generally spicy and hot; if you don't like it hot, then omit the hot peppers or hot paprika.

This dish is wonderful served on individual plates or on a platter, garnished with fresh cilantro and eaten with challah.

Marinated Fish with Onions

❧ MARINATED FISH WITH ONIONS ❧

Ceviche

I think every one of us has what I call "culinary memories," meaning something yummy from the past you can almost savor in your mouth just by thinking about it. That is how I feel about ceviche. It must be kind of how many Ashkenazi Jews feel about herring. Actually, ceviche *is* Latin herring! There are many types of ceviches, but this is the one I love the best because it is so simple. Keep in mind that even though bottled lime juice is convenient, fresh lime juice does taste better.

Tricks of the trade

This fish is cooked by the acids in the lime juice.

1½ pounds skinless white fish, washed, cut into 1" cubes

1½ cups bottled lime juice *or* the juice of 13 limes

¼ red onion, finely sliced

2 red hot peppers, seeded and sliced (optional)

3 garlic cloves, pressed or finely minced

2 teaspoons salt

½ teaspoon pepper

1 cup chopped cilantro (1 bunch, stems discarded), divided

1. Place fish cubes and lime juice into a large bowl.

2. Add onions, hot peppers (if using), garlic, salt, and pepper. Add half the cilantro and marinate, covered, for two hours in the refrigerator so the acids cook the fish and vegetables.

3. Garnish with fresh cilantro and serve very cold.

Yield: 6 servings

❧ WHITE DILL SAUCE ❧

Also an incredible addition to anything! Do you realize that any garnish makes your food look amazing? This sauce will add flavor, color, and the impression that you spend hours at work in the kitchen!

Tricks of the trade

I like using low-fat mayo…who needs the extra calories?

Some Kosher companies make individually frozen cubes of basil, cilantro, garlic, and dill. I use them when I don't have fresh herbs. You can also freeze your own herbs, using an ice-cube tray!

3 garlic cloves

½ cup chopped onions

8 tablespoons low-fat mayonnaise

¼ cup lime juice

½ cup chopped fresh dill *or* 1 tablespoon dried dill

2 teaspoons salt

¼ teaspoon pepper

1. Combine all ingredients, using a small chopper.

2. Serve on the side. Enjoy!

Yield: About 1 cup

❧ FISH STEW WITH A TAMARIND TWIST ❧

Choresh Galieh Mahi

When I started writing this book a few people I know came to me and said I should add this recipe. They all pointed to a Persian "goddess," Liora Youshaei. Liora is famous in all circles in our community because of this dish. Persians, Sephardim, Ashkenazim, kollel members, Aish rabbis—you name them…they all love this dish! It is sublime!

3 onions, chopped

8 garlic cloves, pressed or finely minced

¼ cup olive oil

1½ pounds skinless and boneless salmon, cut into 1"x1" cubes

1 teaspoon salt

¼ teaspoon pepper

2 cups water

1 (6-ounce) can tomato paste

1 teaspoon hot paprika (optional)

4 tablespoons tamarind paste *or*

4 tablespoons of lime juice

2 cups chopped cilantro (2 bunches, stems discarded)

1. In a 6-quart saucepan, sauté onion and garlic in olive oil over medium heat until onion begins to be translucent (about 1 minute). Place fish cubes on onions and cover the pot. Steam fish for 8 minutes over medium/low heat, without stirring. Add salt, pepper, and hot paprika, if using. Stir well.

2. Add water and tomato paste; stir until paste dissolves.

3. Bring to a boil over high heat. Reduce heat to low and simmer, covered, for 10 minutes, stirring occasionally.

4. Add tamarind paste or lime juice and cilantro; stir and simmer for 20 minutes.

5. Serve hot in a casserole dish.

Yield: 6 servings

Tricks of the trade

This dish is sublime when served with *kateh* (see page 185). Some Kosher companies make tamarind paste with a hechsher (kosher certification and symbol); see my website for more details. If you cannot find tamarind paste, just use lime juice instead.

Remind your guests this is to go over *Chelo* (white rice) (page 186).

∽ WHOLE STUFFED FISH WITH TAMARIND SAUCE ∽
(OR NOT!)

This fabulous fish is perfect to make Persians go "Bah, Bah"—which in Farsi means "delicious," or in Yiddish translates to "*gishmak*!" No matter where your guests are from, this dish is always a hit. I don't know what it is about the sight of an animal roasted whole that makes humans joyful…I feel it dates to prehistoric times! But it sure makes everyone's mouth water and everyone's tummy rejoice.

2.5 – 3-pound whole fish (sea bass, red snapper, or any whole white-fleshed fish)

canola oil spray

For the marinade

4 garlic gloves, crushed

½ teaspoon paprika

½ teaspoon salt

¼ teaspoon ground saffron

3 tablespoons olive oil

For the stuffing

Stuff Anything recipe, using rice only (page 133)

2 tablespoons tamarind molasses (optional) *or* 2 tablespoons prune butter combined with 2 teaspoons lime juice

Garnish (optional)

slivered almonds

slivered pistachios

1. Preheat the oven to 400°F. Line a large baking sheet with foil and spray with canola oil. Set aside.

2. Combine all ingredients for marinade and rub all over the fish, inside and outside. Set aside on prepared baking sheet.

3. In the meantime, prepare stuffing as directed on page 133. Add the tamarind or prune butter and lime juice and mix well.

4. Stuff the fish cavity with as much rice as possible. If some stuffing remains, simply wrap in foil and bake alongside the fish to use as a garnish.

5. Bake the fish, uncovered, for 30 minutes or until nicely browned and flesh flakes easily.

6. Serve on a large platter, garnished with remaining baked stuffing, almonds, and pistachios. Wait to hear the crowd's accolades at the wondrous sight!!

Yield: 6-8 servings

Tricks of the trade

This fish is better baked uncovered. However, if it starts to become too brown, cover with foil. You can stuff several small fish if you want to serve them individually or to make it easier to serve from a platter. If you decide you have no time or patience to make the stuffing below, simply stuff with sliced onions and peppers or any stuffing of your choice.

❦ SEARED FISH WITH SCALLIONS AND CILANTRO ❦

This recipe is a hit! It looks so appetizing! I love serving it at *sheva brachot* (meals during the week after a wedding) as the main dish. The *Chattan* and *Kallah* are often bombarded with chicken and beef at most *sheva brachot* and therefore adore the thought of scrumptious fish instead!

5 (5-ounce) skinless salmon fillets

1 teaspoon salt

½ teaspoon pepper

½ teaspoon paprika

1 tablespoon olive oil

canola oil spray

5 scallions, washed and thinly sliced

1 cup chopped cilantro (1 bunch, stems discarded) and additional for garnish

6 tablespoons canola oil, for searing

1. Preheat oven to 350°F.

2. Place fish fillets into a large bowl; season with salt, pepper, paprika, and olive oil. Set aside.

3. Spray a large baking pan or 9"x13" disposable baking pan with canola oil. Set aside.

4. Mix the scallions and cilantro and place into a shallow plate. Dredge each salmon fillet in the cilantro–scallion mixture, making sure to coat well on both sides. Set aside.

5. In a large shallow skillet, heat canola oil until a drop of water sizzles on contact. Sear the fillets in the oil until each side is toasted and brown (approximately 3 minutes). Turn fillets and sear the other side to achieve the same results.

6. Place the seared salmon fillets into the prepared baking pan and bake for 25 minutes.

7. Garnish with fresh cilantro and serve with rice, couscous, or mashed potatoes.

Yield: 5 servings

❧ PERSIAN CHICKEN SOUP ❧
WITH DEHYDRATED LIME AND CUMIN SEED
Ab Goosht

I cannot even start telling you how many old-wives' tales Persians believe! In fact, it is almost a rule that every time we visit my in-laws and go to gatherings, my mother-in-law would later come and wave a handful of salt over our heads and make us spit on her hand to keep the evil eye away!

My wonderful friend Liora Youshaei brought me this soup after I had one of my babies and she said it would make me have lots of milk. I thought it was one of those old-wives' tales. Surprisingly, not only was she right, but also I insist this soup has the powers of bringing one back to life!

1 skinless chicken, cut into pieces *or* 8 skinless chicken thighs
approximately 12 cups water
6 potatoes, peeled and quartered
1 cup yellow split peas

1 teaspoon cumin seeds
1 teaspoon turmeric
1½ tablespoons salt
5 dehydrated Persian limes (*lemon omani*), crushed *or* ½ cup lime juice

1. Place the chicken in an 8-quart saucepan and cover with water to 5 inches above the poultry (approximately 12 cups.) Bring to a boil. Use a small strainer or slotted spoon to remove the scum that rises to the surface.
2. Lower the heat and simmer, covered, for 30 minutes.

3. Add potatoes, split peas, cumin seeds, turmeric, and salt. Return to a boil; then reduce heat to low and simmer, covered, for 1 hour.
4. Add crushed dehydrated limes (*lemon omani*) or lime juice. Simmer for 30 minutes. Serve hot with Chelo (white rice), (page 186), if desired.

Tricks of the trade

I like using the dark meat of the chicken because it is so much more tender than the breast. The *lemon omani* really gives this soup the perfect Persian flavor, but you can certainly use lime juice instead.

❧ PERSIAN EGGPLANT SOUP ❧
WITH POMEGRANATE TWIST

I love to serve this soup on Rosh Hashana! It looks so beautiful garnished with pomegranate seeds and fresh basil. Persians will go crazy for this soup; you can trust me on that! Even my husband, who does not consider soup to be "real" food, loves it!

Soup

1 onion, chopped (about 1 cup)

4 garlic cloves, pressed or finely minced

¼ cup olive oil; plus 1 additional tablespoon if necessary

2 eggplants, peeled and cubed into ½" squares

2 teaspoons salt

1 (28-ounce) can diced or stewed tomatoes

1 tablespoon chicken consommé powder

1 teaspoon cumin

1 cup water

½ cup packed fresh basil leaves chopped or 1 tablespoon dried basil

½ cup pomegranate paste or 1½ cups pomegranate juice

Garnish

splash of lime juice

pomegranate seeds and/or basil leaves

1. In a medium saucepan, fry onion and garlic in the olive oil until translucent. Add the eggplant and sauté, stirring frequently. Add an additional tablespoon of oil if the eggplant absorbs all the oil. Keep the pot covered to help the eggplants soften without having to add more oil.

2. Add salt, diced tomatoes with their liquid, chicken consommé powder, cumin, water, basil, and pomegranate paste or juice. Return to a boil over medium/high heat; then lower heat and simmer, covered, for 30 minutes.

3. Process in the pot with an immersion hand blender for a creamy texture, or leave as is.

4. Garnish with fresh basil or a few pomegranate seeds.

Yield: 6 servings

You are what you eat

Pomegranates are amazing fruit! Did you know some claim that it was indeed a pomegranate and not an apple eaten by Eve (and shared with Adam) in the Garden of Eden?

It is brought down that pomegranates have as many seeds as there are commandments (*mitzvot*): a total of 613! I always wondered if this was true, but most of all I wondered if anyone had the patience to count them! Believe it or not, Alexander Haubold (who holds a Ph.D. in computer science from Columbia University) did a formal research study and counted the seeds of 206 pomegranates originating from 6 different countries. His research indicated that while the number of seeds in a pomegranate is correlated to its size, the average number of seeds from all 206 pomegranates was 613! (See the bibliography for more about this research.) Because of its many seeds, the pomegranate became a symbol of fertility and abundance, making it a staple at the Rosh Hashana table!

∾ PERSIAN NOODLE SOUP ∾

Ash'e Reshte

This is the most popular Persian soup. My husband's grandmother used to make the noodles for this soup from scratch! It was so much work. My mother-in-law suggested I should do the same; G-d bless her, there is no way. I buy ready-made noodles.

Back in Iran this soup was made in huge pots and shared with all the neighbors and friends in the event of a *simcha*.

Soup

1 onion, diced

3 tablespoons canola oil

dash turmeric

9 cups water

4 teaspoons chicken consommé powder (parve)

1 (15.5-ounce) can red kidney beans, drained and rinsed

½ cup lentils, checked and washed

1 (15.5-ounce) can chickpeas, drained and rinsed

2 teaspoons salt

¼ teaspoon pepper

1 cup chopped parsley (1 bunch, stems discarded)

1 cup chopped cilantro (1 bunch, stems discarded)

4 oz. (about 2 cups) linguine noodles broken into 2" pieces *or* Kluski egg noodles *or* Japanese fresh noodles

Garnish (optional)

caramelized onions (see page 188)

crushed mint

dollop of yogurt or Tofutti® sour cream

1. In a 6-quart saucepan, sauté onions in oil and turmeric until translucent. Add water, consommé powder, kidney beans, lentils, and chickpeas. Bring to a boil over high heat. Reduce heat to low and simmer, covered, for 20 minutes.

2. Add salt, pepper, parsley, and cilantro. Return to a boil; then lower the heat and simmer, covered, for 10 minutes.

3. Add noodles and boil until noodles are done (approximately 15 minutes).

4. Garnish with yogurt or *parve* sour cream, dried mint, and caramelized onions. If desired, you can also add little meatballs to this soup; see page 103 for the recipe.

Yield: 8-12 servings

Tricks of the Trade

Keep in mind that this soup can become dairy if you decide to add a spoonful of yogurt to it…it is divine. If you want to keep it *parve* to serve it at a meat meal and still want the whimsical white look of the yogurt, then add a spoonful of Tofutti® brand *parve* sour cream!

∾ PERSIAN SOUR GRAPE SOUP ∾

Ash'e Gureh

There is something about Persians and their obsession with sourness…you would never guess, because these people are just so nice and sweet! Would you believe I have spotted a few people, who will remain nameless, squeezing fresh lime right into a spoon and then into the mouth? Just like that! Does it surprise you they needed to make a sour soup?

Soup

6 cups water

2 teaspoons chicken consommé powder (*parve*)

¼ teaspoon turmeric

1 teaspoon salt

¼ teaspoon pepper

1 cup American rice (medium grain), checked and washed

1½ cup chopped parsley (1 large bunch, stems discarded)

1½ cup chopped cilantro (1 large bunch, stems discarded)

1 tablespoon dried mint

½ cup sour grape juice (*ab gureh*) *or* lime juice

½ cup whole *gureh* (optional)

Meatballs (optional)

1 pound ground beef

½ teaspoon salt

¼ teaspoon pepper

1 onion, grated

Garnish

caramelized onions (see page 188)

1 spoonful yogurt (optional for dairy meals) or Tofutti® sour cream, optional

1. In a 6-quart saucepan, bring water, consommé powder, turmeric, salt, pepper, and rice to a boil over high heat. Add chopped parsley, cilantro, and dried mint.

2. Return to a boil over medium/high heat. Reduce heat to low and simmer, covered, for 10 minutes, stirring occasionally.

3. Add sour grape juice or lime juice, and return to a boil over medium/high heat.

4. In the meantime, combine all ingredients for meatballs, if using.

5. Shape ground meat into balls 1" in diameter (the size of chestnuts) and drop into the soup. Cover and simmer for 25 minutes or until the meatballs

are cooked and the rice is soft. You may fry half the meatballs to use as garnish: Fry over medium heat until browned and cooked through.

6. Transfer soup to a serving bowl and garnish with parve sour cream, fried meatballs, and caramelized onions.

Yield: 6-8 servings

Tricks of the Trade

By the way, this little number is absolutely delicious with some *kotlet* (see page 137) dropped in it…if you are adding *kotlet*, don't add the little meatballs.

When preparing the meatballs, you can cook them all in the soup or, if you don't need so many, fry half for the garnish, or freeze half for another time.

Keep in mind that this soup can become dairy if you decide to omit the meatballs and add a spoonful of yogurt to it…it is divine.

If you want to keep it *parve* or serve it at a meat meal, but still want the whimsical white look of the yogurt, then add a spoonful of Tofutti® brand sour cream!

❧

A NOTE ABOUT GUREH

Gureh is a grape that was picked before it ripened, basically, a green grape. This small little fruit has a huge potential for sourness. Many Iranian dishes include *gureh*. Unfortunately, it can be hard to find it in America. Lime juice is an acceptable substitute for *gureh* juice. If you find fresh or frozen *gureh*, you can use it in this soup by adding ½ cup but skipping the juice. In fact, the way to know if you are at a "real" Persian household is by finding bags of frozen *gureh* in their fridge! Visit my website for internet resources.

∾ PERSIAN POMEGRANATE SOUP ∾

Ash'e Anar

Sometimes I make this soup without boiling the meatballs in it but cooking them separately instead. I often broil the meatballs to diminish the amount of guilt and oil frying takes. I then set them aside in a little individual dish for every guest to eat at leisure or prop them on a dollop of parve sour cream floating on the soup for decoration. This soup totally reminds me of Russian Borscht…what is it with Persians and Russian food?!

Soup

6 cups water

4 teaspoons chicken consommé powder (*parve*)

¼ teaspoon turmeric

2 teaspoons salt

1 cup American rice (medium grain), checked and washed

3 large beets, shredded

1 cup chopped parsley (about one bunch, stems discarded)

1 cup chopped cilantro (about one bunch, stems discarded)

1 tablespoon dried mint

2 cups pomegranate juice (or ¼ cup pomegranate paste mixed with ¾ cup water)

Meatballs (optional)

1 pound ground beef

½ teaspoon salt

¼ teaspoon pepper

1 onion, grated

Garnish

caramelized onions (page 188)

1 spoonful of yogurt (optional for dairy meals) or Tofutti® sour cream

Pomegranate seeds (optional)

1. In a 6-quart saucepan, bring water, consommé powder, and salt to a boil over high heat. Add rice and shredded beets.

2. Return to a boil over medium/high heat; reduce heat to low and simmer, covered, for 15 minutes, stirring occasionally.

3. In the meantime, combine all ingredients for meatballs, if using.

4. Add the parsley, cilantro, dried mint, and pomegranate juice or paste to the soup. Return to a boil over medium/high heat.

5. Shape the meat into balls 1" in diameter (the size of chestnuts) and drop into the soup. Cover and simmer for 20 minutes or until the meatballs are cooked through.

6. Transfer soup to a serving bowl and garnish with *parve* sour cream, fried meatballs, caramelized onions, and pomegranate seeds.

Yield: 6-8 servings

Tricks of the Trade

When preparing the meatballs, you can cook them all in the soup or, if you don't need so many, fry half for the garnish, or freeze half for another time.

Keep in mind that this soup can become dairy if you decide to omit the meatballs and add a spoonful of yogurt.

You Are What You Eat

Beets are just gorgeous in this soup! Beet juice will stain your skin, so be sure to wear gloves when making this recipe. Incredibly enough, it is this very crimson-purple pigment that has the fabulous power to fight colon cancer! Beets have so many health benefits, including protection against birth defects, anemia, and heart disease.

Fortunately, although they have the highest sugar content of any vegetable, they are also extremely low in calories…and who doesn't like that!

Poultry and Meat

❧ POULTRY AND MEAT ❧

In Iran, the word "vegetarian" is not listed in the dictionary. A person is meant to be a carnivore, whether he likes it or not. I was once invited to a Persian wedding before Sam and I were married. At the time, I was going through my vegetarian phase. Now, if you have ever been to a Persian wedding, you know that these people serve so much food you could feed a small country in Africa! They had appetizers on station after station of foods from different places in the world, just in case you hadn't made it to China or Japan last summer. They had a sushi station, complete with geisha and all. They had a burrito and taco station with a guy who was probably Mexican-born. They even had a caviar, vodka, and cucumber station so the Russians would not feel left out! It was all fine and dandy—until I saw a sight that I will never forget. There was the Greek station, with mussaka, gyros, and lamb. Not just any lamb. It was a baby lamb, roasted whole in a standing position! I just stood there, open mouthed and terrified, as the attendant sliced some of the "thigh," literally, for the lady standing beside me. I nearly fainted!

Just in case you were wondering, I had no choice but to give up being vegetarian. It was just impossible to survive around Sammy that way. So, I surrendered…not that I am complaining!

A NOTE ON CHOROSH…
Chorosh is a delicious Persian stew and probably the Persian food that is easiest to make—but the food that everyone thinks you spent the most time on! As long as you don't burn it, you almost cannot go wrong. Keep in mind all *choroshes* start and end the same way. They all start with sautéed onion, garlic, and any kind of meat. Then tomato paste, water, or lime juice is added. Then any of the interesting toppings is added. And last, you boil them up and forget about them for an hour…you will love the results every single time!

Everyone who knows me knows how much I enjoy having guests on Shabbat. In fact, if you are ever in Boston, don't hesitate to contact me and come over for a meal! I have had the pleasure of hosting people from all walks of life. So, trust me when I tell you that you must inform any non-Persian guest that *chorosh* goes on top of white rice. In fact, a rule of thumb is that it takes two to tango, so there is never *chorosh* without white rice! The only time you will see white rice without *chorosh* is when we are having a Persian BBQ. If you think Persian BBQ consist of meat, hotdogs, and bread, you are in for a surprise! A Persian BBQ is nothing less than white rice, kebab, roasted onions, tomatoes, and salad. That is the only time you will see white rice on its own. However, it is highly possible you will be offered a delicious purple tangy spice called sumac to sprinkle on your rice. From experience, after eating this spice, make sure to ask a good-hearted person if you have stuff left in your teeth, because I bet you will!!

Chicken Kebab, page 115

❧ CHICKEN IN TOMATO SAUCE AND SAFFRON ❧

The Ultimate Persian Chicken

This is the chicken my mother-in-law serves every single Shabbat dinner. It is so easy to make and so delicious! It freezes very well (as long as it is not embellished with potatoes) and children love it. The marinade works wonders on turkey as well, and…you guessed it…this is also what my mother-in-law's Thanksgiving turkey tastes like! It can also be made using whole chickens, Cornish hens, or even duck. If you want your birds stuffed, refer to the Stuff Anything á la Persian (*Tudeli*) recipe on page 133. I love serving this dish for *Sheva Brachot*, using whole chicken legs stuffed under the thigh skin.

2 whole chickens *or*
2 chickens cut in pieces *or*
1 whole turkey

Marinade
1 (6-ounce) can tomato paste
¼ teaspoon saffron powder
1 teaspoon garlic powder *or*
3 garlic cloves, pressed
¼ cup olive oil
1 teaspoon salt
¼ teaspoon pepper
1 lime, juiced *or*
3 tablespoons lime concentrate

Stuffing, optional
(see page 133)

1. Preheat oven to 350°F.
2. In a small bowl, combine all marinade ingredients.
3. Rub some marinade inside the inner cavity of poultry if using whole birds. Stuff the poultry with desired stuffing, if using. Rub the outside of the poultry with the marinade.

4. Bake, uncovered, for 1 hour. Cover with a sheet of foil to avoid burning the sauce and bake for 45 more minutes or until an instant-read thermometer inserted in the thickest part of the thigh reads 160°F.

Yield: 8 to 10 servings

❧ THE PERSIAN MATZAH BALL ❧

Gondy

I still remember the first time I tried a *gondy*. I was dating Sammy and we went to visit his Uncle Ray in San Francisco. His lovely wife, Homa, *A"H*, offered me a *gondy*. At the time I was going through the vegetarian phase in my life and politely declined. She said "You vegetarian? No problem, you can have my *gondy*…it is not beef, it is made of *torky*!" So, since I didn't want to hurt her feelings, I ate it. Do I even have to mention that was my last day as a vegetarian who only eats turkey?! Just so you sound *gondy*-savvy, Persians from Shiraz make it with ground meat and from Tehran with ground chicken breast. However, you can use whatever you like, even beef. This dish is unique to Persian Jews and it is served every Friday night at the Shabbat table.

For the broth

10 cups water

2 teaspoons salt

2 tablespoons chicken or onion consommé powder

¼ teaspoon turmeric

2 zucchinis, washed and cut into 1-inch chunks

1 (15.5 ounce) can chickpeas, drained and rinsed

For the meatballs

2 pounds ground beef, chicken, or turkey

1 large onion, liquefied

½ cup chickpea flour (if using turkey, substitute 1 cup instead)

2 eggs

3 tablespoons canola oil

½ teaspoon turmeric

1 tablespoon cardamom powder (optional)

1 teaspoon garlic powder

2 teaspoons salt

½ teaspoon pepper

1. In a 6-quart sauce pan, bring the water, salt, consommé powder, and turmeric to a boil.

2. Meanwhile, mix all meatball ingredients together. When water boils, drop in meatballs the size of golf balls. Bring water to a boil again and add the zucchinis and chickpeas. Cover and simmer for 45 minutes.

3. Serve in a casserole dish along with *chelo* (white rice) and *tadig* (crunchy crust).

Yield: approximately 40 *gondies*

Tricks of the Trade

You can use a small food processor or a grater to liquefy the onions. You can use a combination of yellow and green zucchini to give it color. If necessary, wet your hands to prevent the meat from sticking to your skin. If your guests are sensitive to chickpea flour, you can substitute matzah meal, which is my kids' favorite way of eating *gondy*!

By the way, this dish is also heavenly over couscous.

❧ CHICKEN KEBAB ❧

Joojeh Kebab

When I first tasted this absolutely moist and tangy chicken, I could not figure out what gave it that little "kick." When I learned how to make it, I found out it was lime! I never would have thought of marinating chicken in lime! In my country we marinate fish in lime. But, what a clever thing to do, indeed!

1.5 pounds boneless chicken (breast or dark meat) cut into chunks *or* 6 drumsticks

Marinade

1 teaspoon salt

¼ teaspoon pepper

3 cloves garlic

½ onion, grated

½ teaspoon saffron

½ teaspoon turmeric

3 tablespoons lime juice

1 teaspoon parsley flakes

¼ cup olive oil

metal skewers *or* wooden skewers soaked in water for 15 minutes

Place the poultry into a one-gallon ziptop bag. Mix all marinade ingredients and pour into the bag. Shake the bag to coat all the chicken and place into the refrigerator for as little as 20 minutes or as long as overnight.

From this point on there are 2 choices: grilling or broiling.

GRILLING

1. Preheat an indoor or outdoor grill to 400°F.
2. Thread the chicken chunks or drumsticks onto the skewers. Place on the heated grill. Cook each side for about 10 minutes or until no longer pink. You can also check for doneness with an instant-read food thermometer, which should read 160°F.
3. Remove the chicken from the skewers and divide into portions.

BROILING

1. Preheat the oven to broil.
2. Slice the pieces of chicken or drumsticks into chunks and thread them onto the skewers. Place the kebabs on a baking sheet that has been sprayed with oil. Place under the grill and cook each side for about 10 minutes or until an instant-read food thermometer reads 160°F.
3. Remove the chicken from the skewers and divide into portions.

Yield: 6 servings

You are what you eat

To lime or to lemon? That, my friend, is the question—at least in my mind! Limes are closely related to lemons but are smaller, green with a sour pulp, and a bit juicier. Limes are usually cultivated in tropical countries, so they are the most familiar to me. Lemons are larger, with bright yellow skins. In the past, lemons were used as cosmetics to make lips red and acquire a pale complexion.

You might think I am biased toward limes because I grew up consuming them, but research shows that while both fruits have antioxidants and anti-cancer properties, limes in particular contain flavonoids that can prevent the contraction of illnesses such as cholera. Not too bad for such a tiny sour fruit!

✑ PERSIAN GROUND BEEF KEBAB ✑

Kebab'e Kubide

What does a "regular" American mother send in a lunchbox to school? Maybe a peanut butter sandwich? Perhaps a tuna sandwich? Well, guess what my mother-in-law sent inside my husband's lunchbox? *Chelo Kebab*! (rice with *kebab*). When I learned about this I thought to myself… "How cruel! Was it not enough that the poor kid could not speak a word of English? Did she also have to humiliate him in front of the other kids with this crazy 'fresh-off-the-boat' concoction?" Well, after thoroughly investigating the matter, my husband confessed to having been a victim of constant threats at school. That is, constant threats from kids trying to convince him to switch his lunch with theirs…. I guess what I thought was child abuse ended up being what every kid in the school wanted! Today my kids eat *kebabies* galore and I have to beg them to use forks and leave a few behind for *Baba* (Dad, in Farsi)! You can also make *kebab* with ground turkey…much better for your health. *Kebabs* are served over *chelo* (Persian white rice) sprinkled with sumac powder, along with grilled tomatoes, onions, pickles, and Salad *Shirazi*!

Meat Mixture

2 pounds ground beef *or* turkey

1 large onion, grated

3 garlic cloves, pressed *or* 1 tablespoon garlic powder

1 tablespoon salt

½ teaspoon ground pepper

1 teaspoon turmeric *or* ½ teaspoon ground saffron

1 tablespoon olive oil

1 teaspoon *sumac* (optional)

2 teaspoons dried parsley flakes *or* ¼ cup fresh parsley, chopped (optional)

Basting Sauce

2 tablespoons olive oil

¼ teaspoon ground saffron dissolved in 1 tablespoon warm water

pinch of salt

1. In a large bowl, combine all meat mixture ingredients.

2. In a second bowl, combine all basting ingredients.

At this point you have 2 choices.

CHOICE #1: You can grill the *kebab*, shaping it onto ½-inch wide flat metal cooking skewers or by shaping them like Israeli *kebabs* (flattened ellipses) and placing them directly on the grill.

CHOICE #2: You can broil the meat in the oven in the shape of flattened ellipses or by pressing the meat into a lasagna pan and cutting it into strips before broiling it.

Directions for Choice #1:

1. Preheat the grill without the metal grid.

2. Make balls of meat the size of an orange. Pierce the meat with the skewer and shape firmly around the metal, flattening it to resemble a large flat sausage.

3. Place 3 inches from flame and grill for about 5 minutes per side, turning constantly to prevent the meat from falling into the flames. When ready, remove from the skewers with a piece of flatbread or a wrap. Baste with basting sauce and serve the meat immediately with white Persian rice (*Chelo*, see page 186).

If you don't have flat metal skewers, you can also shape the meat into flattened torpedoes and cook right over the grill grid for about 5 minutes per side. If you use an instant-read thermometer to check doneness, the temperature should read 140°F. Remove from the grill, baste with basting sauce, and serve immediately.

Directions for Choice #2:

1. Preheat oven to broil. Spray canola oil over a baking sheet if you want to shape the meat like flattened torpedoes or spray a 9"x13" lasagna pan if you want to cut it into strips.

2. Wet your hands and shape meat torpedoes. Make the ellipses about 2"x4"x1" each; these will shrink dramatically as you broil them. Place the torpedoes side by side on the baking sheet or press all the meat into the 9"x13" pan and, using a sharp knife, cut the meat into 1½-inch strips. This last method resembles the authentic *Kebab* and, once the meat has cooked, it will be easy to separate the strips from one another.

3. Broil close to the heat source for 7 minutes or until the meat has nicely browned. Take the baking sheet out, turn the *kebabs* over and continue cooking for 8-10 more minutes, farthest from the heat. If you used the 9"x13" pan, you do not have to turn the *kebabs* over. If you use an instant-read thermometer, the meat will be done at 140°F.

4. Baste with basting sauce and serve immediately with over white Persian rice (*Chelo*, see page 186).

Yield: 11 *Kebabs*

You are what you eat

Sumac is probably the most exotic and interesting spice I have ever encountered. It originates from Turkey; some varieties are from Italy. The shrub's petals and berries are dried up and ground into a purple burgundy powder with a strong acidic taste. When mixed with water it can be used for the same purposes as lime juice, but will tint everything, including your teeth, purple!

Tricks of the Trade

If using metal skewers, make sure they are dry and cold before pressing meat onto them. Do not use dirty skewers. I like using metal skewers with wooden handles because the metal gets very hot. Do not oil the metal skewers, as this will prevent the meat from attaching. Also, keep your hands wet when handling ground beef and it will not stick to your hands.

∾ MEAT KEBAB ∾

Kebab'e Barg

There is nothing more entrancing than a juicy piece of meat on the grill (as long as you are not vegetarian!). The well-known scent and the sight of the fire dancing and prickling the flesh makes it almost impossible to resist. Scents take us back in time. My husband insists that the reason man is so prone to grilling is because such practice was a must in the Holy Temple. "It is in our DNA!" he says.

2 pounds beef fillet or lamb fillet (do not trim the fat)

1 onion, grated

4 garlic cloves, pressed

¼ cup olive oil

½ teaspoon powdered saffron threads

2 teaspoons salt

½ teaspoon black pepper

1. Cut the beef into 1"x2" cubes and place inside a one-gallon ziptop bag or a medium bowl. Combine remaining ingredients and pour over the meat, mixing thoroughly. Marinate in the refrigerator, covered, for 4 hours or overnight.

2. When ready to cook, preheat an outdoor or indoor grill without the metal grid to 400°F or use the oven broiler.

3. If using the grill, thread the beef onto metal *kebab* skewers and cook for about 7 to 10 minutes per side, basting occasionally with the marinade juices and turning frequently. If broiling, place onto a greased baking sheet closest to the heat for 7 to 10 minutes per side until the meat looks browned or an instant-read thermometer reads 140°F.

Yield: 6 to 8 servings

You are what you eat

Garlic is another scent and taste that transports us to divinity! It originated in central Asia and it has been known since ancient times. In the past, garlic was not only used in the kitchen, but also utilized for its medicinal qualities. Even today, one can find homeopathic stores selling garlic drops to alleviate ear infections.

♣

Tricks of the Trade

Serve with white Persian rice (*Chelo*), along with grilled tomatoes, onions, pickles, and Salad *Shirazi*. It is customary to sprinkle *sumac* over the white rice to give it a mildly sour taste. Also, some people offer a basket with fresh herbs, including cilantro, tarragon, scallions, and steeped white onions. It might feel very weird to eat raw onions with your meat, but after a while you will love it!

❧ ISRAELI KEBAB ❧

In the Persian, and I dare to say, most of the Sephardic world, the ways of measuring a woman's greatness are what I would call a little unorthodox—in the whole sense of the word! Let me illustrate. My in-laws had come into town for Pesach and I really wanted them to eat well and feel welcomed. So, knowing they love Kebab, I decided to take a little risk and make them this version instead of the usual Persian Kebab.

There I was dutifully chopping my onions for this dish when all of a sudden my mother-in-law yelled "Ezzy, Ezzy, come see this!" (Ezzy is my father-in-law's nickname because his real name, well, just takes too long to pronounce). My heart just dropped! For a second I thought I was doing something very wrong! When Ezzy *Khan* (*Khan* means Mister) arrived at the scene, his jaw just dropped! "Do you know what this means?!!" he said to me. I stared at him; I look down and see my chopped onion…. "Oh my gosh, I don't know!" That is when he finally notifies me that, after over 10 years of marriage, I perfectly qualify to be the wife of a Persian man. In sum, my onions looked so perfectly chopped and were so tiny that I had finally passed the test!!

2 pounds ground beef

1 onion, very finely chopped (you can use a mini food processor)

2 teaspoons paprika

1 tablespoon garlic powder

2 teaspoons ground cumin

2 teaspoons salt

½ teaspoon pepper

3 tablespoons olive oil

⅓ cup fresh parsley, chopped (stems removed)

¼ cup flavored breadcrumbs

1. Preheat the broiler to high. Spray a baking sheet with canola oil.

2. In a bowl, combine the beef, chopped onion, seasonings, oil, parsley, and breadcrumbs.

3. Shape the meat into flattened "torpedoes" about 4 inches long and 1 inch thick. Place them right next to each other on the greased cookie sheet or disposable aluminum pan.

4. Broil close to the heat for 7 minutes or until the meat has nicely browned. Turn *kebabs* over and continue cooking for 8-10 more minutes, farthest from the heat. If you use an instant-read thermometer to check for doneness, the temperature should read 140°F.

Yields: 12 *Kebabs*

Tricks of the Trade

Even if that qualifies you to marry a Persian man, you do not have to chop this onion by hand; you can use a mini food processor. You can substitute 1 teaspoon dried parsley flakes instead of using fresh parsley. Also, I like using Italian Herbs Coating Crumbs® by Manischewitz, but any flavored breadcrumbs will do.

Keep in mind that the meat will not stick to your hands as long as you keep them moistened with water. At first, the "torpedoes" will seem huge, but they shrink dramatically while cooking.

Be very vigilant when making these *kebabs*; broilers are very good at burning food (not you of course!).

This recipe can be doubled and it freezes really well, whether it is cooked or raw.

❧ VEAL OR LAMB ROAST ❧
WITH DATES AND APRICOTS

This is definitely not a Persian recipe, but I had to share this one with you. I just had to! I love how easy is to make a roast—whether beef, lamb, or veal, a roast is the easiest thing to make and a real crowd pleaser.

Persians are not into roasts. Roasts take ovens to cook and back in Iran people preferred cooking over an open fire. Also, take it from my painful experience, Persians do not use knives as part of their cutlery. So, cutting a roast with a fork and spoon alone would be a bit of a challenge. However, now that I think of it, this roast is so tender that you will probably not need a knife!

The dates and apricots give it an exotic flair and look beautiful next to the juicy meat. Keep in mind this recipe is very versatile and you can adapt it to your mood. For the preserves, I love using apricot, but quince or strawberry preserves, or even date honey work beautifully. Also, instead of using Coke®, I have also used beer and even sweet *kiddush* wine! You can experiment and play around with choices… after all, isn't that the fun of cooking?

My friend Gila Cohen taught me how to make this roast…she is an Ashkenazi *tzadeket* married to a very lucky Bukharian man!

1 cup dried apricots	1 teaspoon salt
6 dates, pitted	1 teaspoon garlic powder
1 (3-pound) veal roast (*or* lamb *or* beef)	½ cup onion soup powder
	1 cup non-diet Coke®
1 cup apricot preserves	

1. Preheat oven to 375°F.

2. Place the apricots and dates into the middle of a medium-size roasting pan.

3. Rub the veal on all sides with the preserves, salt, garlic, and onion soup powder. Place the veal onto the dates and apricots. Pour the Coke® over the veal.

4. Place the veal into the oven and roast, uncovered, for 1½ hours or until an instant-read thermometer reads 135°F. If the pan looks dry, add some water, ½ cup, and cover with foil. Allow to stand for 10 minutes before slicing. Serve with Chelo (white Persian rice), dates, apricots, and pan juices.

Yield: 6 servings

Tricks of the Trade

Trying to cook a roast based on times given by a recipe or based on constant monitoring is a mistake that I have committed several times. It is nearly impossible to know when your meat is ready by those methods because there are so many variables, such as weight and temperature. Professional chefs can probably tell when something is done, but most of them still rely on instant-read thermometers. My instant-read thermometer is my best friend and makes sure my meat is always perfect. I give you approximate times in this recipe, but the best you can do is to get yourself an instant-read thermometer.

Also, if you are going to warm this roast over a *blech*, keep in mind to cook it one step below your doneness preference, since exposure to the heat will tend to overcook it. Visit my blog for a meat doneness chart.

∽ STUFFED CORNISH HENS ∽
WITH ROSE PETALS

This dish also doesn't really exist in Persian cuisine, but you know it totally sounds Persian! Even Persians will think it comes from an ancient Persian cookbook! In fact, I got this idea from the book *Like Water for Chocolate*, by Laura Esquivel, but reinvented it with a Persian flair. The rose petals look stunning next to the poultry, but I use them only as garnish. If you want to eat them you need to find edible roses, which come free of pesticides and you must also check the petals for bugs—way too much work for me!

4 Cornish hens *or* 2 whole chickens *or* 2 cut up chickens

Marinade

2 garlic cloves, pressed *or*
2 tablespoons garlic powder

1 teaspoon salt

¼ teaspoon pepper

1 teaspoon cardamom

1 teaspoon cinnamon

½ teaspoon cumin

3 tablespoons rose water

1 tablespoon lemon juice

¼ cup olive oil

Stuffing (optional)

3 tablespoons canola oil

1 onion, finely chopped

2 garlic cloves, crushed *or*
2 teaspoons garlic powder

¼ cup dried barberries (optional)

¼ cup currant raisins *or*
regular black raisins

2 tablespoons slivered almonds

2 tablespoons lime juice

pinch saffron powder

1 cup leftover rice

1 teaspoon salt

Rose Petal Sauce (optional)

1 cup pan juices

½ cup rose jam *or* quince jam

1 tablespoon olive oil

¼ teaspoon ground cinnamon

½ teaspoon garlic powder

½ lemon, juiced *or*
1 teaspoon lemon concentrate

Garnish

fresh rose petals
(from about 2 roses)

¼ cup slivered pistachios

Tricks of the Trade

You can use whole chickens or even ducks for this fantastic recipe! The stuffing is totally optional, but making it puts leftover rice to good use. In fact, whenever I have leftover rice I make stuffing right away and freeze it to have stuffing always available.

Visit my website for information on buying rose water, edible rose buds, and rose jam. However, you can use quince or apricot preserves instead of rose jam.

1. Preheat oven to 350°F.

2. Combine all marinade ingredients and rub all sides of the Cornish hens. Place into a dish and marinate for 2 hours, overnight, or not at all.

3. Meanwhile, make the stuffing. In a small saucepan, sauté the oil, onion, garlic, barberries, raisins, slivered almonds, lime juice, and saffron for 1 minute. Mix in the rice and remove from heat. Check seasoning and add ½ teaspoon salt if necessary. Stuff the poultry; there is no need to sew the cavities.

4. Bake, uncovered, for 1½ hours or until the meat is no longer pink and an instant-read thermometer reads 160°F when inserted the thickest part of the thigh. If the hens still look pale, put under the broiler for 5 minutes or until desired color is reached.

5. Mix all ingredients for the rose petal sauce and drizzle over the hens. Garnish with fresh rose petals and slivered pistachios.

Yield: 4 to 8 servings, depending on the size of the hens.

∾ PERSIAN MUSSAKA ∾

This dish became famous after it was referred to as "moose caca" in the movie *My Big Fat Greek Wedding*. Since I love *mussaka*, I came up with my own easy version of the dish. I then taught it to my personal assistant, Corina Lemus. Just in case you are wondering what a full-time mom is doing with a personal assistant…if you are a full-time mom you will agree that your babysitter IS your personal assistant! When it came time to write this book I had to ask her back for the recipe because she got so good at it that her version became better than mine!

Here I give you the "healthy" version I allow myself to eat. However, the fried version is indeed better. It is up to you to make the choice! If you want it fried, simply fry the breaded eggplants in a large skillet filled with enough canola oil. Make sure the oil sizzles at the touch of a drop of water before frying the eggplant so they don't absorb all too much oil. Here I go again…I can't stop thinking of everyone's arteries! When all your eggplants are fried, simply assemble the *mussaka*. You can make this dish vegetarian by omitting the meat and using only pasta sauce right from the jar…it is absolutely delicious!

You are what you eat

Eggplant, eggplant, eggplant! That is what you find all over my kitchen! Did you know that, in botanical terms, an eggplant is actually a fruit? The name derives from the early European types, which looked like eggs. Interestingly, eggplant originated in India. Choose eggplants that are firm to the touch, dark, shiny, and heavy.

Eggplant

5 eggs

2 cups flavored breadcrumbs, and some additional for garnish

½ teaspoon salt

½ teaspoon pepper

3 eggplants, peeled and cut lengthwise into ½-inch slices

Meat Sauce

(can be made vegetarian)

1 pound ground beef

1 tablespoon Lawry's seasoned salt®

1 teaspoon Ortega Taco Seasoning® (optional)

2 (24-ounce) jars pasta sauce

1. Preheat the oven to broil. Have ready 2 baking sheets sprayed with oil. Also, have ready a 9"x13" lasagna oven-proof dish sprayed with oil.

2. Break the eggs into a small bowl and slightly beat them with a fork; put the bread-crumbs, salt, and pepper in a separate shallow dish. Dip each eggplant slice in egg and then dredge in the breadcrumbs.

3. Place the breaded eggplant slices next to each other in a single layer on the prepared baking sheets and spray with oil. If you decide to use the frying method, simply fry in 1 inch of hot canola oil in a large skillet and skip to step 5.

4. Broil closest to the flame for 5 to 7 minutes or until the eggplant slices are slightly brown. Turn eggplant over, spray with oil, and broil until brown. Remove from the oven and set aside.

5. Set the oven temperature to 350°F.

6. In a 6-quart saucepan, brown the meat over medium heat. Add the seasonings and pasta sauce. Mix well. Set aside.

7. Make layers of eggplant and meat sauce in the ovenproof dish, starting and ending with sauce. Drizzle some breadcrumbs on top. Bake, uncovered, for 1 hour.

Yield: 8 to 10 servings

✿ VEAL OR LAMB CHOPS WITH PERSIAN PESTO ✿

I can still remember my in-laws' faces the first time I served this dish. The taste of this pesto is so Persian, thanks to the dehydrated lime (*lemon omani*), that they were totally fooled into believing I had found it in an ancient Persian cookbook! Let's just say it was concocted very far from Iran!

6 large veal chops

Pesto

4 garlic cloves

1 cup parsley, washed and chopped

1 cup dill, washed and chopped

½ cup olive oil

3 scallions chopped

1 lime, juiced *or*

2 tablespoons bottled lime juice

1 teaspoon salt

¼ teaspoon pepper

1 teaspoon ground cumin

1 teaspoon *lemon omani*
(dehydrated limes)

Optional Garnish

1 tablespoon *ziadune* (nigella) seeds *or* black sesame seeds

fresh parsley

1. Preheat oven to broil. Spray 2 large baking trays with canola oil. Set aside.

2. Using a small food processor, mix all pesto ingredients together until fully combined.

3. Place the chops on the baking trays and spread pesto on both sides. Reserve some pesto for garnish.

4. Broil the chops for 8 minutes. Carefully remove pans from oven, turn over the chops, and broil for 5 more minutes or until nicely browned.

5. Serve on a platter, garnished with some of the pesto sauce, ziadune seeds, and fresh parsley.

Yield: 6 servings

Tricks of the trade

You can substitute the veal chops for lamb chops or chicken breast. By the way, make extra pesto because your guests will like it so much they will want to dip every bite of veal in it!

✃ PERSIAN MEGA MEATBALLS ✃

Kufteh Sabsi

I have to be totally honest with you. I love all things Persian, but I used to dislike this dish. I am the type of person who eats with her eyes and feels food should look as pretty as it tastes. *Kufteh Sabsi* is not the most handsome dish, so I was always apprehensive when trying it. Well, they say you should not judge a book by its cover! *Kufteh Sabsi* is the ugly "cover" for a magnificent "book"!

1 cup rice

1 pound ground beef (if using turkey, add 1 tablespoon of oil)

1 teaspoon salt

½ teaspoon pepper

1 teaspoon garlic powder

¼ teaspoon turmeric

1 onion

1 bunch parsley (1 cup, stems removed)

1 bunch dill (1 cup, stems removed)

½ cup tarragon leaves

water as needed

1 tablespoon onion soup mix

1 tablespoon tomato paste

Garnish

lemon wedges

Tricks of the trade

If you are using turkey to make this recipe, add 1 tablespoon of oil to the mix. To prevent the meat from sticking to your hands, keep them moist with water.

1. In a medium bowl, mix the rice, meat, salt, pepper, garlic, and turmeric. Set aside.

2. In a food processor, liquefy the onion, parsley, dill, and tarragon together. Add to the meat mixture, combine well, and set aside.

3. Fill a medium skillet halfway with water. Add the onion soup mix and tomato paste. Bring to a boil over high heat. Make 2-inch diameter balls with the meat mixture. Carefully place the meatballs into the boiling water. The skillet should be big enough so that all the meatballs are about an inch apart, to give them space to expand. Do not stir.

4. Return to a boil. Cover; simmer over low heat for 45 minutes.

5. Transfer meatballs to a serving dish and garnish with lemon wedges. These meatballs are delicious served with warm bread and a drizzle of lemon.

Yield: 6-8 servings

❧ STUFF ANYTHING Á LA PERSIAN! ❧

Tudeli

This stuffing is so good that you are going to want to eat it un-stuffed! Don't worry, because the recipe gives you enough to stuff 3 peppers, 1 eggplant, 5 tomatoes, and your mouth a few times, too! Make sure to hollow the veggies with a melon baller or a tool named in Arabic *ma'vdeh*, which you can find at any Middle Eastern shop. Don't feel funny asking for this tool…the people at the store will love your accent!

3 tablespoons canola oil

1 onion, finely chopped

2 garlic cloves, crushed *or*

2 teaspoons garlic powder

1 pound ground meat

½ cup cooked or raw basmati rice

½ cup water (if using raw rice, substitute 1 cup instead)

1 teaspoon salt

¼ teaspoon ground saffron

¼ cup dried barberries (optional)

¼ cup currant raisins *or* regular black raisins

2 tablespoons slivered almonds

1. In a small saucepan sauté oil, onions, and garlic for 1 minute. Add the meat and stir well. Cook for 2 minutes or until meat is browned.

2. Add the rice (cooked or raw), water, salt, saffron, barberries, raisins, and almonds. If using cooked rice, stir for a few more minutes over medium heat. Remove from heat and set aside—you are ready to start stuffing! If using raw rice, cook for 5 to 6 minutes, covered, over medium heat or until rice is al dente. Turn off and set aside—you are ready to start stuffing!

Yield: Enough stuffing for two chickens, 2 ducks, or a turkey—or veggies, as noted above

Tricks of the trade

Feel free to play around and to add or substitute any of the last 3 ingredients for golden raisins, slivered pistachios, pine nuts, cut up dried peaches, or sour cherries. I always use leftover rice to make stuffing, even if I have nothing to stuff! I simply put it into a freezer bag and defrost it any time I need it! It is a great shortcut. You can make this stuffing vegetarian, obviously, by omitting the meat. Actually, I do often make this stuffing vegetarian because I love to use it to stuff fish. The barberries are optional, but really give it a delicious tangy flavor.

❧ CHICKEN WITH EGGPLANTS ❧

Joojeh Budemjune

You should have seen how long it took to make this chicken the "authentic" Persian style. *Momonbosorgue* taught me this dish and it took us the whole afternoon! She is the sweetest little lady and she really knows her food. I closely watched her while tending to this dish and measured her every move while she sang *basunak* (wedding songs).... However, there was no way I was going to spend all that time in my kitchen making just chicken! So, here is the non-Persian-bride-friendly version. It tastes the same!

1 chicken, cut in pieces

1 onion, finely chopped

½ teaspoon turmeric

1 tablespoon salt, plus extra for the eggplant

¼ teaspoon pepper

2 garlic cloves, pressed

½ cup water

1 eggplant, peeled and cut lengthwise into ½ inch slices

2 potatoes, peeled and sliced into ¼ inch rounds

¼ cup canola oil, for frying

1 (6-ounce) can tomato paste

¼ teaspoon saffron powder

½ cup *gureh* (sour grapes) (optional)

1. Preheat oven to 350°F.

2. In a 9"x13" roaster, place the chicken pieces skin side up and sprinkle with onions. Rub the chicken with turmeric, salt, pepper, and garlic. Add the water, cover with foil, and bake for 1 hour.

3. In the meantime, sprinkle eggplant with salt. When they have sweated (about 15 minutes), rinse and dry them. Fry the eggplant in a medium skillet until browned. Set aside.

4. Remove the chicken from the oven, uncover, and use food tongs to transfer the chicken pieces from the roaster to a bowl. Add the tomato paste and saffron to the chicken juices in the roasting pan and mix well. Add the potatoes, covering the bottom of the roaster. Return the chicken pieces, skin side up, and drape the fried eggplant slices on top. Drizzle with *gureh*, if using. Return to oven and bake, uncovered, for another hour.

Yield: 6-8 servings

Tricks of the trade

If you don't want to fry the eggplants, feel free to broil them. Although it is optional, *gureh* gives this recipe a great tangy taste and a very exotic look. *Gureh* is available at Middle Eastern shops, or visit my website for internet resources.

❧ PERSIAN MEAT LATKES ❧

Kotlet

I have to admit that even though I love my in-laws, sometimes there are "cultural" moments that can be a little embarrassing. Every time we leave LA to come back home to Boston, my mother-in-law makes these delicious meat latkes and packages them into incredible pita sandwiches that we take along on the flight. When mealtime arrives, the whole airplane start smelling like delicious *kotlet* and I can't stop blushing every time the people sitting in front look back between the seats to get a glimpse of what we are eating! I can see them salivating over our food.

These "meat latkes" are fabulous served inside pita bread along with babaganoush, chummus, and Shirazi salad. Also, these are a delicious accompaniment to the sour soup *"Ash'e Gureh"* on page 103.

It is important to note there is another version of this recipe called *Shami* (also known as *Tapalak* in Shiraz) that is round and calls for half the meat in this recipe. *Shami* was originally served in Iran as the afternoon snack before Shabbat began. To make *Shami*, simply follow the directions below, but omit half the ground beef and shape them round.

Tricks of the trade

These "meat latkes" are shaped like a flattened torpedo to differentiate them from their otherwise look-alike meatless counterpart, *kookoo sibzamini* on page 229.

Make sure to drape a few sheets of paper towel on the serving platter to absorb the extra oil after frying.

5 Yukon Gold potatoes (about 1½ pounds) with skin, washed

1 pound ground beef

½ onion, grated

1 egg

2 teaspoons salt

½ teaspoon pepper

1 teaspoon garlic

½ teaspoon turmeric

For frying

canola oil

1 cup breadcrumbs (optional)

1. Place the potatoes into a 6-quart saucepan and cover with water. Bring to a boil, cover, and simmer until potatoes are fork tender (about 25 minutes).

2. In the meantime, in a medium bowl, combine the ground beef, grated onion, egg, and seasonings.

3. Drain the potatoes; peel and mash them. Combine with ground beef until a smooth consistency is achieved.

4. Fill a medium skillet with ½ inch canola oil. Set over medium heat until the oil sizzles in contact with a drop of water.

5. Shape the beef/potato mixture into flattened-oval ellipses about ½-inch thick, 2 inches long, and 1½ inches wide. Dredge each *kotlet* in the breadcrumbs. Fry for 5 minutes on each side until a nice brown and crispy crust has formed. Transfer to a serving platter.

Yield: about 25 *kotlets*

❧ MOMONBOSORGUE'S DELICIOUS STUFFED GRAPE LEAVES ❧

دلمه

Dolmeh

These little bundles of joy are among the classic staples of Persian cuisine. I was extremely lucky to have my husband's grandmother, *Momonbosorgue Sultanat*, teach me the art of *dolmeh* making. She is a superb cook. *Duset daram Momonbosorgue!* You can find many types of canned *dolmeh* today, but nothing comes close to the sweet-and-sour taste of this recipe. Keep in mind Persians tend to mystify their cooking, but there is nothing to making *dolmeh*…. If I can do it, so can you!

For sauce

1 onion, finely diced

3 tablespoons canola oil

½ teaspoon turmeric

½ cup water

¾ cup pomegranate paste combined with 1 cup hot water and 3 tablespoons canola oil

For stuffing

1 (16-ounce) jar grape leaves, stems cut off

1 pound ground beef

1 onion, ground

1 bunch cilantro, washed and ground

1 bunch mint, washed and ground

1 cup pitted prunes, ground *or* ½ cup prune butter

1 cup American rice

1 cup raisins

½ teaspoon salt

¼ teaspoon pepper

⅓ cup red wine

½ cup pomegranate paste

3 tablespoons sour cherry preserves in heavy syrup (optional)

SAUCE

In a large saucepan, sauté diced onion, oil, and turmeric until translucent. Remove from heat and set aside.

STUFFING

1. In a large bowl, thoroughly combine all stuffing ingredients except the grape leaves.

2. Set one grape leaf on a flat surface, vein side up. Place 1 teaspoon of stuffing in the center of the leaf. Roll the leaf, starting from the stem edge and wrapping the stuffing within. As you roll, fold the sides of the leaf toward the center to prevent stuffing from pouring out, just as one would do when wrapping a Mexican burrito.

3. Repeat with remaining leaves and stuffing. Place *dolmeh* into the saucepan on top of the onions, seam side down, to prevent them from opening while cooking.

TO COOK

1. Return the *dolmeh*-filled saucepan to the stovetop over medium heat. Add ½ cup water and cover.

2. When steam starts rising, reduce heat to low and simmer for 30 minutes.

3. Pour mixture of pomegranate paste, hot water, and oil all over the *dolmeh*.

4. Return to a simmer and cook for 1 hour. Baste *dolmeh* occasionally with the juices.

5. Serve warm, at room temperature, or cold.

Yield: 8-10 servings

Tricks of the trade

There are shortcuts to making *dolmeh*. Cut grape leaf stems a bunch at a time. Use already washed and checked frozen cilantro and mint or even dried herbs. Instead of raw rice, use leftover white rice; it cuts cooking time by almost half! You can use a food processor to grind all the ingredients for the stuffing together (except the grape leaves, ground beef, and rice).

Since I am obsessed with organization, I find it helpful to set up a "stuffing station" on a clean surface (such as a cutting board or clean countertop). Place the saucepan with the stuffing near you so you can easily fill the *dolmeh*.

You can freeze *dolmeh* for your convenience. These can be served as an appetizer, a side dish, or meat entrée. And you cannot eat just one!

∾ STUFFED ARTICHOKE HEARTS ∾

These are so cute—I like calling them little soldiers! A couple of stuffed artichokes with sauce make a really nice appetizer or even great finger food for a party. They also look gorgeous in a platter as a main dish on the Shabbat table.

My friend Michal Bessler likes to make them with zucchini instead of artichoke hearts.

1 (16-ounce) bag frozen artichoke hearts

Baking Sauce

1 (8-ounce) can tomato sauce

½ cup water

½ teaspoon salt

½ teaspoon sugar

juice of 2 lemons *or* 6 tablespoons bottled lemon juice

Meat Filling

1 pound ground beef *or* turkey

1 heaping teaspoon *baharat or* allspice

1 teaspoon salt

1 egg

1. Thaw artichoke hearts. Preheat oven to 350°F.

2. Combine ingredients for baking sauce. Pour baking sauce into a 9"x9" oven-to-table casserole dish. Set aside.

3. In a small bowl, combine ingredients for meat filling. Shape meatballs and press each meatball into the concave side of the artichoke hearts. Custom size the meatballs according to artichoke size. If you have leftover meat, shape into regular meatballs.

4. Place each filled artichoke heart meat side up, on the tomato sauce in the prepared casserole dish. Add any meatballs formed from remaining filling.

5. Bake, uncovered, for 45 minutes. Do not baste with the tomato sauce; you want them to look as neat as possible. Serve with sauce under each artichoke or on the side.

Yield: 8 servings

Tricks of the trade

There are a few brands of frozen kosher artichoke hearts, so take advantage of this super-convenient product.

If you don't have energy to make the baking sauce, use ¾-jar of marinara sauce instead! I do that most of the time.

❧ LAMB WITH PRUNES STEW ❧

This is a super-popular dish I love making for both Pesach and Rosh Hashana. It fits Pesach perfectly because of the lamb offering our ancestors brought during the Exodus from Egypt, and it fits Rosh Hashana really well because it calls for honey. The prunes are incredibly delicious and become so tender that they melt in your mouth. Not to mention the obvious benefits of consuming prunes during Pesach! This stew is also very fragrant and handsome.

1 large onion, chopped

3 garlic cloves, pressed

3 tablespoons olive oil

4 pounds lamb stew *or* shoulder

1 cup water

½ teaspoon salt

¼ teaspoon pepper

½ teaspoon ground saffron

1 teaspoon dried ginger

¼ teaspoon nutmeg *or* allspice

2 cups pitted prunes

2 teaspoons cinnamon

1 tablespoon honey (optional)

Garnish (optional)

1 tablespoon toasted sesame seeds

1. In a 6-quart saucepan, sauté the onion and garlic in the olive oil until the onion starts to look translucent (about 1 minute). Add the lamb; cover and cook until it no longer looks red, stirring occasionally.

2. Add the water, salt, pepper, saffron, ginger, and nutmeg. Stir well. Return to a boil and simmer, covered, for 40 minutes.

3. Add the prunes, cinnamon, and honey, if using. Cover and simmer for 30 more minutes, stirring occasionally.

4. Garnish with sesame seeds and serve with rice, mashed potatoes or couscous.

Yield: 8-10 servings

You are what you eat

Prunes can help you lose weight—I am not even joking! Prunes are rich in soluble fiber. Foods rich in soluble fiber reduce the speed at which food leaves the stomach, making you feel satisfied for a longer time. Not to mention other benefits of consuming fiber-rich foods, such as prevention and treatment of Type 2 Diabetes.

❧

Tricks of the trade

I love using lamb shoulder or neck with bones because it looks better than just lamb stew.

For the garnish and any other dish that calls for it, buy already toasted sesame seeds…It will make your life so much easier!

❧ LAMB WITH SQUASH AND ZUCCHINI ❧

I served this dish at a Sukkah party I hosted for my friends from the Sephardic synagogue…There were people from all over, but I was worried because a few incredible Moroccan cooks were going to be there. Fortunately, they LOVED this dish! They went on and on talking about it and how it reminded them of good old Morocco….

1 large onion, diced

3 garlic cloves, pressed

3 tablespoons olive oil

2 pounds lamb *or* veal stew

6 cups water

2 teaspoons salt

½ teaspoon pepper

3 tablespoons onion soup mix

1 butternut squash, peeled and cut into 1-inch cubes

1 (15.5-ounce) can chickpeas, drained and rinsed

2 zucchinis, 1 yellow and 1 green, washed and cut into 1-inch chunks

¾ cup golden raisins

1 teaspoon pumpkin spice

1 teaspoon cinnamon

4 cups cooked instant couscous to serve

1. In a 6-quart saucepan, sauté the onion and garlic in the olive oil until the onion starts to look translucent (about 1 minute). Add the lamb or veal; cover and cook until it no longer looks red; stirring occasionally.

2. Add water, salt, pepper, and onion soup mix. Cover and simmer for 30 minutes.

3. Add the squash, chickpeas, zucchinis, raisins, pumpkin spice, and cinnamon. Cover and simmer for another 30 minutes or until lamb is tender.

4. Serve over a bed of couscous.

Yield: 8-10 servings

❧ ROSH HASHANA TONGUE ❧
WITH TOMATO AND MUSHROOMS
Zaban

You have to trust me when I tell you that I have eaten the grossest things in the world! Every summer my family would take a trip to Zaraza, the town where my father was born. Many members of the family would gather together at the family farm and cook many interesting dishes. Have you heard of a stew made from an animal that is related to rodents called capybara? How about turtle quiches? How about crocodile or iguana stew? I have eaten them all! However, I never, ever ate tongue! It was not until I became acquainted with Persians that I was put to the test of eating tongue once a year on Rosh Hashana.

The truth is that originally the most authentic dish to serve is a lamb's head, but it is very hard to find. Instead they use a tongue (part of the head)…What a relief, right?! We eat it to symbolize that we would be at the "head" and not the "tail." Well, I am glad it is not the other way around, since I don't even want to know what exactly we would have to eat instead!

Tongue Broth

1 beef tongue

water as needed

1 onion, diced

4 garlic cloves

Sauce

3 tablespoons olive oil

1 onion, thinly sliced

dash turmeric

1 (13-ounce) can mushrooms, sliced or stems and pieces, drained

1 cup reserved tongue broth

3 tablespoons tomato paste

½ teaspoon salt

¼ teaspoon pepper

fresh flat leaf parsley, for garnish

1. Place the tongue into a 6-quart saucepan and cover with water until it reaches about 3 inches above the meat. Add the onion and garlic and bring to a boil. Reduce heat and simmer, covered, for 3½ to 4 hours, checking periodically and using a small strainer or slotted spoon to remove the scum that accumulates on the surface of the water.

2. Remove tongue from broth and set aside to cool. Reserve one cup broth and set aside. To make sauce, sauté olive oil, onion, and turmeric in a skillet until onion is translucent. Add mushrooms and toss together for one minute. Add tongue broth, tomato paste, salt, and pepper, and cook for about 3 minutes.

3. While the tongue is still warm, peel the surface skin off and discard. Cut tongue into ¼-inch-thick slices and arrange on a serving platter. Pour the mushroom sauce on top and sprinkle with chopped parsley for garnish.

Yield: 6-8 servings

Persian Stews
and
Sephardic
Shabbat Stews

❧ EGGPLANT AND POMEGRANATE STEW ❧

Choroshté Budemjune

This is my sister's favorite stew. It calls for pomegranate paste, but I often use pomegranate juice because it is available today at any supermarket. Also, I broil the eggplant to avoid using large quantities of oil. In other words, this is a healthier version of the old favorite and tastes the same! This dish looks nice with long and skinny Chinese eggplant, but those are hard to find. You can use your regular eggplant and cut it in quarters lengthwise…now you've got an American/Chinese-looking eggplant in a Persian stew–talk about being international!! Remember, you can use any kind of meat you would like or even make it meatless for your vegetarian friends by using *seitan* (wheat "meat") instead of meat. I love using veal, but you can use lamb or beef.

3 large eggplants, peeled and quartered lengthwise *or* 7 Chinese eggplants, peeled (leave the stem end attached)

canola oil spray

1 large onion, chopped

3 garlic cloves, pressed

¼ cup olive oil

2 pounds stew meat

2 teaspoons salt, plus extra for the eggplant

1 teaspoon pepper

2 cups water

1 (6-ounce) can tomato paste

¾ cup pomegranate paste *or* 2 cups of pomegranate juice

8 ounces (½ of a 16-ounce bag) frozen cut-up green beans (optional)

1. Preheat the oven to broil.

2. Place the eggplant into two 9"x13" aluminum pans. Spray with oil and rub with 1 tablespoon of salt. Place under the broiler and brown for 10 minutes. Turn over and broil 10 more minutes to make sure most sides of the eggplant become brown. Remove from the oven and set aside.

3. In a 6-quart saucepan, sauté onion and garlic in olive oil until onions start to become translucent (about 1 minute). Add the meat; cover and cook until meat no longer looks red, stirring occasionally. Add salt and pepper.

4. Add water, tomato paste, pomegranate paste or juice, and frozen green beans, if using. Simmer, covered, for 20 minutes.

5. Uncover and add the eggplant, reserving 3 slices for garnish. Simmer for additional 45 minutes or until meat is tender. Serve hot in a casserole dish and drape the remaining eggplant on top for garnish.

Yield: 8-10 servings

You are what you eat

Last time I went to LA, my father-in-law started telling my husband how pomegranate prices are rising. "Saman *joon, Amrikayai* (Americans) have finally discovered what we have known for ages about pomegranates! Now they are so expensive! It is not fair!" What a "comeback" for pomegranates! What PR! Growing up, our neighbors had a pomegranate tree, and we were constantly eating the yummy fruit while my mother was constantly reminding us not to stain our clothes.

Pomegranates were always popular in Judaism. There is no Rosh Hashana that can go by without a pomegranate. Not only that, the Kohen Gadol's outfit had decorative pomegranates embedded in its hem. Even the Greeks agreed that it was a symbol of fertility and love due to its many seeds. It was mostly used as medicine until the Renaissance and then started appearing in recipes in European cookbooks at the time of Louis XIV. Believe or not, research reveals pomegranate juice has one of the most powerful levels of antioxidants compared to any other juice, even wine!

❧ HERB STEW WITH DEHYDRATED LIMES ❧

Chorosh Sabsi

When I first saw this dish being served at my in-laws' home I started to panic. I thought it looked awful and I was convinced it must taste awful too. After all, this is a green stew with black dried limes floating in it. I thought this was the Persian version of *Green Eggs and Ham*. To my surprise, this dish was fabulous! In fact, the smell of this dish brings me good memories, since its aroma has permeated my mother-in-law's kitchen. The best part is that, if you have dehydrated greens (*sabsi*) in cans, this is probably the easiest stew (*chorosh*) around!

1 large onion, chopped

3 garlic cloves, pressed

¼ cup olive oil

2 pounds stew meat

2 teaspoons salt

1 teaspoon pepper

1 (2-ounce can) dehydrated greens (*sabsi*) *or*

    2 bunches parsley

    2 bunches cilantro

    1 leek, chopped

    ½ bunch mint

    ½ cup spinach (optional)

2 stalks celery, finely diced

½ cup lime or lemon juice *or* the juice of 3 limes

3 cups water

5 whole dehydrated limes (*lemon omani*), pierced

1 (15-ounce) can red kidney beans, drained and rinsed (optional)

⅓ cup *gureh* (sour grapes) (optional)

1. In a 6-quart saucepan, sauté onion and garlic in olive oil until the onion starts to become translucent (about 1 minute). Add the meat; cover and cook until meat no longer looks red, stirring occasionally. Add salt and pepper.

2. If using fresh herbs, grind in a food processor.

3. Add to the saucepan the dehydrated greens (no need to soak) or ground fresh greens, celery, lime juice, water, dehydrated limes, kidney beans, and *gureh*, if using. Bring to a boil; then simmer, covered, for 1½ hours or until meat is tender. Serve hot in a casserole dish.

Yield: 8-10 servings

Tricks of the trade

Keep in mind that *Shirazis* do not add red kidney beans, while *Tehranis* do. I personally add them for a splash of color! Also, the dehydrated limes give it a great taste and an authentic look, but you can get away with not adding them too. If all you have available are ground dehydrated limes, use 1 tablespoon instead. You can order dehydrated limes online. See kosherpersianfood. com for internet resources.

❧ QUINCE STEW ❧

Chorosht'e Be

My mother-in-law makes this stew almost every Shabbat because it is my sister-in-law's favorite! Whenever I buy quinces, I have to hide them because my children love to eat them raw! This fruit is not really meant to be eaten raw…it is meant for jams and stews. I guess my kids must be "hard-core" Persians!

The quince tree originates from Iran and Caucasus. The Romans used its oil for perfume, while the Greeks enjoyed it cooked.

1 large onion, chopped

3 garlic cloves, pressed

¼ cup olive oil

2 pounds stew meat

2 teaspoons salt

1 teaspoon pepper

3 cups water

1 (6-ounce) can tomato paste

2 quinces (do not peel; just slice like an apple and make sure to remove the entire core)

¼ cup lime or lemon juice *or* the juice of 3 limes

¾ cup pitted prunes

2 potatoes, peeled and diced

1. In a 6-quart saucepan, sauté the onion and garlic in olive oil until the onion starts to become translucent (about 1 minute). Add the meat; cover and cook until meat no longer looks red, stirring occasionally. Add salt and pepper.

2. Add water, tomato paste, lime juice, quince, prunes, and potatoes. Simmer, covered, for 1 hour, stirring occasionally.

3. Serve hot in a casserole dish.

Yield: 8-10 servings

❦ WALNUT STEW ❦

Chorosht'e Fesenjune

I consider this dish to be a delicacy in Persian cuisine. You can expect to eat it at fancy weddings and special occasions. However, when Sammy first introduced me to it I was appalled to taste it. It looked like someone had a bathroom accident on my plate! I honestly thought he was playing a bad joke on me. I know this is exactly what you will think when you see this dish and, if you are Persian, you know exactly what I mean. Be brave, give it a try, and—if you love walnuts—you are in for a fabulous surprise! If you can't find ground walnuts, you can grind them in a food processor; see below right for instructions.

1 large onion, chopped

3 garlic cloves, pressed

¼ cup olive oil

2 pounds stew meat

2 teaspoons salt

1 teaspoon pepper

¾ cup pomegranate paste *or*

2 cups pomegranate juice

2 cups water

2 (4-ounce) bags ground walnuts (about 2 cups ground walnuts)

½ teaspoon saffron powder

whole walnuts and pomegranate seeds for garnish (optional)

1. In a 6-quart saucepan, sauté the onion and garlic in olive oil until the onion starts to become translucent (about 1 minute). Add the meat; cover and cook until meat no longer looks red, stirring occasionally.

2. Add the pomegranate paste or juice, water, ground walnuts, and saffron. Cover and simmer for 1½ hours or until meat is tender.

3. Serve hot in a casserole dish. You can garnish with whole walnuts and pomegranate seeds.

Yield: 8-10 servings

You are what you eat

The latest medical studies show that nuts in general, but especially walnuts, are extremely healthful. In several studies nuts have been shown to lower cholesterol levels. You might be thinking…but nuts are fattening! You are right, but the fat in them is mono and polyunsaturated and rich in Omega-3 acid. Not only are nuts good fat, but they are also high in fiber and vitamin E!

♣

Tricks of the trade

Make sure to check any nuts you are going to use to avoid ruining your dish with rancid nuts. It is best to store nuts in the freezer or refrigerator.

If you cannot find ground walnuts (or any ground nut), first bring whole nuts to room temperature and then grind them in the food processor with a tablespoon of sugar to avoid forming a nut paste.

Raw nuts do not need kosher certification. For more information, contact your local rabbi.

❧ OKRA AND TOMATO STEW ❧

Chorosht'e Bamieh

A lot of people have never tasted okra. Not because there is anything wrong with it, but because most people don't know how to cook it. I belonged to the last group. I always wondered what to do with this funky-looking veggie. You must know, this stew is not only exotic-looking but also very easy to make!

1 large onion, chopped

3 garlic cloves, pressed

¼ cup olive oil

2 pounds stew meat

2 teaspoons salt

1 teaspoon pepper

4 cups water

1 (6-ounce) can tomato paste

1 large tomato, diced

½ cup bottled lime juice *or* juice of 3 fresh limes

1 (16-ounce) bag frozen whole okra

1. In a 6-quart saucepan, sauté the onion and garlic in olive oil until the onion starts to become translucent (about 1 minute). Add the meat; cover and cook until meat no longer looks red, stirring occasionally. Add salt and pepper.

2. Add water, tomato paste, diced tomato, lime juice, and frozen okra. Cover and simmer for 1½ hours or until meat is tender and okra is still whole. Serve hot in a casserole dish.

Yield: 8-10 servings

You are what you eat

Okra is also known as "lady's fingers" due to its likeness to, I guess, lady fingers! The word *bamieh* is actually an Arabic word with French origins (as in *boudoir* biscuits), which takes us back to the large influence of French in the Farsi language. The right time for picking okra is before it ripens. In the past, okra seeds were used as a substitute for coffee! Okra has the quality of thickening any substance with which it is cooked if added at the beginning of the cooking process. If added at the end, it will remain crisp and intact.

❦

Tricks of the trade

I like using baby okras for this stew. I find they are less likely to fall apart while cooking. Keep in mind that you do not need to defrost the okra before using it. It will cook beautifully in the stew and defrost in the juices to perfection!

❧ YELLOW SPLIT PEA STEW ❧

Chorosht'e Lape

Probably one of the most popular Persian stews, *Chorosht'e Lape* is a meal in itself! It has an extraordinary texture and a delicious tangy taste. It is sublime on a canvas of white rice and sprinkled with very thin French fries (which you can make from scratch if you have the time…but since I don't, I use canned potato sticks instead).

1 large onion, chopped

3 garlic cloves, pressed

¼ cup olive oil, plus 1 tablespoon extra to fry the split peas

2 pounds stew meat

2 teaspoons salt

1 teaspoon pepper

2 cups yellow split peas

1 teaspoon ground cinnamon

4 cups water

1 (6-ounce) can tomato paste

1 large tomato, diced

5 whole dehydrated limes (*lemon omani*) (3 pierced and 2 crushed)

½ cup bottled lemon juice *or* the juice of 3 fresh limes

½ cup canned potato sticks or narrow French fries (optional)

1. In a 6-quart saucepan, sauté the onion and garlic in olive oil until the onion starts to become translucent (about 1 minute). Add the meat; cover and cook until meat no longer looks red, stirring occasionally. Add salt and pepper.

2. In the meantime, sauté split peas in 1 tablespoon of oil for 1 minute. Add the cinnamon and mix well. Set aside.

3. Uncover the browning meat and add the water, tomato paste, diced tomato, dehydrated limes, lime juice, and sautéed split peas. Cover and simmer for 1½ hours or until meat is tender and split peas are soft but still whole.

4. Serve hot in a casserole dish. Garnish with potato sticks or French fries, if desired.

Yield: 8-10 servings

Tricks of the trade

Remember how a Persian's cook reputation can be ruined by over-cooking basmati rice? Well, if a Persian cook's yellow split peas are all mushy and shapeless, that reputation is down the drain as well! But there is nothing to worry about, since the trick of whole-yet-tender split peas is simply sautéing them in a bit of oil with a dash of cinnamon. I know what you are thinking… don't try it with the rice…the trick doesn't work there!

❧ MINI MEATBALLS AND ZUCCHINI STEW ❧

Chorosht'e Gime ba Gorje Farangi

This is my husband's favorite stew! Of course you know that the way to a man's heart is through his stomach, so I was very determined to learn this stew and make my way into his heart—and so I could get him to buy me a really nice bracelet I fell in love with at the mall! This dish can be eaten with bread or rice.

Stew

1 onion, diced

4 garlic cloves, pressed

¼ cup canola oil

1 (28-ounce) can stewed tomatoes

2 potatoes, peeled, cut into one-inch dice

2 zucchini cut into one-inch-thick slices

1 tablespoon salt

½ teaspoon saffron

2 limes, juiced, and lime wedges to garnish

Meatballs

1 pound ground beef

1 onion, ground or very finely chopped

½ teaspoon salt

¼ teaspoon pepper

1. In a 6-quart saucepan, sauté the onion and garlic in oil until translucent. Add the stewed tomatoes with their liquid, potatoes, and zucchini; stir well. Simmer, covered, for 15 minutes.

2. In the meantime, make the meatball mix by combining all ingredients very well.

3. Uncover the saucepan and add the salt, saffron, and lime juice. Mix well. Bring back to a boil and shape meatballs 1 inch in diameter (the size of chestnuts). Gently drop onto the surface of stew, making sure not to stir it at all or they will lose their shape.

4. Reduce the heat and simmer, covered, for 10 minutes. Uncover and gently stir the stew, detaching the mini meatballs from one another. Continue to cook, covered, for 20 minutes or until the meatballs are fully cooked and the vegetables are whole but tender.

Yield: 6-8 servings

Tricks of the trade

Interestingly, it happens that my mother-in-law, also known as Superwoman, shapes the mini-meatballs for this stew 2 at a time! I was very impressed and actually learned to do it too—it really cuts the time in half! Simply place two portions of meat the size of chestnuts in your left palm (if you are a righty), one in the middle of the palm and another over the middle finger. Roll both meatballs simultaneously using your right hand over your left hand as usual.

❧ VEAL STEW WITH BASIL AND PARSLEY ❧

I am very blessed to have what they call a "Pesach Kitchen." Since not many people I know have one, I let my friends borrow it. One year my good friend Celine Sellam was about to give birth and needed to get Pesach done beforehand. So, she came to cook in my Pesach kitchen. The aromas coming from her cooking were so incredible that I had to come down there and "check" on her! This dish is one of her incredible array of Sephardic dishes…did I mention she is Ashkenazi?! Ever since, this dish is part of my Pesach Seder and many Shabbat meals all year round. It is also great with lamb, and I have even made it using cubed leftover roast.

1 large onion, chopped

3 garlic cloves, pressed

¼ cup olive oil

2 pounds veal *or* lamb stew

2 teaspoons salt

1 teaspoon pepper

1 (16-ounce) can stewed crushed tomatoes

2 large tomatoes, peeled and diced

3 dried bay leaves

1 cup chopped fresh basil, stems discarded *or* ⅓ cup dried basil

1 cup chopped fresh parsley, stems discarded *or* ⅓ cup dried parsley flakes

1. In a 6-quart saucepan, sauté the onion and garlic in olive oil until the onion starts to become translucent (about 1 minute). Add the meat; cover and cook until meat no longer looks red; stirring occasionally. Add salt and pepper.

2. Uncover and add canned tomatoes with their liquid, diced tomatoes, and bay leaves. Cover and simmer for 40 minutes.

3. Uncover and add the fresh basil and parsley, reserving some for garnish. Simmer for 10 more minutes. Remove bay leaves and serve warm over white rice or couscous and garnish with parsley and basil.

Yield: 6-8 servings

One Friday afternoon, a young Jewish man named David went to visit Rabbi Zuber to witness all his pre-Shabbat preparations. David was well versed in spiritual techniques such as meditation and other esoteric wisdoms, but not in Judaism. He had been told there was much spirituality involved in his own religion, so he decided to find out. He thought that he would find Rabbi Zuber preparing for Shabbat while in a deep trance, possibly floating in mid-air, legs crossed and hands clasped. When he arrived at the Zuber's residence, he enthusiastically asked Rabbi Zuber what kind of extracorporeal prepping was necessary for the enjoyment of such a holy day. Rabbi Zuber looked him in the eye, reached out his hand, and handed him a potato peeler with a wink. "David, we prepare for the holy Shabbat by making good old *cholent*!"

Our Ashkenazi brothers call this magical concoction *cholent*. In the Sephardic world, it has many names and many different recipes, but it is mostly known as *Hamim*, which means *hot* in Hebrew. Shabbat stews are a real treat for the senses. There is nothing like the aroma and warmth of this stew on a cold winter Shabbat morning—not to mention the hypersomnia qualities that seem to send everyone to take the coveted Shabbat nap!

Shabbat stews originated as a defense against rebellion. The Torah states that Jews are not allowed to kindle a flame on Shabbat. However, according to the Oral Law, the Torah does not prohibit using a flame which was ignited before Shabbat began to keep cooked foods warm (since we are not permitted to cook on Shabbat). Nevertheless, at the time of the Second Temple, a sect of Jews called Sadducees rebelled by disregarding the Divine origin of the Oral Law. These people would sit all Shabbat in cold and darkness, and eat cold and sad foods. The rest of the Jews defended the Oral Law by consuming warm stews on Shabbat that were left to cook overnight on a covered fire that was lit before Shabbat started. As you can imagine, there are no Sadducees around anymore!

In Iran, *Chale Bibi* (*Shirazi cholent*) was left over the covered flames of a brazier. The pot was covered with several blankets to keep the food warm as the flames died down and it was left unhandled until the moment came to serve it for Shabbat lunch. In many families, this was the main dish, served along with several smaller side dishes, lavash bread, herbs, and fruits. Today, thanks to modern equipment, we use slow cookers and *Chale Bibi* became one of the many side dishes for a Shabbat lunch feast.

☙ TURKEY SHABBAT STEW ☙

Halim

This is a typical Persian porridge served hot with sprinkle of cinnamon on top, and two little bowls on the side, one filled with sugar and the second with caramelized onions.

This is by far one of my favorite Shabbat stews (I have a sweet tooth), not only because of the sugar but also because wheat is so healthy! Wheat is actually healthier than rice and couscous. The difference between wheat and bulgur is that bulgur is wheat that has been "precooked," making it easier and faster to cook, giving it a nutty flavor and a longer storage life. However, since Shabbat stews cook for so long I decided to use cracked wheat (broken-up wheat grains) instead of bulgur.

2 cups cracked wheat

2 turkey thighs (2 pounds), whole and without skin

1 cup chopped leeks

9 cups water, divided

1 teaspoon cumin

2 teaspoons salt

Garnish

sugar

cinnamon

Caramelized Onions (see page 188)

1. About 4 hours before Shabbat, place the cracked wheat, turkey, leeks, 5 cups water, cumin, and salt in a 6-quart slow cooker. Turn cooker on high and cook, covered, until right before Shabbat.

2. Before lighting Shabbat candles, check seasoning and add 4 more cups hot water.

3. Reduce temperature to low, cover, and continue cooking over low heat until Shabbat lunch (about 18 to 20 hours).

Yield: About 6 servings

Tricks of the trade

Note that when adding water to the slow cooker before Shabbat, the water should be quite hot so that the slow cooker doesn't crack!

❧ SHIRAZI SHABBAT STEW ❧

Chale Bibi

This Shabbat stew literally means "aunt and grandmother," denoting that in this stew there is a little of everything. Perhaps the name derived from the fact that during Shabbat many Persian families get together—aunts, grandmothers, cousins, more cousins; here again—a little of everything. *Chale Bibi* is the classic Shirazi Shabbat stew. It tastes more like regular Ashkenazi *cholent* than any other Sephardic Shabbat stew I have tried.

½ cup red kidney beans

½ cup lentils

½ cup mung beans *or* green split peas

2 turnips, peeled and quartered

½ small red cabbage, shredded (about 2 cups)

½ cup American rice or barley

3 eggs, whole (optional)

1 pound stew meat

6 cups water, or more as needed

1 tablespoon salt

1 teaspoon pepper

½ teaspoon turmeric

1. About 4 hours before Shabbat, place the kidney beans, lentils, mung beans or green split peas, turnips, cabbage, rice, meat, and eggs (if using) into a 6-quart slow cooker.

2. Add 6 cups water, salt, pepper, and turmeric.

3. Cook on high, covered, until right before Shabbat starts.

4. Before lighting Shabbat candles, check seasoning. Add more water if the water has mostly cooked out and the stew looks dry. Turn heat to low, and cook until Shabbat lunch (about 18 to 20 hours.)

Yield: about 8 servings

You are what you eat

Never heard of mung beans before? You might recognize them as bean sprouts. Yes, these are the dried beans from which bean sprouts originate.

This recipe calls for red cabbage, which is actually more healthful than the white variety. Red cabbage is regarded as a super-healthful cruciferous vegetable! In only 3½ ounces it contains nearly 100% of the recommended daily allowance of vitamin C.

Also, as you can see, this recipe calls for turnips instead of potatoes. I find this to be ideal because this root is not only a great low-carbohydrate substitute for potatoes, but, when cooked, it looks exactly the same!

Tricks of the trade

Note that when adding water to the slow cooker before Shabbat, the water should be quite hot so that the slow cooker doesn't crack!

❧ PERSIAN CHICKEN SHABBAT STEW ❧

Code

The first time I tried this dish, I could not have enough of it. It is absolutely delicious, and my children love it. It is so much more merciful to one's stomach than *cholent*, and it still tastes delicious when reheated. I used to throw away so much *cholent* after lunch it hurt! Today, all I make is *Code*, nothing gets trashed, and everyone (including our tummies) is happy!

1 whole broiler chicken (about 3-4 pounds), without skin

1 (15.5-ounce) can chickpeas *or* ½ cup raw chickpeas

4 garlic cloves, chopped

1 (15-ounce) can tomato sauce

1½ cups basmati rice

4 cups water, or more as needed

1 tablespoon salt

1 teaspoon pepper

½ teaspoon turmeric

½ teaspoon cumin (optional)

1. About 2 hours before Shabbat, place the whole skinless chicken in a 6-quart slow cooker, breast side up.

2. Add the chickpeas, garlic, tomato sauce, rice, water, and spices.

3. Cook on high until right before Shabbat.

4. Before lighting Shabbat candles, check seasoning and add more water if the water has mostly cooked out and the stew looks dry. Reduce temperature to low and cook until Shabbat lunch (about 18 to 20 hours).

Yield: about 6 servings

You are what you eat

Turmeric is probably the most widely used spice in Persian cookery. Did you know turmeric is a root? It actually looks very much like ginger but with bright yellow flesh and dark skin. When dried it is reduced to a powder also known as curcumine. Turmeric is used in many countries—mostly in India, Iran and Southeast Asia—and it is one of the ingredients of curry powder. It has an earthy flavor, and it makes everything bright yellow, even your fingers. So be careful!

❧

Tricks of the trade

Note that when adding water to the slow cooker before Shabbat, the water should be quite hot so that the slow cooker doesn't crack!

❧ MOROCCAN SHABBAT STEW ❧

Dafina

This recipe is from my friend Jenny Ohana, a "non-Moroccan bride" who really mastered her beloved's natal food! *Dafina* is unlike any Ashkenazi *cholent* because the ingredients are set up separately in the slow cooker and served separately as well. I love this dish so much! *Dafina* is a complete meal that is not only beautiful to the eyes, but absolutely delicious to the stomach. Although it might seem the list of ingredients is overwhelming, it is surprisingly easy to make. The meatloaf bundle is completely optional and the recipe can easily be made vegetarian. Most people add eggs that cook along with the stew to a beautiful tan perfection and a creamy yolk.

Tricks of the trade

Note that when adding water to the slow cooker before Shabbat, the water should be quite hot so that the slow cooker doesn't crack!

Stew

¼ cup canola oil

1 cup chickpeas *or* 1 (15.5-ounce) can chickpeas, drained and rinsed)

4 small Yukon Gold potatoes, peeled and quartered

2 sweet potatoes, peeled and quartered

4 dates

3 whole eggs (optional)

2 tablespoons honey

1 teaspoon garlic powder

1 teaspoon ginger powder

1 teaspoon cumin

1 teaspoon paprika

½ teaspoon hot paprika or harrisa (optional)

1 teaspoon nutmeg

1 teaspoon salt

water as needed

Sweet rice bundle

1 large Reynolds® oven bag (16"x17"x½")

1 onion, chopped

¼ cup sugar

1 teaspoon salt

¼ teaspoon pepper

¼ teaspoon turmeric

¼ cup canola oil

2 cups water

Barley bundle

1 large Reynolds® oven bag (16"x17"x½")

1 cup barley

1 tablespoon canola oil

1 teaspoon paprika

½ teaspoon cumin

1 teaspoon salt

2 cups water

Meatloaf bundle

2 (12"x12") foil squares

1 pound ground meat

½ teaspoon cumin

½ teaspoon paprika

½ teaspoon salt

½ teaspoon pepper

½ teaspoon garlic powder

¼ cup flavored breadcrumbs

1 egg

1. In the bottom of a 6-quart slow cooker, layer first the oil, then chickpeas and potatoes.

2. Combine all ingredients for the sweet rice bundle in the oven bag and tie with a knot, pricking the top of the bag with a fork a few times to allow the steam to escape. Place bundle over potatoes, knot side up.

3. Combine all ingredients for the barley bundle in the oven bag and tie with a knot, and prick top to allow steam to escape. Nestle next to the sweet rice bundle, knot side up.

4. Make the meatloaf bundle by mixing all the ingredients very well, dividing the mixture into two, and wrapping each half firmly in the foil squares, like burritos; nestle them next to the other two.

5. Add remaining ingredients (dates, eggs if using, honey, and seasonings). Fill to the rim with water.

6. Cook on high until before lighting Shabbat candles. Add more water if the water has mostly cooked out and the stew looks dry. Turn to low and cook until Shabbat lunch.

Yield: 6-8 servings

❧ HAMIM EGGS ❧

Tochmomorque Shabbati

These eggs are a staple in every Sephardic Shabbat stew. Eggs can be easily added, shell and all, to any of the previous stews. These eggs will cook and caramelize to a beautiful brown color and a creamy delightful yolk. Here I give you the "express" recipe I use when I have many guests and am unable to fit the eggs into the slow cooker. The oil will prevent the water from evaporating as the eggs cook. Do not peel until ready to serve. To make the color even deeper, you can add a tea bag, some coffee, or even a piece of red cabbage.

6 white eggs, room temperature

skin of 3 onions

water as needed

1 teaspoon canola oil

Place the eggs and the onion skins into a 4-quart saucepan. Cover with water and bring to a boil. Reduce heat and simmer for at least 1 hour, but no more than 3 hours. Serve warm along with any Sephardic Shabbat stew.

Yield: 6 servings

Persian Rice

∾ PERSIAN RICE TUTORIAL ∾

Rice (*berenj* in *Farsi*) to Persians is like spaghetti to Italians or sushi to the Japanese! There is no life without it. Rice is equivalent to bread and in fact comes before bread in the Persian diet. Rice is everything Persian. My husband claims that it doesn't matter how much food there is; if there is no rice, a person will not feel satisfied. And, when it comes to Persians, he is right!

There are many ways to cook Persian rice, but there is only one main type of rice that is used in Persian cuisine: Basmati rice. Fortunately, this type of rice is available in many supermarkets nowadays. The word *basmati* means "the fragrant one" in Sanskrit (Hindi)—and it is a very accurate name at that. Basmati rice has a delicious aroma and a very elegant, elongated grain. Rice may have been brought to Iran from Southeast Asia or the Indian subcontinent in ancient times. There are many types of rice used in Iran, depending on the results the cook is trying to achieve; however, for the sake of convenience I have decided to use only basmati rice in the following recipes. Here is a brief synopsis of the different rice recipes traditionally made in Persian cuisine. Recipes for each can be found on the following pages.

KATEH

Traditionally, this is Persian rice in its simplest form. *Kateh* is what most Persians would call "sticky rice," and it is cooked without draining it afterward. Because of its compact consistency, this rice is often mixed with yogurt, salt, and pepper for a quick dinner or fed to children with stew or soup. *Kateh* was originally made in Iran with a type of rice called *champe* (which is similar to American rice). To keep things simple, I make it with basmati rice. In addition, since this rice is not drained, it is very tasty and the *tadig* that results is not oily. Instead, it is extremely crunchy and delicious. Nowadays anyone can enjoy the convenience of cooking *kateh* in Persian rice cookers (different from your regular rice cooker—see my website for shopping information).

CHELO

Chelo is as simple as basmati rice that has been parboiled and then steamed. It is the equivalent to bread on the Persian table. When it comes to *chelo*, it takes two to tango! On its own, *chelo* is just a blank canvas. Therefore, it will always call for a partner—unless it is used to accompany *kebab*. *Chelo* is the "bed" for all kinds of amazing Persian stews called *choroshes*, and it contains the most sought-after, incredible, crunchy piece of heaven...*tadig*!!

TADIG

The burnt bottom of the rice? Hardly! *Tadig* is made with absolute forethought! It is not the by-product of steaming rice, but the whole purpose of the creation of the world...to Persians, that is!! You will, in fact, be witness to countless fights for this uncanny treasure and will find yourself conducting your own inner battle as you try not to eat a piece before taking the platter out to the table!

POLO

This is *chelo*, but with all kinds of delicious fruits, vegetables, and/or nuts added to it. *Polo* is a dressed up *chelo*. *Chorosh* (Persian stew) is not to be put on *polo*, since this special rice is a dish on its own. Many *polos* come cooked with meat, but in order to use them mainly as side dishes, I have omitted the meat from most of the recipes. *Tadig* is also made while steaming *polo*.

I can almost read your mind…I know you are thinking there is no way your rice will turn out like the Persian rice you have had before. I know you think that to make *tadig* you have to have Persian blood. In the beginning, it might seem like an uphill battle. However, I guarantee that if you follow my easy steps, you too can make *tadig*!

Jeweled Rice, page 211

❧ MAKING TADIG TUTORIAL ❧

All Hail to the King, Tadig

Did you know that Persians make amazing poets? In fact, arguably the most famous German writer, Goethe, said, "One Persian poet is as good as seven European ones." I am not going to start telling you how many poets we have in our own family. Many times we get together for *mehmuni* (family parties) and all the aunts and uncles show up, along with the first, second, and third cousins to have a poetry recital. The famous poet in the family is *Chaleh Shuku* (that is Farsi for Aunty Shuku). I cannot understand her poems to save my life, but I can appreciate the beauty of her words and her passion as she relates—for the most part—the story of a platonic love. I can see the longing in her eyes; I can hear the pain in her voice. It is similar to when you go to the opera and cannot understand a word, but for some reason tears start leaking from your eyes! So, my theory was that the reason Persians make great poets is because they all overdosed on *tadig*! But, after trying to fill myself with *tadig* and only ending up a few pounds heavier, I dropped the theory. There is simply nothing like a piece of *tadig*, nothing!

Tadig can be served in two ways. It can be broken into pieces and set on a plate alone or around rice. Or it can be detached from the bottom of the pan and turned out onto a platter (just like getting a cake out of the pan). Keep in mind that you will need nonstick cookware to do this; otherwise the *tadig* will stick to the bottom of the pan. When presented like this, I guarantee you that all the Persians in your table will "ohh" and "ahh" about it. Actually, I take that back—if your guests are real Persians, they will make a strange remark. They will say "Bah, Bah." In Farsi, this means, "Man, this *is* good!!!"

You can be very creative when making *tadig*. Here are some great ideas; just keep in mind that all of the following ingredients are to be added to the bottom of the pan **after** the oil and the turmeric have been heated but **before** pouring the rice like a pyramid (see basic recipe on page 187). Visit my blog for more ideas and great pictures.

- Slice a few potatoes ¼-inch thick and add to the hot oil. These slices will become delicious and crunchy along with the rice.
- Slice onion rings and add to the oil. These will become caramelized and absolutely delicious.
- Cut a pita into 6 pizza-like triangles. Place on top of the oil, forming a Star of David. When turned out onto a platter, the *tadig* will have the design embedded in it.

- Get the kids involved and bring out the cookie cutters. Cut shapes from slices of regular or whole grain sandwich bread and add to the oil. You can use themes, such as flowers in spring or Hebrew letters for Shabbat. Or you can make it a family tradition to create the surprise *tadig* of the week!
- Add coriander seeds (also called cilantro seeds) to the oil. It will taste like heaven!
- Add one flour tortilla to the oil. (Hey, there has to be something Latin, since this book is for me too!)

Making *tadig* is like riding a bicycle. It is hard in the beginning and you might fall a few times. However, once you have learned, you will never forget. I have provided you with all the important tips. So, I want to hear those teeth crunching! And, you if need extra help, take a look at my website (kosherpersianfood.com) for a video on *tadig* troubleshooting!

❧ PERSIAN STICKY RICE ❧

Kateh

Kateh is embedded in every Persian child's taste buds. It is the easiest and fastest way to make Persian rice. The first time I tried *kateh* was when my husband (back then my boyfriend) was foraging around in his mother's refrigerator looking for leftovers to eat. He found this bowl of what looked like fancy Persian rice gone wrong. He warmed it up and added yogurt, salt, and pepper. I had never seen anyone add yogurt to rice, so you can imagine the look of revulsion on my face. He somehow convinced me to try his concoction—and my life was never the same!

Kateh is very tasty and its *tadig* is heavenly; the longer you steam this rice, the crunchier and yummier the *tadig* will be. If you are having guests, please serve them *chelo*, but if it's just family and you want something yummy, simple, and soothing, then make a bowl of *kateh*!

5 cups water

3 cups rice, checked and rinsed

¼ cup canola oil

1 tablespoon salt

1. Add water, rice, oil, and salt to a 6-quart nonstick saucepan. Bring to a boil, uncovered, over high heat.

2. Reduce heat to medium and cook, uncovered, stirring occasionally, until water evaporates (5–7 minutes).

3. With a spoon, shape the rice into a pyramid. Cover tightly, placing two paper towels (one on top of the other) or a clean dishtowel between the lid and the pot. Reduce the heat to low and simmer for at least 45 minutes.

4. Turn the rice out onto a flat serving platter by inverting the pot, as you would invert a cake pan—or simply eat it directly from the pot!

Yield: 6 servings

Tricks of the Trade

Be sure to use a nonstick saucepan so the delicious *tadig* doesn't stick! When you invert the pan over your serving platter, the *tadig* will come out of your nonstick pan just like a cake topping.

Chelo

Many people become extremely intimidated when it comes to making Persian rice. You have to trust me when I tell you it is really not a big deal—just don't tell anyone Persian I said that! All you need to do is to imagine that instead of making rice, you are making pasta. Most of us know how to make pasta; it is probably what you ate every day when you went to college! You are going to cook this rice in boiling water with oil and salt, just like pasta. You are going to wait until the rice is "al dente" (when you bite a grain of rice it should still have a white dot in the middle), just like pasta. Do not overcook Persian rice or your reputation as a Persian cook will suffer! And last, you are going to drain it, just like pasta.

The difference comes next: Persian rice has one cooking step that pasta doesn't have. Persian rice gets steamed. Think of it this way: since this rice is fancy, it requires a "spa treatment." What is the result when you pamper yourself at the sauna? A new you! What is the result when you treat your rice to a "spa treatment"? Each and every grain of rice becomes its own entity and a pearl from heaven! What is the best after-effect of a "spa treatment" for a woman? It makes her a better wife, a better mother—and a better cook! What is the best after-effect of a "spa treatment" for Persian rice? The most scrumptious, crunchy, golden crust: *TADIG*!

To make this rice you will need a colander—and the smaller the openings, the better. You don't want your precious rice to slip out! Also, many Persian cooks wash and soak the rice as if it were dirty laundry…I am sorry, I keep my laundry in the basement and I don't have time for all that soaking, so trust me when I tell you that you don't need to do it!

The quantities in the recipe below might seem large, but considering that Persians breathe rice, it goes really fast. **If you want to make a smaller quantity, try only 3 cups rice, 8 cups water, ¼ cup oil, and 1 tablespoon salt.** Also, any basmati rice will do. Basmati rice is also available in whole-grain brown; although it is a little stickier, it is absolutely delicious and healthful! Visit my website for a video of this recipe.

Part 1:

COOKING THE RICE

5 cups basmati rice, checked and rinsed

12 cups water

½ cup canola oil

3 tablespoons salt

Part 2:

STEAMING THE RICE AND MAKING TADIG

¼-inch canola oil poured into the bottom of the saucepan

2 tablespoons water

¼ teaspoon turmeric or powdered saffron (optional, for a more authentic flavor)

TO COOK THE RICE

1. Fill a large nonstick saucepan (at least 6 quarts) with 12 cups water; add oil and salt. Cover and bring to a brisk boil over high heat.

2. Add the rice and continue cooking over medium to high heat, stirring occasionally.

3. After 3–5 minutes, use a slotted spoon to scoop some grains from the water. Break one grain in half to make sure it is "al dente" (see above). Turn off the heat and pour rice into the colander to drain; set aside.

TO STEAM AND MAKE TADIG

1. Place the empty 6-quart saucepan back onto the stovetop over medium heat. Add ¼-inch canola oil and 2 tablespoons water. Add turmeric and/or saffron powder. Stir together.

2. Add the drained rice and shape it into a pyramid. Cover the pot and cook for 5–7 minutes until rice begins to steam.

3. Uncover and place 2 paper towels (one on top of the other) over the rice. The ends will extend outside the pot. Replace the lid tightly.

4. Reduce heat to low and simmer, covered, for 45 minutes. Turn off the heat and tilt the lid until ready to serve.

5. With a wide spatula, scoop the rice from the pot, making sure not to disturb the crust (*tadig*) that formed on the bottom of the pot. Serve the rice on a flat serving platter, mounding it into the shape of a pyramid. Turn the *tadig* out onto a flat serving platter by inverting the pot, as you would invert a cake pan, or cut it into pieces and serve around the rice.

Yield: 8 servings

Optional garnish:

SAFFRON RICE

1. To make saffron water, mix together 1 teaspoon crushed saffron threads and ¼ cup hot water. Steep for a few minutes, until the water becomes yellow.

2. Mix saffron water with steamed white rice. Use this intensely yellow rice to make designs on the Chelo.

Yield: Up to 8 servings, depending on whether your guests are Persian!

To reheat this rice:

Pour ½ cup water mixed with ¼ cup canola oil onto the pyramid in a large pot. You can also freeze this rice, as long as you do not stir it until it is completely defrosted. You can even cook it, freeze it, and later steam it as it defrosts. I know I will have to spend time in "rice hell" for admitting to freezing Persian rice, but it is worth it to make my life easier!

Tricks of the Trade

Chelo cooks very quickly. Therefore, when I make *Chelo*, I always make sure to have a colander ready in the sink to drain the rice so I do not overcook it. Also, when you steam the rice by placing the paper towels between the lid and the pot, make sure these are safely away from the heat. After this rice is steamed, it is important to tilt the lid to allow any extra steam to escape so that the crunchy bottom does not become soggy.

I often cook this rice on Thursday and have it ready to steam on Friday a few hours before Shabbat.

برنج ایرانی PERSIAN RICE 187

❧ FANCY PERSIAN RICE TUTORIAL ❧

پلو

Polo

Women know that a very simple outfit can look like a fancy ensemble if the accessories are right. For Persians, white rice is the same way. There are myriad ways to dress up simple rice that will make it look stunning! Just remember that fancy rice requires boiling in water tinted with turmeric (except rice with dill and lima beans). Or, simply combine saffron-tinted rice with plain white rice for a stunning duo! The specific Persian recipes that follow will teach you how to combine these toppings to make authentic Persian *polo*. But, don't be intimidated! Where is the fun of cooking without experimenting? Have fun mixing things up and playing with colors, textures, and flavors.

FANCY PERSIAN RICE TOPPINGS

Caramelized Onions

Persians love to caramelize onions. My husband's aunt keeps a large plastic container filled with caramelized onions in her refrigerator so that they are handy and can be used on demand! Caramelized onions look best when cut "*a la julienne*," which translates to "thin strips."

To caramelize 2 onions:
Combine ¼ cup canola oil and a dash of turmeric. Heat flavored oil in a large skillet over medium heat; add julienned onions and fry for approximately 30 minutes, stirring occasionally to avoid burning. The result will be scrumptious sweet and crunchy onions…the stuff Persian dreams are made of!

Fried Dried Fruits

There is nothing like seeing a tiny currant raisin go from wrinkled to plump in the heat of the fire! It happens so fast that you must be right there to recue it from burning. All these dried fruits turn into flavorful indulgences when fried—almost like a frog turning into a prince after the kiss!

To fry dried fruits: Use one tablespoon canola oil for every cup of dried fruit. Heat oil over medium heat and add fruit(s) as desired. Watch carefully to prevent fruit from burning; remove from heat as soon as the fruit plumps in the oil.

You can fry these and set aside for hours until ready to use; simply keep them covered at room temperature. Some good choices are:
• Currant raisins (or regular raisins)
• Golden raisins
• Barberries (*zereshk*) (for every 2 cups of barberries, add 2 tablespoons of sugar)
• Dried apricots, chopped (use an oiled knife to make chopping easier)

Toasted Slivered Almonds and Slivered Pistachios

Here is another staple of Persian rice toppings. Toast slivered almonds in the oven or fry in a tablespoon of oil. Slivered pistachios are not fried.

To toast almonds or pistachios: Place nuts on a baking sheet and toast in the oven at 350°F for 10 minutes or until golden brown.

To fry almonds: For every cup of nuts, add one tablespoon canola oil to a large frying pan, over medium heat, Add nuts and stir periodically to avoid burning. Remove from heat when nuts are golden brown.

Toasted or fried nuts can be stored in a dry cold place, covered, for months!

Boiled Legumes and Frozen Vegetables
• **Yellow split peas and lentils**: Using a ratio of ½ cup legumes to 1½ cups water, boil until "al dente" or partially tender, for about 7 minutes.
• **Lima beans, green beans and green peas**: I always keep these frozen until after the rice has been drained. I mix the frozen veggies into the hot rice. The steaming process will defrost them and they will automatically cook to perfection.
• **Slivered orange peel and carrots**: Orange peel is very popular, but it must be boiled with sugar to tame the bitterness. Simply use a vegetable peeler to peel 2 oranges as if they were apples, leaving behind the white pith. Sliver peels with a sharp knife. Buy carrots already slivered if you don't want to peel and slice them. Add orange peels, 1 cup slivered carrots, and 2 cups sugar to 2 cups water; boil together for 10 minutes.

White Rice Tinted with Saffron
Use this intensely golden-yellow rice to make designs on the white rice.
To make saffron water: Add 1 teaspoon crushed saffron threads to ¼ cup hot water. Steep for a few minutes until the water becomes orange/yellow. Mix saffron water into 1 cup cooked rice. You can make stripes of saffron rice over the white rice, or mix saffron rice into white rice to give it a dramatic look!

Advieh (the secret spice)
Advieh is a mixture of spices Persians add to polo. My mother-in-law is not a lover of *advieh*, but her sister, Aunt Shuku, is! I actually really like this spice but, since my husband does not love *advieh*, I rarely use it. *Advieh* is the same as *baharat* and allspice. It is a mixture of ground cloves, cardamom, ginger, cinnamon, and other spices. Sometimes *advieh* can also include dried rose petals and cumin. Fortunately, allspice is a great substitute and is available in most supermarkets. For authentic *advieh*, mix equal parts of ground cardamom, nutmeg, cinnamon, dried rose buds and half cumin (optional). Keep it in an airtight container.

❧ SAFFRON ❧

The golden threads of Persian cuisine

I was first introduced to saffron when I started cooking Persian food. Back at home we never used it, even though my favorite Spanish dish, *paella*, calls for it. It was too hard to find! We used other means, like turmeric, to dye the rice yellow. But there is nothing like the color, smell, and taste of real saffron. I still remember when one of Sammy's aunts sent us a thank-you gift of four 2-ounce bags of saffron…It was so much! It looked very authentic, red and crisp, with Farsi written all over it. I called her to thank her and told her it was so much saffron that I would have enough to last until my kids got married! She laughed so much, and today I know she thought I was joking. Persians use so much saffron that those bags are long gone and enjoyed!

Even though saffron is used almost as much as salt in Persian food, from appetizers to desserts, it comes in tiny quantities and does go a long way. This is because it usually is dissolved and a few threads can make the dullest *sholezard* (Persian rice pudding) as golden as the sun! So, although it might seem expensive, it ends up being worth it. In fact, there is even a *Gemara* that documents that even in the time of the Talmud saffron was expensive. Did you know that saffron threads are the delicate stigmas of saffron crocus flowers? Each flower has only three stigmas! These have to be handpicked and then dried. In fact, to obtain just one pound of saffron requires an orchard the size of a football field and 40 hours of labor! The lower end of the stigma (the style) is yellow and has no culinary value. However, it is often added to commercial saffron to increase its weight. Unfortunately, saffron often comes in dark containers to avoid sunlight damage, so it makes it impossible to check the color of the threads.

Saffron comes both in threads and in powder form. The powder form is more convenient, but it takes away the fun of crushing the threads, and it can hide all kinds of impurities. I like to buy threads rather than powder, and I use a small mortar and pestle to crush a pinch or two if I want to use it in powder form. Use saffron threads when you want it to show in your recipes and powder form when you want to keep it hidden. For the most part, I like to keep it hidden. To make liquid saffron, combine 1 teaspoon powdered saffron and ¼ cup hot water and steep till water becomes orange/yellow.

Keep in mind that saffron quality and price vary depending on origin. Persians will tell you the best saffron in the world is Iranian saffron; however, what you purchase depends on your taste and budget. The better quality your saffron, the less you need to use. For your convenience, the recipes in this book are based on the saffron readily available in American supermarkets, which unfortunately do not always carry the best-quality saffron. However, if you have top-quality saffron, you will need about half the amount suggested in my recipes. The reason is that quality saffron has a stronger flavor and greater coloring power. There are a few criteria that will help you realize the quality of the saffron you are using. First, the aroma should be strong, not musty. Second, the threads should be dried and brittle to the touch. And third, the color should be bright red all over. When you buy saffron, check the packaging to see if the ISO (International Organization for Standardization) is listed. This number will disclose the coloring strength of the saffron you are purchasing. Be sure it is not much lower than 190.

❧ SWEET RICE WITH ORANGE AND CARROTS ❧

Shirin Polo

This is by far my favorite Persian rice. Every time I go to New York, my husband and I make sure to stop by *Colbeh*. They make the best *Shirin Polo*!! This is my version of this yummy dish. For the orange peel, simply use a vegetable peeler to peel 2 oranges as if they were apples, leaving behind the white pith. You can eat this orange after you make the rice! With a knife, cut the peel into slivers (¼-inch x ⅛ -inch). For the carrot slivers, buy them at the vegetable department of your regular grocer (who has patience to start cutting carrots into such tiny slivers?) The *tadig* in this recipe is guaranteed to be a hit and looks beautiful as a garnish around the rice.

Tricks of the Trade

Don't worry about the oil in this recipe; it will be drained out before serving! Make sure to have a colander ready in the sink to drain the rice. When cooking the *tadig*, make sure the paper towels are safely away from the heat. I often make double of *Shirin Polo* topping and freeze half the batch to use later.

For the rice

3 cups basmati rice, checked and rinsed

8 cups water

2 tablespoons salt

⅛ teaspoon turmeric

½ cup canola oil

For the rice topping

2 cups water

¾ cup slivered orange peel (peel of 2 oranges)

1 cup slivered carrots

2 cups sugar

½ teaspoon cinnamon

1 teaspoon cardamom

½ cup slivered almonds (optional)

½ cup slivered pistachios (optional)

To steam and make *tadig*

canola oil

2 tablespoons water

⅛ teaspoon turmeric and/or saffron powder

2 potatoes, peeled, sliced into ¼-inch rounds

1 onion, cut in ¼-inch rounds

TO COOK THE RICE AND MAKE THE TOPPING

1. Fill a 6-quart nonstick saucepan with 8 cups water. Add oil, salt, and turmeric. Cover and bring to a brisk boil over high heat.

2. Meanwhile, fill a small saucepan with 2 cups of water, slivered orange peel, carrots, and sugar. Bring to a brisk boil over high heat, reduce the heat to low and simmer for 10 minutes.

3. When the turmeric water boils, add the rice and continue cooking, uncovered, over medium to high heat, stirring occasionally.

4. After 3–5 minutes, use a slotted spoon to scoop some grains from the water. Break one grain in half to make sure it is "al dente". Turn off heat and pour rice into the colander to drain; set aside.

5. Drain the orange peel/carrot mixture. Gently stir the orange-carrot mixture, cinnamon, cardamom, almonds, and pistachios into the rice. Reserve some almonds and pistachios for garnish.

TO STEAM AND MAKE TADIG

1. Place the empty 6-quart saucepan back onto the stovetop over medium heat. Add ¼-inch canola oil and 2 tablespoons water. Add turmeric and/or saffron powder. Stir together.

2. Add potatoes and onions in a single layer. Add the drained rice and shape it into a pyramid.

3. Cover the pot and cook for 5–7 minutes until rice begins to steam. Uncover and place 2 paper towels (one on top of the other) over the rice. The ends will extend outside the pot. Replace the lid tightly.

4. Reduce the heat to low and simmer, covered, for 45 minutes. Turn off the heat and tilt the lid until ready to serve.

5. Serve on a shallow platter, mounding the rice into a pyramid and garnishing with the *tadig*.

Yield: 8 servings

❧ RICE WITH LIMA BEANS AND DILL ❧

Baghala Polo

Wouldn't it be nice if we all had a beautiful vegetable garden where we could pick fresh dill whenever we needed…just a dream! Of course this recipe is superior with fresh dill, but we all know the convenience of dried dill is even better. So, I give you a choice: you can garden, shop fresh at the greengrocer, or simply get dried dill at the store. Traditionally, this rice is made with *fava* beans (broad beans), but I like to make it with lima beans or also green peas. I love to use onions for the *tadig* of this rice.

For the rice

3 cups basmati rice, checked and rinsed

8 cups water

2 tablespoons salt

½ cup canola oil

1 (16-ounce) bag frozen baby lima beans (do not defrost)

1 cup fresh chopped dill or ⅓ cup dried dill

To steam and make tadig

canola oil

2 tablespoons water

⅛ teaspoon turmeric and/or saffron powder

1 onion, cut into ¼-inch rounds.

TO COOK THE RICE

1. Fill a 6-quart nonstick saucepan with 8 cups water; add oil and salt. Cover and bring to a brisk boil over high heat. Add rice and continue cooking, uncovered, over medium to high heat, stirring occasionally.

2. After 3–5 minutes, use a slotted spoon to scoop some grains from the water. Break one grain in half to make sure it is "al dente". Turn off heat and pour rice into the colander to drain; set aside.

3. Gently stir frozen baby lima beans and dill into the rice in the colander.

TO STEAM AND MAKE TADIG

1. Place the empty 6-quart saucepan back onto the stovetop over medium heat. Add ¼-inch canola oil and 2 tablespoons water. Add turmeric and/or saffron powder. Stir together.

2. Add a double layer of onions. Add the drained rice, mounding it into a pyramid. Cover the pot and cook for 5–7 minutes until rice begins to steam. Uncover and place 2 paper towels (one on top of the other) over the rice. The ends will extend outside the pot. Replace the lid tightly.

3. Reduce the heat to low and simmer, covered, for 45 minutes. Turn off the heat and tilt the lid until ready to serve.

4. Serve on a shallow platter, mounding the rice into a pyramid and garnishing with the *tadig*.

Yield: 8 servings

Tricks of the Trade

Don't worry about the oil in this recipe; it will be drained out before serving! Make sure to have a colander ready in the sink to drain the rice.

When cooking the *tadig*, make sure the paper towels are safely away from the heat.

برنج ایرانی PERSIAN RICE 195

❧ PERSIAN RICE WITH BARBERRIES ❧

Zereshk Polo

Iran is the largest producer of *zereshk* (barberries) in the world. These tiny dried berries are rich in vitamin C and give a tart flavor to many Persian dishes. Many Persians use the word *zereshk* as an expression for what would translate into English as "Yeah, right!" Also, in the story of *Purim*, which took place in Persia, Haman's wife's name is *Zeresh*, perhaps derived from the Persian name for the barberries, which means *tart* or *sour*.

You can find dried barberries in most Middle Eastern stores. Sugar is often added to barberries to tame their sharp flavor. If you don't have barberries around, feel free to substitute currant raisins instead of barberries; however, as a result the rice will be sweet instead of sweet and sour. When you buy dry barberries, make sure that they still retain some redness; dark barberries have been sitting on the shelf for a while.

To make the rice

3 cups basmati rice, checked and rinsed

8 cups water

2 tablespoons salt

⅛ teaspoon turmeric

½ cup canola oil

To make rice topping

1 onion, caramelized (see page 188)

2 tablespoons oil

2 cups dried barberries, checked and rinsed

2 tablespoons sugar

To steam and make *tadig*

canola oil

2 tablespoons water

⅛ teaspoon turmeric and/or saffron powder

3 potatoes, peeled and sliced into ¼ inch rounds

TO COOK THE RICE AND MAKE THE TOPPING

1. Fill a 6-quart nonstick saucepan with 8 cups water. Add oil, turmeric, and salt. Cover and bring to a brisk boil over high heat.

2. Meanwhile, make the topping: In a small skillet, sauté the barberries in 1 tablespoon oil until they are shiny and bright red (about 45 seconds). Add sugar and stir; cook until sugar has dissolved. Remove from heat and set aside.

3. When the turmeric water boils, add the rice and continue cooking, uncovered, over medium to high heat, stirring occasionally.

4. After 3–5 minutes, use a slotted spoon to scoop some grains from the water. Break one grain in half to make sure it is "al dente". Turn off heat and pour rice into the colander to drain; set aside.

TO STEAM AND MAKE TADIG

1. Place the empty 6-quart saucepan back onto the stovetop over medium heat. Add ¼-inch canola oil and 2 tablespoons water. Add turmeric and/or saffron powder. Stir together.

2. Add sliced potatoes in a single layer. Add the drained rice and shape it into a pyramid. Cover the pot and cook for 5–7 minutes until rice begins to steam. Uncover and place 2 paper towels (one on top of the other) over the rice. The ends will extend outside the pot. Replace the lid tightly.

3. Reduce the heat to low and simmer, covered, for 45 minutes. Turn off the heat and tilt the lid until ready to serve.

4. Serve on a shallow platter, mounding the rice into a pyramid and garnishing with stripes of saffron rice (see page 189), fried barberries, caramelized onions, and tadig.

Yield: 8 servings

Tricks of the Trade

To ensure that the barberries retain their color and crispness, I like adding them at the end of the steaming process instead of steaming them with the rice. This rice is so beautiful because of the contrasting colors…It looks like a rose garden! Also, be careful when cooking barberries because they burn easily.

Don't worry about the oil in this recipe; it will be drained out before serving! Make sure to have a colander ready in the sink to drain the rice. When cooking the *tadig*, make sure the paper towels are safely away from the heat.

If you are caramelizing onions for this recipe, make a large batch and keep some in the fridge ready to use. Caramelized onions are amazing over anything!

RICE WITH YELLOW SPLIT PEAS
AND CURRANT RAISINS
Polo Lape

This was the first Persian rice I ever made…boy, did I make mistakes! I cooked the split peas for too long and I didn't caramelize the onions. My husband was so gracious that he didn't complain. (Or was it that we were both starving students and anything that at least looked like Persian food was better than nothing?!)

To make the rice

3 cups basmati rice, checked and rinsed

8 cups water

2 tablespoons salt

⅛ teaspoon turmeric

½ cup canola oil

To make rice topping

1 onion, caramelized (see page 188)

1 tablespoon oil

1 cup currant raisins

½ cup yellow split peas

1 cup water

1 tablespoon *advieh* (optional)

To steam and make *tadig*

canola oil

2 tablespoons water

⅛ teaspoon turmeric and/or saffron powder

3 potatoes or one onion, peeled, sliced into ¼-inch rounds

Optional topping

carmelized onions (see page 188)

TO MAKE THE RICE AND THE TOPPING

1. Fill a 6-quart nonstick saucepan with 8 cups water; add oil, salt, and turmeric. Cover and bring to a brisk boil over high heat.

2. Meanwhile, make the topping: In a small skillet, sauté the raisins in 1 tablespoon oil until they look shiny and plump (about 45 seconds). Remove from heat and set aside.

3. In a small saucepan, bring water and yellow split peas to a boil over high heat. Simmer, uncovered, for 7 minutes or until peas are "al dente" (see page 189). Drain, remove from heat and set aside.

4. When the turmeric water boils, add rice and continue cooking, uncovered, over medium to high heat, stirring occasionally.

5. After 3–5 minutes, use a slotted spoon to scoop some grains from the water. Break one grain in half to make sure it is "al dente". Turn off heat and pour rice into the colander to drain; set aside.

6. Gently stir the raisins, tender split peas, and *advieh* –if using– into the rice in the colander.

TO STEAM AND MAKE TADIG

1. Place the empty 6-quart saucepan back onto the stovetop over medium heat. Add ¼-inch canola oil and 2 tablespoons water. Add turmeric and/or saffron powder. Stir together.

2. Add sliced potatoes or onions in a single layer. Add the drained rice and shape it into a pyramid. Cover the pot and cook for 5–7 minutes until rice begins to steam. Uncover and place 2 paper towels (one on top of the other) over the rice. The ends will extend outside the pot. Replace the lid tightly.

3. Reduce the heat to low and simmer, covered, for 45 minutes. Turn off the heat and tilt the lid until ready to serve.

4. Serve on a shallow platter, mounding the rice into a pyramid, and garnishing with *tadig* and caramelized onions, if desired.

Yield: 8 servings

You are what you eat

Split peas are a great source of protein. They come in yellow and green varieties and, to speed the cooking process, they are mechanically split after their skin is removed.

♣

Tricks of the trade

Don't worry about the oil in this recipe; it will be drained out before serving. Make sure to have a colander ready in the sink to drain the rice. When cooking the *tadig*, make sure the paper towels are safely away from the heat.

When cooking the raisins, keep the heat low and pay attention because raisins burn easily.

You can use potatoes for the *tadig*, or you can use some of the rice before mixing it with the toppings.

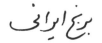

❧ RED RICE WITH ONIONS ❧

Polo Germez

This is my husband's favorite rice. The children love it as well. When people ask me how many kids I have, I usually tell them I have five boys (thank G-d). That was the case until one day I caught my husband eating this rice and snatching some from the children's plates while they were not looking. From then on, if people ask me how many kids I have, I answer, "I have five boys and a husband!"

3 cups basmati rice, checked and rinsed

1 (28-ounce) can crushed tomatoes

3 cups water

½ cup canola oil

1½ tablespoons salt

¼ teaspoon ground saffron (optional)

1 large onion, chopped into small dice

1. Fill a 6-quart nonstick saucepan with rice, tomatoes, water, canola oil, salt, saffron, and onion. Mix together. Cover and bring to a boil over high heat. Reduce heat to medium/low. Simmer for 10 minutes.

2. Uncover and place 2 paper towels (one on top of the other) over the rice. The ends will extend outside the pot. Replace the lid tightly. Reduce heat to low and simmer for 30 minutes.

3. Turn off the heat and tilt the lid to allow the steam to escape so that the crunchy bottom does not become soggy.

4. Serve on a shallow platter, mounding the rice into a pyramid, and garnishing with the *tadig*.

Yield: 8 servings

Tricks of the trade

When cooking the *tadig*, make sure the paper towels are safely away from the heat.

❧ RICE WITH TOMATO SAUCE, MEAT, AND GREEN BEANS ❧

Istanbuli Polo

Why is this rice called *Istanbuli Polo*? Could it have originated in Istanbul? Nobody seems to know, and nobody seems to care. People just want to eat it! This rice is not the usual fluffy Persian rice that characterizes "polo." This is more like sticky rice, so don't panic when you see the results. Try it with a drizzle of lime juice on top.

1 onion, chopped (about 1 cup)

4 garlic cloves, pressed

¼ cup olive oil

2 pounds short ribs, cut between the bones *or* 1 pound flanken, cut into 1-inch cubes.

3 cups water

2 teaspoons salt

3 cups basmati rice, checked and rinsed

1 (28-ounce) can crushed tomatoes

1 heaping teaspoon *baharat (advieh)* spice *or* allspice

½ teaspoon ground saffron

½ teaspoon cinnamon (optional)

2 cups frozen French-cut green beans

Tricks of the trade

When cooking the *tadig*, make sure the paper towels are safely away from the heat.

No need to cook the frozen green beans before adding to the pot; they will cook in the steam from the rice.

1. In a 6-quart nonstick saucepan, fry the onion and garlic in the olive oil until translucent (about 3 minutes). Add the meat and brown, stirring occasionally, for about 10 minutes or until no longer pink. Add water and salt, cover and bring to a boil over medium/high heat. Reduce heat to low, and simmer for 1½ hours or until meat is tender.

2. Pour the meat broth from the saucepan into a measuring cup. Add enough water, if necessary, to equal 3 cups liquid. Return liquid to the saucepan. Add the rice, tomatoes, saffron, *baharat*, and cinnamon, if using. Stir well. Cover and simmer over medium/low heat for 10 minutes.

3. Use a spoon to mound the rice in the pot into a pyramid. Drape frozen green beans over the pyramid. Place 2 paper towels (one on top of the other) over the rice. The ends will extend outside the pot. Replace the lid tightly. Reduce the heat to low and simmer for 30 minutes.

4. Turn off the heat and tilt the lid until ready to serve.

5. Serve on a shallow platter, mounding the rice into a pyramid.

Yield: 8 servings

✒ OVEN-BAKED SUPER-EASY BASMATI RICE ✒
WITH DRIED CRANBERRIES AND SAFFRON

This extremely easy rice is a hit! My good friend and fabulous cook, Ninoska Ravid, gave me this recipe. I am warning you: This rice will stick together; therefore Persians will not necessarily consider it a success. Also, since this rice is baked, there will not be *tadig*. However, this rice is wonderful in Ashkenazi circles, and it has the Persian flavor in it. I like to serve it plated at *Sheva Brachot* and I use a metal ice-cream scoop to give each serving a round and tailored look!

9"x13" disposable or oven-to-table roaster, sprayed with canola oil

4 cups basmati rice, checked and rinsed

6 cups water

½ cup chicken consommé powder (*parve*)

1 stick *parve* margarine (4 ounces), cut into pieces

1 cup sweetened dried cranberries

½ teaspoon ground saffron

½ teaspoon turmeric

1 teaspoon salt

1. Preheat oven to 350°F.
2. Spread rice in the bottom of the pan. Add water, chicken consommé powder, margarine, dried cranberries, saffron, turmeric, and salt. Stir together and cover with foil.
3. Bake for 1½ hours, or until rice is tender and water has evaporated.
4. Fluff rice with a fork and serve on a shallow platter, mounding rice into a pyramid.

Yield: 8 servings

Tricks of the trade

If you cannot find sweetened dried cranberries, this rice can also be made with black or golden raisins.

❧ RICE WITH LENTILS AND CARAMELIZED ONIONS ❧

Adas Polo

There is a morbid side to this rice: It is commonly served at funeral receptions. In fact, the first time I had this rice was at a funeral. Lentils contain high levels of protein and are also among the best vegetable sources of iron. Also, lentils are a common food for mourners in Judaism because they are round, symbolizing the life cycle from birth to death. The good news is that you can also eat it all year long!

I love serving this rice when *Parshat Toldot* is read. This Torah portion describes the time when Jacob purchases the birthright from Esau with red lentil soup. This is the soup Jacob served Isaac while mourning for Abraham.

Tricks of the trade

Don't worry about the oil in this recipe; it will be drained out before serving. Make sure to have a colander ready in the sink to drain the rice.

When cooking the *tadig*, make sure the steam stays inside the pot and the paper towels are safely away from the heat.

To make the rice

3 cups basmati rice, checked and rinsed

8 cups water

2 tablespoons salt

⅛ teaspoon turmeric

½ cup canola oil

To make rice topping

½ cup brown lentils, checked and rinsed

1½ cups water

1 onion, caramelized (see page 188)

To steam and make *tadig*

canola oil

2 tablespoons water

⅛ teaspoon turmeric and/or saffron powder

3 potatoes, peeled and sliced into ¼-inch rounds

TO COOK THE RICE AND MAKE THE TOPPING

1. Fill a 6-quart nonstick saucepan with 8 cups water; add oil, salt, and turmeric. Cover and bring to a brisk boil over high heat.

2. Meanwhile, make the topping: In a small saucepan, bring the water and lentils to a boil. Reduce heat to medium/low and cook for 7 to 10 minutes or until the lentils become "al dente". Remove from heat, drain, and set aside.

3. When the turmeric water boils, add the rice and continue cooking, uncovered, over medium to high heat, stirring occasionally.

4. After 3–5 minutes, use a slotted spoon to scoop some grains from the water. Break one grain in half to make sure it is "al dente". Turn off heat and pour rice into the colander to drain; set aside.

5. Gently stir cooked lentils into the rice in the colander.

TO STEAM AND MAKE TADIG

1. Place the empty 6-quart saucepan back onto the stovetop over medium heat. Add ¼-inch canola oil and 2 tablespoons water. Add turmeric and/or saffron powder. Stir together.

2. Add sliced potatoes in a single layer. Add the drained rice and shape it into a pyramid.

Cover the pot and cook for 5–7 minutes until rice begins to steam.

3. Uncover and place 2 paper towels (one on top of the other) over the rice. The ends will extend outside the pot. Replace the lid tightly.

4. Reduce the heat to low and simmer, covered, for 45 minutes. Turn off the heat and tilt the lid until ready to serve.

5. Serve on a shallow platter, mounding the rice into a pyramid and garnishing with caramelized onions and *tadig*.

Yield: 8 servings

❧ RICE WITH CHERRIES IN HEAVY SYRUP ❧

Albaloo Polo

When I first saw this rice I couldn't believe it was edible! The cherries give it such a beautiful purple color! Unlike sweet cherries, sour cherries are often mixed with sugar to tame their acidity and are rarely eaten alone (unless you are Persian!). Hence, this rice calls for sour cherries in heavy syrup, which will give it a sweet and sour taste. Persians are in love with sour cherries, and this tiny fruit is used in many Persian dishes and drinks.

To make the rice

3 cups basmati rice, checked and rinsed

8 cups water

2 tablespoons salt

⅛ teaspoon turmeric

½ cup canola oil

To make rice topping

1 (15.5-ounce) jar sour cherries, pitted, preserved in heavy syrup

caramelized onions for garnish (optional)

To steam and make *tadig*

canola oil

2 tablespoons water

⅛ teaspoon turmeric and/or saffron powder

3 potatoes, peeled and sliced into ¼-inch rounds

TO COOK THE RICE

1. Fill a 6-quart nonstick saucepan with 8 cups water; add oil, salt, and turmeric. Cover and bring to a brisk boil over high heat.

2. When the turmeric water boils, add the rice and continue cooking, uncovered, over medium to high heat, stirring occasionally.

3. After 3–5 minutes, use a slotted spoon to scoop some grains from the water. Break one grain in half to make sure it is "al dente". Turn off heat and pour rice into the colander to drain.

4. Transfer rice to a bowl and use a large spoon to stir the entire jar of cherries into the rice. Set aside.

TO STEAM AND MAKE TADIG

1. Place the empty 6-quart saucepan back onto the stovetop over medium heat. Add ¼-inch canola oil and 2 tablespoons water. Add turmeric and/or saffron powder. Stir together.

2. Add sliced potatoes in a single layer. Add the drained rice and shape it into a pyramid. Cover the pot and cook for 5–7 minutes until rice begins to steam.

3. Uncover and place 2 paper towels (one on top of the other) over the rice. The ends will extend outside the pot. Replace the lid tightly.

4. Reduce the heat to low and simmer, covered, for 45 minutes. Turn off the heat and tilt the lid until ready to serve.

5. Serve on a shallow platter, mounding the rice into a pyramid and garnishing with caramelized onions.

Yield: 8 servings

Tricks of the trade

Don't worry about the oil in this recipe; it will be drained out before serving. Make sure to have a colander ready in the sink to drain the rice. When cooking the *tadig*, make sure the paper towels are safely away from the heat.

Try to handle cooked basmati rice gently and use wide spoons to avoid breaking the elegant elongated grains, which are the pride of perfect Persian rice.

❧ JEWELED RICE ❧

Javaher Polo

Persian women, in general, love jewelry. When I realized there was a rice recipe with the word "jeweled" in its name, it didn't surprise me at all! This rice really looks like a gastronomic jewelry box. It contains edible rubies (barberries), emeralds (pistachios), and onyx (currant raisins). It is a gorgeous display of color and tastes. The good thing about it is that you can use a mixture of anything you might have on hand and make it into *Javaher Polo*. See page 188 for a large array of options that will make your rice look as gorgeous as the Empress's crown!

To make the rice

3 cups basmati rice, checked and rinsed

8 cups water

2 tablespoons salt

⅛ teaspoon turmeric

½ cup canola oil

To make rice topping

The following are good choices for *Javaher Polo* (see page 188 for specifics):

• Yellow split peas, currant raisins, barberries, pistachios, fried slivered almonds

• Barberries, orange peel, slivered carrots, caramelized onions

• 1 tablespoon *advieh* (optional)

To steam and make *tadig*

canola oil

2 tablespoons water

⅛ teaspoon turmeric and/or saffron powder

3 potatoes, peeled and sliced into ¼-inch rounds

TO MAKE THE RICE

1. Fill a 6-quart nonstick saucepan with 8 cups water; add oil, salt, and turmeric. Cover and bring to a brisk boil over high heat.

2. When turmeric water boils, add rice and continue cooking, uncovered, over medium to high heat, stirring occasionally.

3. After 3–5 minutes, use a slotted spoon to scoop some grains from the water. Break one grain in half to make sure it is "al dente". Turn off heat and pour rice into colander to drain. Set aside.

TO STEAM AND MAKE TADIG

1. Place the empty 6-quart saucepan back onto the stovetop over medium heat. Add ¼-inch canola oil and 2 tablespoons water. Add turmeric and/or saffron powder. Stir together.

2. Add sliced potatoes in a single layer. Add drained rice and shape it into a pyramid. Cover the pot and cook for 5–7 minutes until rice begins to steam. Uncover and place 2 paper towels (one on top of the other) over the rice. The ends will extend outside the pot. Replace the lid tightly.

3. Reduce the heat to low and simmer, covered, for 45 minutes. Turn off the heat and tilt the lid until ready to serve.

4. In the meantime, prepare your choice of garnishes listed above. See page 188 for instructions and more ideas. Add advieh–if using.

5. Serve on a shallow platter, mounding the rice into a pyramid and garnishing with the toppings of your choice. You can mix them into the rice or lay them in separate stripes over the rice.

Yield: 8 servings

Tricks of the trade

Don't worry about the oil in this recipe; it will be drained out before serving. Make sure to have a colander ready in the sink to drain the rice. When cooking the *tadig*, make sure the paper towels are safely away from the heat.

When cooking the dried fruit, keep the heat low and pay attention because these burn easily.

I often make this rice when I have leftover toppings in the fridge. It looks as if I labored for hours, but in fact everything was already made!

You can use potatoes for the *tadig*, or you can use some of the rice before mixing it with the toppings.

☙ RICE WITH CABBAGE AND BLACK-EYED PEAS ☙

Kalam Polo

This rice is indigenous to Shiraz, the city where my husband was born. Did you know each city in Iran has a different reputation? Shiraz is known for its happy and spirited people who love to party with *ghaliun* (water pipe) and *arak*! If you met my husband, you would realize he fits right in. This dish features delicious black-eyed peas and green cabbage. Black-eyed peas are originally native to India and really look as if they had a little black eye. Interestingly, black-eyed peas are considered a "good-luck" symbol at the *Rosh Hashana seuda* (New Year's feast). Hence, eating these foods on *Rosh Hashana* has remained common practice among Sephardic Jews all over the world. Apparently, some American non-Jews adopted this practice around the time of the Civil War.

To make the rice

3 cups basmati rice, checked and rinsed

8 cups water

2 tablespoons salt

⅛ teaspoon turmeric

½ cup canola oil

To make rice topping

1 onion, chopped into small dice

dash turmeric

3 tablespoons canola oil

3 cups shredded green cabbage

1 teaspoon salt

1 (15.5-ounce) can black-eyed peas

To steam and make *tadig*

canola oil

2 tablespoons water

⅛ teaspoon turmeric and/or saffron powder

3 potatoes, peeled and sliced into ¼-inch rounds

TO MAKE THE RICE TOPPING

1. Fill a 6-quart nonstick saucepan with 8 cups water; add oil, salt, and turmeric. Cover and bring to a brisk boil over high heat.

2. In the meantime, fry onion and turmeric in the oil over medium heat, stirring periodically for about 7 minutes or until onion is translucent. Add cabbage and salt and cook over medium heat until cabbage has wilted. Turn off the heat and set aside.

3. Drain and rinse the black-eyed peas in a small colander and set aside.

4. When the turmeric water boils, add the rice and continue cooking, uncovered, over medium to high heat, stirring occasionally.

5. After 3–5 minutes, use a slotted spoon to scoop some grains from the water. Break one grain in half to make sure it is "al dente". Turn off heat and pour rice into the colander to drain.

6. Stir the cabbage/onion mixture and the peas into the rice in the colander. Set aside.

TO STEAM AND MAKE TADIG

1. Place the empty 6-quart saucepan back onto the stovetop over medium heat. Add ¼-inch canola oil and 2 tablespoons water. Add turmeric and/or saffron powder. Stir together.

2. Add sliced potatoes in a single layer. Add the drained rice and shape it into a pyramid. Cover the pot and cook for 5–7 minutes until rice begins to steam. Uncover and place 2 paper towels (one on top of the other) over the rice. The ends will extend outside the pot. Replace the lid tightly.

3. Reduce the heat to low and simmer, covered, for 45 minutes. Turn off the heat and tilt the lid until ready to serve.

4. Serve on a shallow platter, mounding the rice into a pyramid and garnishing with *tadig*.

Yield: 8 servings

Tricks of the trade

Don't worry about the oil in this recipe; it will be drained out before serving. Make sure to have a colander ready in the sink to drain the rice.

When cooking the *tadig*, make sure the paper towels are safely away from the heat. In the picture at left, I garnished the rice with nigella seeds to add contrast.

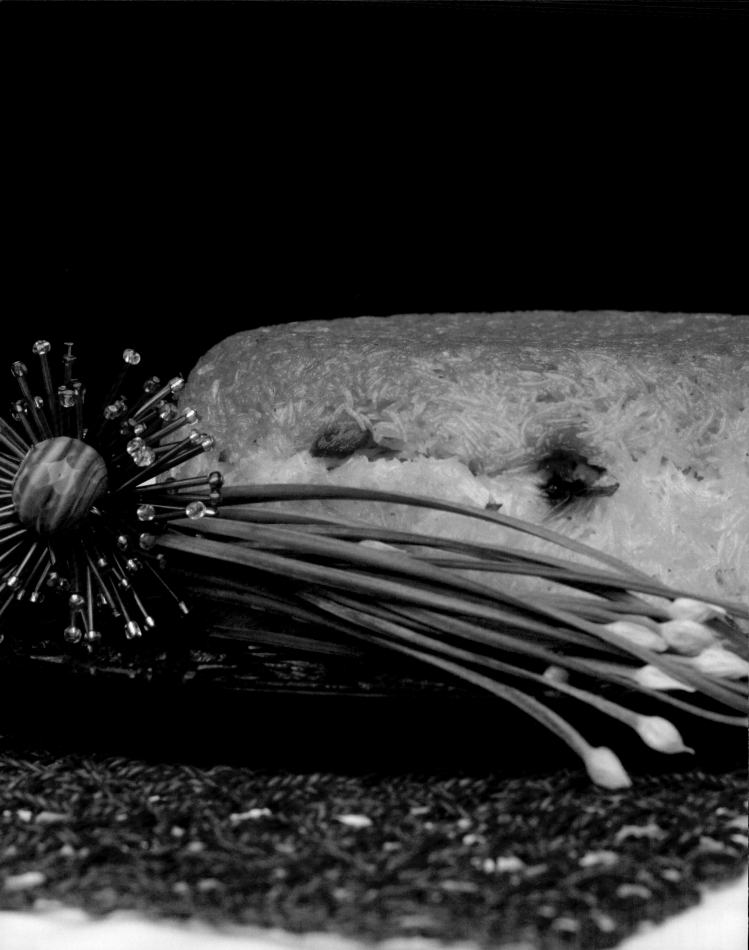

❧ STUFFED RICE CAKE ❧

Tah Chin

This recipe is beautiful! It is a one-pot meal and children love it. It reminds me very much of *arroz con pollo* (a Latin dish with chicken and rice). If you decide to use barberries, this dish will be sour, but if you use currant raisins it is sweet. It is really up to you! Traditionally, in the non-Jewish world, this dish is made with yogurt. However, thanks to Mrs. Melamed, we are able to enjoy it in a *parve* way. We can also stuff it with chicken or beef (*kashrut* laws do not allow the mixing of milk and meat), and it still tastes delicious!

Rice

3 cups rice, checked and rinsed

8 cups water

¼ cup canola oil

1 tablespoon salt

Sauce

4 eggs

3 tablespoons mayonnaise

¼ teaspoon saffron

3 tablespoons lime juice

½ teaspoon salt

¼ teaspoon pepper

1 tablespoon canola oil

Stuffing

2 tablespoons canola oil

1 onion, diced

2 cups diced cooked chicken *or* beef

¼ cup barberries *or* currant raisins

Tadig

canola oil

2 tablespoons water

¼ teaspoon turmeric

TO MAKE THE RICE

1. Fill a 6-quart nonstick saucepan with 8 cups water; add oil and salt. Cover and bring to a brisk boil over high heat.

2. In the meantime, make the sauce: Mix the eggs, mayonnaise, saffron, lime juice, salt, pepper, and oil in a medium bowl. Set aside.

3. When the water boils, add the rice and continue cooking, uncovered, over medium to high heat, stirring occasionally.

4. After 3–5 minutes, use a slotted spoon to scoop some grains from the water. Break one grain in half to make sure it is "al dente". Turn off heat and pour rice into the colander to drain.

5. Pour the cooked rice over the sauce and mix together very well until well coated. Set aside.

6. **Make the stuffing**: In a small skillet, fry the onion with the oil over medium heat until translucent. Add the diced chicken or any other stuffing of your choice and the barberries or raisins and cook over medium heat, mixing it, for about one minute. Turn off heat and set aside.

TO STEAM AND MAKE TADIG

1. Add ¼-inch canola oil and 2 tablespoons water to a 4-quart nonstick saucepan. Add ¼ teaspoon turmeric and stir. Place over medium heat and warm the oil. Pour half the rice mixture in and flatten with a spoon.

Pour stuffing in and flatten as well. Pour in the rest of the rice mixture and flatten again.

2. Cover the pot and cook for 5–7 minutes until rice begins to steam. Uncover and place 2 paper towels (one on top of the other) over the rice. The ends will extend outside the pot. Replace the lid tightly.

3. Reduce heat to low and simmer, covered, for 45 minutes. Turn off the heat and tilt the lid until ready to serve.

4. Invert pot and turn rice out onto a platter, just as you would a cake.

Yield: 8 servings

Tricks of the trade

I recommend having a colander ready in the sink to drain the rice. Persian rice cooks really fast!

I love using leftover chicken or even meat to make this rice. Make sure to remove any bones and simply dice. I have even used leftover *moussaka* to stuff this dish!

The longer this rice steams while simmering, the crunchier the *tadig* surrounding it will be. So, if you can spare more than 45 minutes, it will be superb!

Dairy Foods, Egg Dishes and Persian Snacks

I have never been to Iran and to be honest with you, I don't know if I will ever be able to go. I would love to visit the Persepolis ruins and witness the site of the grave of Queen Esther and Mordechai in Hamadan…But rest assured: having lived in LA, there are certain elements of Iran, specifically of Shiraz, that I have definitely experienced without putting a foot on its soil!

Persians are thrilled when they see a park filled with flowers and fitted with barbecue stands, tables, and running water. By "running water" I don't mean drinking fountains; I mean a stream. When Sammy invited me for the first time to "the park" with his family, I never thought I would feel transported to Iran! When we arrived, the park was already overflowing with Persians, to the point that most Americans must have felt like foreigners in their own backyards! All of a sudden, Sam's mom whipped out a small barbecue, a large pot of *Chelo* (Persian White Rice), freshly made *Chai* (tea), fresh cut-up fruit, nuts—and a mini reproduction of her kitchen. I was stunned! I looked to my side, and to my amazement Sam's dad had already set up several feet of sitting room…meaning several blankets on the ground, along with a few cushions and, of course, a giant backgammon board and a deck of cards. In the blink of an eye, Sam's mom was already shaping *Kebab* into large (and slightly scary) swords, and the smell of Persian cuisine was filling the air.

I have lived this experience many times. I have seen innumerable Persian men, old and young, take their shoes off and stick their feet into a stream of questionable water while smoking water pipes as I would hold my breath, hoping the police would not come—because, even though it is just tobacco, it looks too much like something else! I have seen random people in the park coming and sharing their *Kebab* with us because they felt like they belonged to the same big family. I have seen the same old man, whose clone appears in every park, playing the violin while Sam's grandmother sings *basunak* (wedding songs). I have witnessed many poem recitals that neither Sam nor I could understand because the Farsi is so advanced that only a few people in the park have the intellect to comprehend it. I have been harassed by cute old Persian ladies trying to convince me their son is a good candidate for marriage—until the moment they realize I am not Persian! So, although I honestly do not look forward to the swarm of flies, the mosquito bites, the leaves that fall on my rice, and the general mayhem of being in a park filled with Persians, I still can't help being mesmerized at this people's ability to transport me to the private gardens of Shiraz!

Many of the dishes in this section are appropriate to bring to a picnic—and these do not require you to "shlep" your whole kitchen along!

❧ PERSIAN BREAKFAST ❧

Just like Jews are the people of the book, Persians are the people of the food! They make every meal an extraordinary pleasure for the taste buds and the eyes, and breakfast is no different. You may be used to having a quick bowl of cereal, but when it comes to Persian food the fast-breakfast meal goes beyond cornflakes and milk…. Persian breakfast takes you far away to an exotic dimension where fresh Bulgarian cheese and scrumptious nuts are bundled together, making it impossible to forget–and impossible to resist.

Since life is quite busy and there is not often time for a sit-down breakfast during my crazy weekdays, I often indulge on Sundays with a Persian breakfast. I make an "omelet," which to Persians means sautéed vegetables with egg. Also, I set the table with toasted bread (Barbari or Lavash – see page 33, 35) and Bulgarian feta cheese. Some other nice additions are a bowl of walnuts and cut-up honeydew and yogurt. Last, but certainly not least, I serve a steaming glass of sweet Persian tea (see page 265). However, if you cannot wait for Sundays, as long as you have some barbari (or pita) bread, feta cheese, and walnuts, you can totally indulge in a breakfast a lá Persian!

Persian Breakfast Omelet

∽ CHEESE AND WALNUTS ∽

Panir'o Gerdu

This is a very common and easy breakfast in Persian homes. It consists of:

Lavash or barbari (see page 33, 35)
Bulgarian feta cheese
Walnuts *and/or* honeydew melon

Enjoy wrapping cheese with pieces of walnuts or melon in slices of bread.

Panir'o Gerdu image featured on previous page.

❧

∽ PERSIAN BREAKFAST OMELET ∽

1 medium onion, finely sliced into half-circles
2 tablespoons olive oil
¼ teaspoon turmeric
2 tomatoes, finely sliced into half-circles

½ teaspoon salt
¼ teaspoon pepper
4 eggs, whisked together

In a medium skillet, sauté onions in olive oil and turmeric over medium heat for 10 minutes. Add tomatoes and sauté for an additional 5 minutes until soft. Combine eggs with salt and pepper. Pour over onion-tomato mixture and cook over medium/low heat, covered, for 10 minutes or until eggs set.

Yield: 4 servings

❧ PERSIAN EGGPLANT OMELET ❧

Kookoo Budemjune

If you are an eggplant fan, this dish will be absolutely delicious! A *kookoo* is nothing more than a Persian *latke*. This recipe makes 5-inch *kookoos* (imagine a *latke* on steroids) or you can also make the usual 2-inch bite-size portions. These are great stuffed into a pita with chummus and vegetables.

1 large eggplant

½ onion, finely diced

½ teaspoon salt

¼ teaspoon pepper

1 egg

½ cup flour

dash turmeric

1 tablespoon canola oil, for frying

1. Roast the eggplant on a grill *or* directly over medium heat on your stovetop *or* broil in the oven on high in a 9"x13" aluminum pan until the skin is blistered and black on all sides. Make sure to turn the eggplant so all the sides become blistered. Set aside for 10 minutes or until it looks heavy and sinks in.

2. In the meantime, combine remaining ingredients (except oil) in a medium bowl.

3. Peel the eggplants, mash with a fork, and add the pulp to the bowl. Keep mixing until it looks like a creamy batter.

4. Heat oil in a small skillet (5-inch diameter) over medium/high heat. Use a ladle to pour one-fifth of the batter into the skillet; it should be about 2 inches thick. Cook, covered, over medium heat until the edges brown. With the help of a large spatula or a small plate, turn the *kookoo* over and cook the other side until it is brown.

5. Repeat with remaining batter.

6. Serve with pita bread, tomatoes, and onions.

Yield: 5 *kookoos*

Tricks of the trade

If you do not have a spatula large enough to flip this *kookoo*, do not panic. Simply use a dinner plate instead of a spatula. Position the plate upside-down firmly on top of the skillet, just like a lid. Hold the skillet handle with your left hand and place your right hand firmly flat on the plate. Rapidly flip the skillet over, supporting the plate with your right hand, and lift the skillet off the plate. The *kookoo* will be sitting on the plate, ready to be slipped back into the skillet to brown on the other side!

✿ PERSIAN HERB OMELET ✿

Kookoo Sabsi

This is another favorite! Although this *kookoo* is fried, it is impossible to feel you are not eating pure goodness! The vegetables in this dish not only give it a gorgeous color but also an irresistible smell! It can also be stuffed into pita bread or eaten on its own. I like making it into a large round and then cutting it like pizza. An 8-inch nonstick skillet is ideal for this recipe.

1 (16-ounce) bag frozen spinach
1 bunch scallions (8 stems), finely chopped
1 tablespoon dried mint
1 tablespoon dried dill (dill weed)
⅓ cup dried parsley flakes

3 eggs
1½ teaspoons salt
½ teaspoon turmeric
½ teaspoon pepper
2 tablespoons canola oil, for frying

1. In a medium bowl, combine all ingredients except oil and toss well. Set aside.

2. In an 8-inch nonstick skillet, heat 1 tablespoon of oil over medium/high heat.

3. Pour in the entire mixture and flatten with a spoon.

4. Reduce heat to medium, cover, and cook for 7 to 10 minutes or until the edges of the *kookoo* start browning.

5. Turn *kookoo* over and continue cooking, uncovered, for another 10 minutes.

Yield: 1 8-inch *kookoo*

Tricks of the trade

If you do not have a spatula large enough to flip this *kookoo*, do not panic. Simply use a dinner plate instead of a spatula. Position the plate upside-down firmly on top of the skillet, just like a lid. Hold the skillet handle with your left hand and place your right hand firmly flat on the plate. Rapidly flip the skillet over, supporting the plate with your right hand, and lift the skillet off the plate. The *kookoo* will be sitting on the plate, ready to be slipped back into the skillet to brown on the other side!

❧ PERSIAN POTATO LATKES ❧

Kookoo Sibzamini

Persians have their own shuls, neighborhoods, schools—but I'll bet you never imagined Persians have their own version of potato latkes! These are crunchy on the outside, soft on the inside, and look more tailored than the old favorite. However, it doesn't need to be Chanuka to enjoy *kookoo sibzamini*! In fact, I would dare to say this *kookoo* is the Persian falafel! My mother-in-law loves making it as a quick lunch stuffed into pita bread. Keep in mind this kookoo is round, not oval. To avoid confusion, Persians designated the oval shape only for any *kookoo* with meat added.

4 medium potatoes, unpeeled and scrubbed

2 eggs, lightly beaten

1 teaspoon salt

½ teaspoon pepper

canola oil, as needed, for frying

1. Place clean potatoes in a medium saucepan and cover with water. Bring water to a covered boil over high heat. Simmer until fork tender (about 25 minutes).

2. Drain potatoes and return to saucepan. Cover with cold water. When the potatoes are cold enough to handle, peel them by hand and mash. Mix potatoes with egg, salt, and pepper until a smooth consistency is achieved.

3. Fill a medium skillet with ½-inch oil and heat over medium heat until oil sizzles in contact with a drop of water.

4. Wet your hand and shape potato mixture, about 2 tablespoons at a time, into flattened rounds about ½-inch thick and 2 inches in diameter or use falafel tool to shape. Fry for 5 minutes per side until a brown and crispy crust has formed. Transfer each *kookoo* to a paper-towel-lined platter until ready to serve.

Yield: approximately 10 *kookoos*

Tools of the trade

Next time you are at a falafel restaurant (probably the most common kosher establishments after kosher Chinese restaurants), pay attention when they make your falafel. There is a really cool tool that is used to shape it. This tool is also commonly used to shape *kookoos*; it is called "*ghaleb'e kookoo*." In the case of falafel, the batter blows up into a consistent flattened ball. In the case of *kookoo*, the shaper forms identical perfect rounds. A treat to the eye and a relief for perfectionists!

غذای تخم مرغ EGG DISHES   229

❦ TRADITIONAL CHANUKA LATKES ❦

Levivot

How can one make a kosher cookbook without mentioning the quintessential Chanuka dish? Every year I make sure to starve a little before Chanuka so I can indulge in the pleasure of latkes with tons of sour cream and not much guilt. My children love helping to peel the potatoes…It is a wonderful way of integrating the family into the magic of Chanuka and making sure (in my case) that the boys stay close to the kitchen!

2 large potatoes, peeled and shredded

1 egg

1 teaspoon salt

¼ cup flour

canola oil, as needed, for frying

1. In a medium bowl, mix the potatoes, eggs, salt, and flour to form a wet batter. Set aside.

2. Fill a medium skillet with ½-inch oil and heat over medium heat until oil sizzles in contact with a drop of water.

3. Using a large spoon or ¼-cup measure, drop batter into oil to form patties about 2 inches wide. Fry for about 2 minutes on each side or until the latkes are brown and scrumptious.

4. Place on the platter draped with paper towels until ready to serve.

5. Serve warm or at room temperature along with sour cream and applesauce.

Yield: approximately 15 latkes

Tools of the trade

I love, absolutely love, perfection. It is a problem, I know. However, let me just share with you a little trick to help your latkes all look the same. You can use either an ice-cream scoop or a ¼-cup measuring cup to scoop up the batter and then drop it into the oil. All the latkes will be the same size and picture perfect!

My obsession with: Paper towels!

Back at home (Venezuela) we did not use paper towels. They were just not available and not part of our culture. In America, paper towels are everywhere! So the first time I used them, I was very uneasy about it. I felt it was such a waste of paper, so I would cut off the exact amount I needed. Today, I have grown accustomed to them and use them for everything from writing quick messages (although sometimes these end up in the garbage by mistake) to using them as toe separators for applying nail polish! However, when I use them to soak up the extra oil from my fried food, I feel I have indeed accomplished something! Never forget to line any platter with a good old paper towel and let it soak up the extra oil—instead of letting your arteries do it!

❧ SOUR APPLE LATKES ❧

Kookoo sib'e torsh

I bet you never imagined Persian food could be as original as this—talk about killing two birds with one stone! As you know, latkes are traditionally eaten with applesauce and sour cream… Here is a latke with the applesauce included! These are absolutely delicious and, contrary to what one might think, they are savory with a hint of sweetness.

2 large green apples, with skins,
cored and shredded

1 egg

½ teaspoon salt

¼ cup flour

canola oil, as needed, for frying

1. In a medium bowl, mix the apples, eggs, salt, and flour to form a wet batter. Set aside.

2. Fill a medium skillet with ½-inch oil and heat over medium heat until oil sizzles in contact with a drop of water. Drape a platter with a few sheets of paper towel to absorb the extra oil after frying.

3. Using a large spoon or ¼-cup measure, drop batter into oil, forming patties about 2 inches wide. Fry for about 2 minutes on each side or until the *kookoos* are brown and scrumptious. Place on the paper-towel-covered platter to drain excess oil.

4. Serve warm or at room temperature.

Yield: 13 *kookoos*

A "FRIENDLY" WORD ABOUT YOGURT

We have a tradition in my country that the woman who consumes yogurt will enjoy a "porcelain-like" face. As a child, I was never sure if that meant I was supposed to "shmear" yogurt on my face or eat it. Don't worry; I did eventually learn that I was supposed to eat it. But what does a porcelain face look like, anyway? Perhaps like a bad botox job? I wasn't sure what to make of it, but one thing was for sure: I always loved yogurt.

Yogurt has been around for a while; in fact, for thousands of years! It was probably discovered by mistake while a Balkan nomad (who of course must have been ultimately Persian…right?!) somehow kept his sheepskin canteen filled with milk at an average of 110°F for a long period of time. To his astonishment, friendly bacteria called *Lactobacillus bulgaricus* and *Streptococcus thermophilus* had invaded his milk and fermented it. The results proved to be incredible, a smooth creamy-textured paste with a sour yet surprisingly pleasant taste. The nomad was so happy—but when I found out the result of his scientific research, my love for yogurt went down the drain! After discovering my beloved yogurt was bacterial, I could not stop looking at the motionless white blob…as if waiting for it to move a little and show me how alive it was! But fortunately, my sister (who, by the way, is a scientist), explained to me that this very bacteria is what has given yogurt its claim to fame!

You see, friendly bacteria (or *probiotics*), are more beneficial to the body than anyone ever imagined… even the Balkan nomad! Probiotics are able to survive the severe acidic environment of our stomach and ultimately reach all the way down the intestinal tracts. Probiotics (being good old friendly bacteria) make peace between the other kinds of bacteria that live there. Incredibly enough, as a result of all this bacterial cooperation, the body is able to better break down foods, process hormones, and synthesize vitamins. The results are good digestion, a cure for antibiotic-induced diarrhea, and helping people with lactose intolerance by breaking down dairy food. Yogurt can also boost immunity, reduce osteoporosis, treat yeast infections, and even prevent cancer! After hearing all my sister's arguments—and seeing that the white blob never did move on its own—I embraced yogurt again…starting with frozen yogurt, of course!

❧ REFRESHING YOGURT DIP ❧
WITH SHREDDED CUCUMBER AND MINT
Must'o Chiar

This dish is probably the most popular Persian dairy dip there is. It is fantastic with potato chips! It is very low fat and incredibly healthy—well, as long as you don't eat a whole bag of potato chips with it! My husband and I love eating it for a light, informal dinner.

I am sure you have probably been to a spa, and if you haven't, please make it a point to visit one soon and pamper yourself a little. Any great spa will often have a whirlpool, and any decent whirlpool will have a little bowl filled with finely sliced cucumber to place over your eyes while indulging in the swirling warm waters. Did you ever wonder why? Why not offer sliced carrots...after all, aren't those good for the eyes?! The reason is that cucumbers have two compounds (ascorbic acid and caffeic acid) which prevent water retention, and reduce swelling! Not only that, but since cucumbers are mostly water, they are also a great source of hydration. Their skin contains silica, potassium, magnesium, and a ton of fiber.

1 large English cucumber, peeled
and shredded

½ cup onion, finely chopped
(1 small onion)

1½ cups low-fat plain yogurt

1 tablespoon dried mint

½ teaspoon pepper

1 teaspoon salt

1. In a medium bowl, combine all ingredients.

Yield: 2 pints

2. Serve in a bowl and decorate with fresh or dried mint. This dish is absolutely delicious accompanied by potato chips.

❧ EGGPLANT WITH WHEY OR YOGURT ❧

Kashk'e Budemjune

I like using low-fat yogurt in this recipe instead of *kashk* (whey) because it is easier to find with kosher certification and because it is healthier. Some people use sour cream instead. However, *kashk* tastes different from yogurt or sour cream. If you want the look of *kashk* but cannot find it, you can use *tehina* as a substitute. However, *tehina* does not taste like *kashk* and, sadly, there is no real substitute for it. So, if you are lucky enough to find kosher *kashk*, go ahead and have a treat!

2 large eggplants, roasted (about 1½ cups pulp)

2 cups onions, finely chopped

2 garlic cloves, pressed

3 tablespoons canola oil

¼ teaspoon turmeric

1 teaspoon salt

½ teaspoon pepper

1 cup low-fat plain yogurt or *kashk*

1. Roast eggplant on a grill or directly over medium heat on your stove top, or broil in the oven on high on a cookie sheet covered with parchment paper, until the skin is blistered and black in all sides. Make sure to turn the eggplant so all sides become blistered.

2. Once eggplant is roasted, set it aside for 10 minutes or until it looks heavy and sinks in.

3. In the meantime, using a large sauté pan or skillet, fry onions, turmeric, and garlic in oil until slightly golden (about 10 minutes).

4. Peel eggplant, mash with a fork, and add the pulp to the onions in the pan. Add salt and pepper. Mix well, stirring with a spatula. Remove from heat and set aside to cool.

5. Once cooled, add the yogurt and mix well.

6. Serve as a refreshing dip along with lavash (page 35), challah (page 334), or tortilla chips.

Yield: 3 cups

❧ YOGURT WITH SPINACH ❧

Borani Esfanaj

This is my favorite dairy Persian dish! It is so easy to make and so delicious. I feel so healthy when I eat this dish. It is obviously a lot more convenient to make if you already have frozen spinach in the freezer. Spinach can be hard to clean and check for insect infestation, so make sure to get the kosher frozen kind, such as Bodek brand.

2 cups onions, finely chopped

2 garlic cloves, pressed or finely minced

3 tablespoons canola oil

¼ teaspoon turmeric

1 (16-ounce) package frozen chopped spinach, defrosted and drained

1 teaspoon salt

½ teaspoon pepper

2 cups low-fat plain yogurt

1. In a small saucepan, fry onions, turmeric, and garlic in oil until slightly golden (about 10 minutes).

2. Add spinach, salt, and pepper and cook for additional 5 minutes, mixing well. Set aside to cool.

3. Once cooled, add the yogurt and mix well.

4. Serve in a bowl and decorate with fresh or dried mint. This dish is absolutely delicious accompanied by lavash (page 35) and potato chips.

Yield: 3 cups

Tricks of the trade

Some people serve this dish into a "bread bowl" using one unsliced round loaf of bread, slicing off the top and hollowing out bottom, leaving a ½-inch shell.

✂ YOGURT WITH SHALLOTS ✂

Must'o Mooseer

This is probably one of the hardest dairy foods to resist! Imagine tasting a dollop of creamy, refreshing yogurt and then finding that it has been infused with the mild flavor of a shallot. The smooth and crunchy texture of this dish is a joy to behold. Obviously, it tastes better on warm lavash bread, pita, or simply with potato chips.

In this recipe, the shallots must be steeped in order to tame their sharpness. *Steeping* is a technique used by many cooks to draw the flavor from food into liquid. Steeping requires soaking ingredients in water (usually hot) until the flavors from the ingredient are infused into the liquid. Some other foods that are commonly steeped are tea leaves, saffron, and coffee, of course!

½ cup boiling water

½ cup shallots, finely diced (about ½ of 1 large shallot)

1 (16-ounce container) low-fat plain yogurt

½ teaspoon salt

¼ teaspoon pepper

1. In a small bowl, combine boiling water and diced shallots. Set aside for 15 minutes. Drain the shallots in a small colander or sieve.

2. In a large bowl, mix the yogurt, salt, and pepper.

3. Add the shallots to the yogurt mixture and combine thoroughly.

4. Serve in a bowl accompanied by lavash (page 35) and/or potato chips.

Yield: 16 ounces

Roasted Corn on the Cob

❧ PERSIAN YOGURT SOUP ❧

Ash'e Must

When my mother-in-law told me she was going to teach me the typical Persian yogurt soup to serve for the holiday of Shavuot, the first thing that came to my mind was, "I wonder if this soup is served hot or cold?" Well, what do you know? This soup does not look like soup at all! After learning to make this delicious meal, I find that rather than a soup, it looks like a dip. It is served cold and eaten with bread or chips.

3 cups water

1 teaspoon salt

¼ teaspoon pepper

1 stick unsalted margarine (8 tablespoons)

1 cup American rice

2 bunches parsley (stems removed), finely chopped

1 bunch mint (stems removed), finely chopped

3 cups low-fat plain yogurt

Garnish

caramelized onions (page 188)

1. In a 4-quart saucepan, bring water, salt, pepper, and margarine to a boil. Add the rice and herbs and stir. Reduce heat and simmer for 25 minutes or until the rice is soft and runny. Remove from heat and allow to cool.

2. Add the yogurt and combine well. Serve in a bowl and garnish with caramelized onions.

Yield: 6 servings

❧ ROASTED CORN ON THE COB ❧

Balal

Balal is a very popular snack, readily available in the streets of Iran. My husband has fond memories of this treat. My children go crazy for this…and so do I! I make this snack right on my gas stovetop (it will not work on an electric stove). If you can't find corn with a long stem, pierce the stem end with a fork and use the fork to keep your hands away from the heat—or hold the cob with food tongs.

corn ears, peeled, preferably with stems

4 cups water

1 tablespoon salt

1. Combine water and salt in a shallow bowl.

2. Remove the stovetop grids. Turn heat to high and roast the corn, carefully holding the stem, and placing the corn directly on the heat source, turning as it cooks (this should take less than 4 minutes per ear). The corn will make a popping sound and look slightly burned when ready.

3. Immediately submerge corn in salted water. Serve warm.

∙ STEEPED WALNUTS ∙

Gerdu

This is a very popular snack in Iran, and it is available for sale by street vendors. In Iran the steeped walnuts are whole, resembling a brain! Unfortunately, it is nearly impossible to find whole shelled walnuts in America. Using halved walnuts gives the same result.

2 cups whole shelled walnuts

3 cups water

salt

1. Place the walnuts in a glass container and cover with water.

2. Store in the refrigerator overnight.

3. Keep refrigerated; to serve, drain walnuts and present them on a tray, sprinkled with a little salt.

Pumpkin Seeds

❧ ASSORTED NUTS AND DRIED FRUITS ❧

Ajil

Ajil is a medley of roasted nuts and/or raw and dried fruits. Persians love to snack on these, especially over a game of backgammon!

Some ideas are:

Trays bursting with walnuts (*gerdu*), almonds (*badam*), watermelon seeds (*tochme hendune*), chickpeas (*nochkodchi*), pumpkin seeds (*tochme cadu*), and sunflower seeds (*tochme afolagardan*)

Trays bursting with dried fruits such as apricots, apple (*sib*), pear (*golabi*), cranberries, mulberries (*toot*), figs (*angear*), dates, and big raisins

---

❧ SUKKOT CHICKPEA AND SUGAR TREATS ❧

Sar'e Gandak

These are little bundles of chickpea flour and powdered sugar that are hung in the *Sukka* at the beginning of the *Hag* and eaten when the *Sukka* is put away. My mother-in-law has beautiful childhood memories of reaching up to these bundles and eating the treasure inside! Doesn't it sound great? Well, maybe that worked in Shiraz, but we live in a different climate in the US. Where we live, it rains every single *Sukkot*. Also, the squirrels would have a feast the second I hang the treats! So, I decided to hang them right before the *Sukka* is taken down. The kids have a blast looking for them among all the decorations! I like using white paper cone cups, which the kids decorate. This is a great way to reward the children for helping out while putting the *Sukka* away.

½ cup chickpea flour
½ cup powdered confectioner's sugar

paper-cone cups or cone-shaped favor boxes

1. Combine chickpea flour and sugar and fill each cone cup with approximately 2 tablespoons of the mixture.

2. Wrap in foil, attach a string, and hang from the *schach* in the *Sukka*!

3. To serve, pluck cones from the *schach*, and give one to each child (or help yourself to one!). Snip or tear off the pointy end of the cone and suck out the tasty powder.

Yield: 4-5 treats, depending on cone size.

HOT FAVA BEANS

Bagalah Garmak

I can still remember my husband's cousin, Lital, gobbling tons of fava beans while watching TV. She was only a child, but she loved these as much as popcorn! These are a yummy, filling, and healthy snack. Fava beans resemble large lima beans but are not the same. Fava beans come surrounded by a pod that easily peels off once the beans have been cooked.

1 (14-ounce) bag frozen fava beans with shells (also known as broad beans)

8 cups water

2 tablespoons salt

1. In a 6-quart covered saucepan, bring water and salt to a boil over high heat.

2. Drop frozen fava beans into boiling water. Return to a boil over high heat.

3. Reduce heat to medium and cook for 8 to 10 minutes or until soft.

4. Drain and serve warm, seasoned with a pinch of salt.

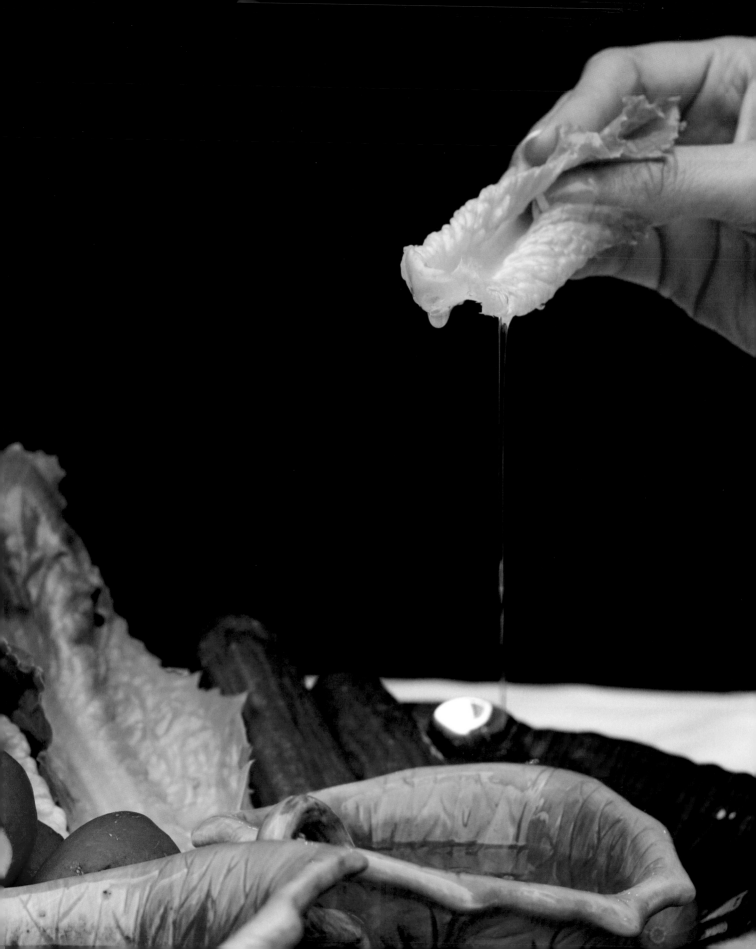

ROMAINE LETTUCE, PICKLED VEGETABLES, AND WINE VINEGAR SYRUP
Kahu Torshi

I have to admit that in the beginning I thought this was a rather strange way to snack. However, today I actually like it very much. It consists of a tray layered with a few hearts of romaine lettuce, a bowl of pickled vegetables (*torshi*; see next page) and vinegar syrup (*sekanjebeen*, page 277) for dipping. All you do is dip the lettuce into the pickled vegetables (sour) or the vinegar syrup (sweet) and eat it, just like that. It is very filling and healthy!

1 romaine lettuce heart
1 cup *torshi* (see next page)
1 cup *sekanjebeen* (see page 277)

Serve on a tray and eat, dipping the lettuce in your choice of dips.

Roasted Garlic

❧ PERSIAN PICKLED VEGETABLES ❧

Torshi

Torshi is nothing more than pickled vegetables. Persians eat torshi as a relish for meats and vegetables. There are several different ways of making *torshi*. Depending on taste, a person can make onion *torshi*, eggplant *torshi*, mixed vegetable *torshi*, garlic *torshi*, and many more. However, even though making *torshi* is very easy, it requires one thing that is not always easy: patience! The vegetables must marinate at least 2 months before they are usable. Hence, I often purchase ready-made *torshi* from Middle Eastern grocers instead of making it myself. The good news is that I was able to get the Immediate-Gratification Marinated Garlic *torshi* recipe from the *torshi* guru: Ronan Armin.

❧ IMMEDIATE-GRATIFICATION MARINATED GARLIC ❧

Torshi'e Seer

6 garlic heads (13.5 ounces)

3 tablespoons water

1 tablespoon olive oil

¼ teaspoon salt

1 cup seasoned rice vinegar

1 cup apple cider vinegar

4 tablespoons honey

You will also need

1 (24-ounce) glass jar with a tight-fitting lid (terrine)

Yields: 24 ounces

Tricks of the Trade

There is not a single Shabbat dinner in my house that goes by without a bowl of roasted garlic! Follow the same directions as step 1 at left, but roast at 350°F for about 1 hour 30 minutes, until the garlic has caramelized and each clove can be easily squeezed out of its shell. Serve warm.

1. Preheat the oven to 350°F. Cut a 12"x12" square of aluminum foil; set aside.

2. With a knife, slice the top from each head of garlic. Separate into cloves and remove excess skin, without peeling each clove.

3. Pile the garlic in the middle of the aluminum square. Pour the water, olive oil, and salt onto the garlic and gather all the aluminum corners, making a bundle.

4. Place in the oven for 45 minutes or until soft enough to almost squeeze out of the shell.

5. Remove from the oven and pour into glass jar. Add apple cider vinegar, white vinegar, and honey. Close the lid tightly and place in a cool, dark place for 1 day.

❧ MARINATED EGGPLANTS ❧

Torshi'e Liteh

Make sure to use a clean spoon every time you remove some marinated eggplant from the jar. As you can see in the picture, this dish can also be made with whole roasted unpeeled Chinese eggplants. Just follow all directions—but do not peel or mash the Chinese eggplant.

2 large eggplants

¼ cup fresh cilantro, washed and chopped

1 teaspoon dried basil

1 teaspoon dried parsley

1 teaspoon dried mint

white vinegar

salt and pepper

You will also need

1 (24-ounce) glass jar with a tight-fitting lid (terrine)

1. Roast the eggplant on a grill or directly over medium heat on your stovetop or broil in the oven on high on a cookie sheet covered with parchment paper, until the skin is blistered and black in all sides. Make sure to turn the eggplant so all sides become blistered.

2. Once the eggplant is roasted, set aside for 10 minutes or until it looks heavy and sinks in.

3. Peel eggplant and mash with a fork. Fill the glass jar with layers of eggplant and herbs.

4. Fill to the top with vinegar and season with salt and pepper to taste.

5. Close the lid tightly. Store in a cool, dry place for at least 2 to 3 months until ready to serve.

❧ MARINATED VEGETABLES ❧

Torshi'e Machloot

This recipe is delicious with *kebab*. Make sure to use a clean spoon every time you remove some marinated vegetables from the jar.

½ cup cauliflower, finely diced

½ cup carrots, finely diced

½ cup celery, finely diced

1 shallot, finely diced

3 garlic cloves, pressed

1 tablespoon dried mint

white vinegar

salt and pepper

You will also need

1 (24-ounce) glass jar with a tight-fitting lid (terrine)

1. Add all vegetables and herbs to the jar.

2. Fill to the top with vinegar and season with salt and pepper to taste.

3. Close the lid tightly. Store in a cool, dry place for at least 2 to 3 months until ready to serve.

Persian Beverages and Desserts

I can still remember the face a prominent Ashkenazi Rabbi made when Sammy (my husband) convinced him to try a *Kuluche* (Chickpea Cookie, page 287). He didn't like it at all! Fortunately, I was right there, laughing out loud and handing him a napkin. How about when one of my guests asked if I had put perfume in the dessert? Someone even thought that the kids might have added dishwashing soap by mistake. You see, most Persian pastries have one ingredient in common: rose water. Now, you might think this is amusing. Or you might politely say this is "an acquired taste," which is a nice way of saying, "How could anyone like this?!" The good news for those who cannot stand the aroma and taste of roses is that, on a Persian table, there is always a platter of beautiful fresh fruit. I love the gorgeous display of fruits that I encounter whenever I am invited to a Persian wedding…It is really a sight to behold!

However, there is one aspect of Persian desserts that you probably were not expecting at all. Many Persian desserts are actually French! Persians "borrowed" French desserts and made them their own by incorporating ingredients that are indigenous to Persian culture, such as saffron, cardamom, and, of course, rose water. Interestingly, Persians also borrowed French words and made them part of their everyday lingo. This process of "modernization" of Farsi and Persian culture in general began in the nineteenth century. At the time, France was seen as the role model for secular culture and behavior. Indeed, French was the language of choice, used not only to discuss cuisine, couture, diplomacy, and etiquette, but was also a second language heard at European royal courts and employed by aristocrats. The inflow of French words was so vast that a study made in 1982 estimated about 3,000 to 4,000 words had been adopted. Hey—at least there is some hope for you to learn Farsi if you took French at school!

Although French-inspired Persian desserts are luscious and stunning, they are often reserved for special occasions. Most of the time, Persians offer actually quite simple yet delicious choices. Many times dessert will include only fresh cut-up fruits such as melon, sweet lemon, tangerines or oranges, sliced apples, watermelon, and sometimes mini-cucumbers. Very often, some fruits will be offered in their dried form, including dates, mulberries, raisins, and apricots. Also, Persians are known for indulging in all kinds of roasted nuts and seeds, such as pistachios, walnuts, watermelon seeds, and pumpkin seeds, to name a few.

Another curious factor is that, no matter what time of day it is, no matter how cold or hot the weather, Persians love their *Chai* (tea). So, make sure to have some available if you want your guests to have a genuine Persian experience. Also, remember that all Persian pastries are now readily available in stores. So, if baking is not your "cup of *Chai*," you can get these in a pinch! However, in general, there is nothing like a batch of fresh cookies or a fabulous-looking homemade Persian *Roulade* (page 305)!

Gaz and Noglh, sweets common in Persian festivities and Smachot

❧ THE STORY OF PERSIAN TEA ❧

Chai

The origin of tea is diluted between history and legend. Nonetheless, stories and formal research seem to point to China as the birthplace of tea. One of my favorite legends takes place 5,000 years ago when Shen Nung, an early emperor, always requested that his water be boiled for hygienic reasons. One fateful day, while he was on an excursion, his servants were boiling water outdoors when dried leaves from a nearby bush landed in the pot—and infused the first cup of tea! The word *tea* (in English) or *chai* (in Farsi) is derived from the word *te* in the Xiamen dialect from the Fujian province of China and the word *cha* in Cantonese. In China today, there still exist wild tea trees that are over 1,000 years old!

It is hard to believe that tea arrived in Iran only at the end of the nineteenth century. After all, nowadays the second a guest walks into a Persian home he is offered *chai*. Before tea became popular, coffee was the main beverage in Iran. However, under the influence of England and Russia, tea became a favorite. The change of heart might have also been influenced by the high taxes and elevated price of coffee at the time, which resulted in a decline of imports. Curiously, teahouses in Iran are still called coffee houses (*kahveh chune*) — but in these establishments there is not a single coffee bean to be found!

♣

YOU ARE WHAT YOU EAT

Incredibly, the switch from coffee to tea was a smart move! Dry tea has more caffeine by weight than coffee does. Nonetheless, more dried coffee is used than dry tea in preparing the infusion. A cup of tea contains drastically less caffeine than a cup of coffee of the same size. In addition, it is thought that tea contains antioxidants. Antioxidants slow the aging process and are beneficial for the body, helping to prevent and fight cancer. It is also notable to mention that tea can normalize blood pressure, preventing coronary heart disease and diabetes. Finally, tea has the ability to preserve the adequate balance of the intestinal flora, providing immunity to various intestinal disorders.

For Persians, tea is equivalent to water. It does not matter if the weather is scorching hot or freezing cold, hot steaming tea is offered to anyone and everyone coming through the door. Persians drink tea at any time. Persian tea is traditionally loose tea that is steeped in hot water. Persians make tea in a beautiful kettle called a *samovar*. Today, it consists of two parts: a small teapot and a kettle. To keep the tea warm, the teapot nestles on top of the hot kettle. Tea is served in small glass cups, along with a couple of sugar cubes on the side. The drinker traps the sugar cube between the tip of the tongue and the front teeth while sipping tea. This way, every sip passes through the sugar, becoming nice and sweet. In Iran, milk is never added to tea; most accompaniments to tea are served on the side. Some popular snacks to have with tea are raisins, medjool dates, wedges of lime, and honey.

Today, Persian tea is available loose and in tea bags for your convenience. It is also available in different flavors, but the closest match in flavor outside of Iran is Earl Grey. Making Persian tea is very easy and drinking it with friends is a great bonding experience.

❧ PERSIAN TEA ❧

Chai

Some people like to flavor their tea by adding a few cardamom seeds or ¼ teaspoon of cardamom powder. Others add 1 tablespoon of rose water or orange blossom water to give it a fresh and delectable fragrance.

3 cups water
1 heaping teaspoon loose Earl
Gray tea leaves

1. In a small stainless steel teapot, bring the water to a brisk boil over high heat. Remove from the heat and add the tea. Let the tea steep for 10 minutes. In the meantime, bring a few cups of water to a boil in a kettle, to dilute the tea if necessary.

2. Serve the tea by filling 5-ounce glass cups half full and adding more tea or hot water, depending on how dark or strong each guest prefers. Offer hot tea along with a few sugar cubes.

Yield: 6-10 (½-cup) servings, depending on dilution

نبات

Nabat

Rock candy, *nabat*, is a staple at most Persian homes. However, it usually does not take the place of sugar. In fact, it is not necessarily used to sweeten any tea or coffee; the real use of rock candy—to Persians that is—is to cure any kind of stomach-related issue!

Candy has been around for ages. The Egyptians, Arabs, and Chinese were the pioneers when it comes to sweets. Sugar is extracted from a reed stalk called sugar cane. This giant grass is mentioned in Sanskrit texts from 1200 BCE. In Farsi and Arabic, the word *kand* means sugar…and a good dictionary will tell you that this is the origin of the word *candy*.

The process of making rock candy is called *crystallization*. This process consists of allowing a saturated solution of sugar and water to cool off, forming crystals around thread, on wooden sticks, or simply into loose "pebbles." It is the same process nature uses to produce diamonds and quartz. (Ladies, don't get too excited—unfortunately, I don't have the recipe for diamonds. Besides, this is a cookbook!) Rock candy is the purest form of sugar because, through this process, all the impurities are left behind as the sugar crystallizes and the water evaporates. Luckily for us, *nabat* is readily available for purchase, so we can make the great recipes that follow!

Thoughout the ages, sugar has been used for different reasons. In the thirteenth century, the Venetians used sugar for decorative purposes, making large statues to decorate the dessert tables of the rich and noble. It was the Venetians who started the tradition of giving little bundles of sweets at parties and weddings. Sugar was also known to be a great preservative. Fruits, nuts, and even flowers were covered with sugar to maintain their freshness. In fact, Persian Jews are notorious for giving bundles of sugar-covered almonds, called *noglh*, at circumcisions and weddings.

However, the most famous use of sugar, specifically sugar candy, is for therapeutic purposes. Rock candy is used to this day to cure multiple ailments such as chest pains, dried lips, and, most of all, stomachaches. Persians are extremely faithful to rock candy's healing properties and use it at the first sign of any stomach problem. As an "outsider," I have to confess it has worked for me several times. How sweet it is to have some *chai* and *nabat*!

❧ RELAXING TEA ❧

Gole Gabzaban

The name of this tea literally means "cow's tongue flower." Yes, the flower from which this tea originates (borage plant flowers), scientifically known as *Echium amoenum*, looks like a cow's tongue. What ever happened to Persians and poetry? I laugh so much every time I offer this tea and visualize a cow sticking out its tongue! Borage is a plant that grows in Europe as well as in the Mediterranean and in Iran. The flowers and leaves of this plant are often used in France and Iran for the treatment of stress and depression, for curing chest colds, and for relieving fever. In fact, studies show that these claims are true, and this tea is indeed a useful treatment for infectious diseases and as an anti-febrile medicine. No wonder Persians swear a warm cup of *gole gabzaban* really does the job!

3 cups water

1 heaping teaspoon loose *gole gabzaban* leaves (dried borage flowers)

4 chunks rock candy (*nabat*)

fresh lime juice (optional)

1. In a small stainless steel teapot, bring water to a brisk boil over high heat. Remove from heat and add tea leaves and rock candy. Steep for 20 minutes.

2. Serve in 5-ounce glass cups. This tea should not be diluted, due to its medicinal purposes. This tea is a beautiful scarlet color, and it tastes better with a drizzle of fresh lime juice.

Yield: 6 (½-cup) servings

Persian Green Tea

↬ PERSIAN GREEN TEA ↫

Chai Sabs

This has become a very popular tea. However, when it comes to Persians, green tea is used to cure—excuse my French—diarrhea. This does not mean it cannot be used for the simple pleasure of having a delicious cup of green tea. Simply skip the nabat and enjoy with sugar instead!

3 cups water

1 heaping teaspoon loose green tea leaves

4 chunks rock candy (*nabat*)

1. In a small stainless steel teapot, bring water to a brisk boil over high heat. Remove from heat and add tea and rock candy. Steep for 20 minutes.

2. Serve in 5-ounce glass cups. This tea should not be diluted, due to its medicinal purposes.

Yield: 6 (½-cup) servings

↬ PERSIAN WHITE TEA ↫

Chai Sefid

When I first heard of white tea I wondered: Does this tea come from a tree with white leaves? In fact, I was quite wrong! Most teas, including black, green, and white teas, originate from the same plant (*Camellia sinensis*) with bright green leaves. The only difference is the way the leaves are processed and the amount of oxidation attained. White tea is processed with minimal oxidation.

I was also under the impression that this clear tea had less caffeine than its counterpart, and I was wrong again! White tea, in fact, has more caffeine than green tea does. However, studies have shown white tea is able to destroy organisms that cause disease and it has many healing properties, including anti-microbial properties. Persians use it specifically to treat stomachaches and nausea.

3 cups water

1 heaping teaspoon of loose white tea leaves

4 chunks rock candy (*nabat*)

1. In a small stainless steel teapot, bring water to a brisk boil over high heat. Remove from heat and add tea and rock candy. Steep for 20 minutes.

2. Serve in 5-ounce glass cups. This tea should not be diluted, due to its medicinal purposes.

Yield: 6 (½-cup) servings

❧ TURKISH COFFEE ❧

Kahveh

Some years ago I had the privilege of meeting a Middle Eastern prince. Don't ask how, but His Majesty ended up at my house, having dessert. I figured I must offer him *chai*, since this is what most Persians crave after sweets. To my surprise, instead of tea, His Imperial Highness wanted coffee! Unfortunately, all I had was tea. I had never been a good coffee-maker, much less a good Turkish coffee-maker. Ever since this episode, I made it a personal goal to learn the secrets of Turkish coffee-making. A few years later I met the expert, Peleg Morris. Peleg learned the art of making Turkish coffee while serving in the Israeli Army and camping in treacherous deserts. He was even appointed the best Turkish-coffee-maker in his division. Turkish coffee is traditionally made in a special long-handled copper jug called *ibrik*. However, a very small saucepan will also do the trick.

This coffee is served in tiny porcelain cups. After drinking this coffee, some people read the future by looking at the patterns the coffee grounds have left behind in the cup. I am not even kidding! We have no real fortune-tellers in the family, but a few aunts are known for making great guesses.

1 cup water

2 teaspoons fine ground Turkish coffee

2 teaspoons sugar

3 cardamom seeds or ¼ teaspoon cardamom powder

1. Place the water in an *ibrik* or very small saucepan with a long handle. Bring to a boil over high heat.

2. Remove from heat and add coffee, sugar, and cardamom. Mix with a spoon.

3. Reduce the flame to medium. Return the *ibrik* to the heat and boil until the coffee rises to the top of the *ibrik* just like lava in a volcano.

4. Immediately remove from the heat before "eruption" occurs and serve.

Yield: 4 (¼-cup) servings

❦ REFRESHING LIME SYRUP ❦

Sharbat'e limoo

This is by far my children's favorite! I have to pretend I don't have any syrup left. It is so refreshing in the summertime. In fact, every summer the kids set up a Persian lemonade stand and sell *Sharbat'e Limoo*…It is the most popular stand on the whole block!

2 cups water

2 cups sugar

½ cup bottled lime juice *or* juice of 5 limes

1 teaspoon lime zest (zest of 1 lime)

Garnish

lime slices

star fruit slices

1. In a 4-quart saucepan, mix the water and sugar together and bring to a boil, uncovered, over high heat. Stir periodically with a spoon.

2. When the water boils and the sugar dissolves, add the lime juice and zest and cook, uncovered, over medium/low heat for 20 minutes or until light, lime-infused syrup has formed.

3. Cool and store in a glass jar until ready to use.

4. This syrup is very refreshing mixed with water in a ratio of three parts water to one part syrup, along with some ice cubes to keep it chilled. Garnish with slices of lime or star fruit.

Yield: 2 cups

Tricks of the trade

It is best to juice limes when they are at room temperature. However, if you keep them refrigerated, you can put them in the microwave for 15 to 30 seconds and they will yield about 30% more juice. The trick of getting juicy limes is to pick the ones with smooth and shiny rinds.

❦

YOU ARE WHAT YOU EAT

Lime versus lemon…that is the question. Back in Venezuela, we do not have any lemons; we only have limes. In fact, my parents had a beautiful lime tree in our backyard. I would collect the limes and go door-to-door selling them to our neighbors to make a little pocket money for myself. Mind you, I was 10! The funniest thing is that almost everyone had a lime tree in his or her own backyard. So, as you can imagine, I prefer using limes instead of lemons. Not only because limes gave me my first few coins to spend, but mostly because I love their intense sour taste. Did you know that limes are responsible for nicknaming sailors? At the time when the British navy ruled the seas, the sailors ate limes to keep scurvy at bay and became known as the "limey." Later on it was discovered that limes are rich in Vitamin C…A lime a day keeps scurvy away, aye, aye, matey!

❧ VINEGAR AND MINT SYRUP ❧

Sharbat'e Sekanjebeen

Persian men bond with each other in peculiar ways. From my experience, nothing causes more of a bonding atmosphere for these men than a running body of water in which to place their feet, a set of backgammon (*sheshbesh*), a water pipe (*kalium*), and a platter filled with romaine lettuce along with a bowl of *sekanjebeen* syrup for dipping. Go figure! Feel free to double the recipe. It can be stored in an airtight jar at room temperature for months.

2 cups water

2 cups sugar

½ cup white vinegar

½ bunch fresh mint (with stems), washed and bundled in a *bouquet garni*

Garnish

mint leaves

1. In a 4-quart saucepan, combine all ingredients except mint and bring to a boil, uncovered, over high heat. Stir periodically with a spoon.

2. When the water boils and the sugar dissolves, drop in the bundle of mint and cook, uncovered, over medium/low heat for 20 minutes or until a light, mint-infused syrup has formed.

3. Set aside to cool. Remove mint sachet and squeeze juices from sachet into saucepan. Store in a glass jar at room temperature until ready to use.

4. Serve this syrup in a bowl along with hearts of romaine for dipping. Also, this syrup is very refreshing mixed with water in a ratio of three parts water to one part syrup. Nothing is as refreshing as a cold, tall glass of *sekanjebeen* on a summer day!

Yield: 4 cups (about 12 servings)

Tricks of the trade

To add flavor, fresh mint leaves are added to this syrup while it simmers. I put the leaves into a small sachet and close the top. This bundle is called *bouquet garni* in French. If you do not have these ready-made sachets (much like coffee bags), you can use cheesecloth to make your own, or see my website for information on how to buy these sachets online.

ᴄ᧞ ROSE WATER ᧞ᴄ

A Sensory Window to the Spirit

Rose water is by far the most exotic, sensuous, and stimulating product I have ever used. This water-like liquid can transport anyone to faraway gardens and faraway times. Rose water has been produced since antiquity and in many different countries by many different peoples. In my culture, as well as in Persian culture, rose water is used for aesthetic purposes. As a teenager, I was taught to spray my face with rose water to keep it radiant and healthy. In Iran, rose water was added to cosmetics for women to beautify themselves and used by men to clean and perfume facial hair.

Persian Jews use rose water for religious purposes. It is taught that during Shabbat every person is granted a second *neshama* (soul) to enjoy this holy day at its fullest. Sadly, that extra *neshama* departs from one's body the second Shabbat has finished, leaving the person spiritually vacant. Therefore, during *havdala* (the ceremony to mark the end of Shabbat) it is customary to smell something fragrant in order to return to one's spiritual senses. It is almost like using smelling salts when one is dizzy. While other cultures use fragrances from cloves or even cinnamon, it is not surprising that Persian Jews use nothing less than rose water to help them return to their spiritual senses.

In Iran, rose water is also used to make refreshing drinks and to add an inconspicuous scent to baked goods. To many people new to this usage, this colorless liquid can be hard to identify at first. However, after a few tries, it becomes obvious that rose water is present. At first, it was hard to appreciate the qualities of this delicate fragrance in my food. After all, I was brought up with using rose water only for aesthetic purposes. I honestly felt the food had perfume in it. And then, suddenly, it all became obvious; a memory that never departed my mind came flashing in front of my eyes. I learned that many poets used to drink perfume while writing romantic poetry, so as to become one with the poem by overwhelming their body with the scent of romance and love. I also learned that many artists would eat fruits they were trying to depict in an effort to conduct the feelings from their taste buds through their brushes and achieve perfection on the canvas. Persians need rose water in their taste buds to be able to continue carrying on the enchantment and mystery, the passion and romance that are characteristic of their people and their culture. That is the magic of rose water!

❧ ROSE WATER SYRUP ❧

Sharbat'e Golab

You would think the first thing I do after the fast of Yom Kippur ends is to eat. Well, not really. The first thing I do is to prepare a tall glass of warm *golab* with *nabat* for my husband. This is the first thing that enters his mouth after any fast. He adopted this custom from his mother. The warmth and aroma of rose water, together with the sweetness and healing powers of *nabat*, make an empty stomach ready for the meal that follows.

Quick *golab* recipe

8 ounces water (hot or cold)

1 tablespoon rose water

Mix ingredients together and enjoy!

Syrup recipe

2 cups water

2 cups sugar

½ cup rose water

¼ cup rose buds, bundled in a *bouquet garni* (optional)

Garnish (optional)

mint leaves *or* rose buds

1. In a 4-quart saucepan, mix water and sugar together and bring to a boil, uncovered, over high heat. Stir periodically with a spoon.

2. When the water boils and the sugar dissolves, add the rose water and rose buds, and cook, uncovered, over medium/low heat for 20 minutes or until light, rose-infused syrup has formed.

3. Set aside to cool. Remove rose bud sachet and squeeze juices from the sachet into saucepan. Store in a glass jar at room temperature until ready to use.

4. This syrup is very refreshing when mixed with cold water and very soothing when mixed with hot water in a ratio of three parts water to one part syrup. Garnish with mint leaves and/or rose buds.

Yield: 2 cups syrup

Tricks of the trade

To add flavor and color, I like adding rose buds to this syrup while it simmers. I put the rose buds into a small sachet and close the top. This bundle is called *bouquet garni* in French. If you do not have these ready-made sachets (much like coffee bags), you can use cheesecloth to make your own, or see my website for information on how to buy these sachets online.

∾ SOUR CHERRY SYRUP ∾

Sharbat'e Albaloo

My husband grew up drinking himself silly with *sharbat'e albaloo*! I sometimes close my eyes and can imagine him, as a child, with his rosy plump cheeks and a *sharbat* mustache painted on his face; running wild through his grandfather's *bach* (garden) in Shiraz…. My kids do the same, but in our front yard!

Quick *Sharbat'e Albaloo* recipe

8 ounces cold water

1 tablespoon sour cherry syrup

Mix ingredients together and enjoy!

Syrup recipe

2 cups water

2 cups sugar

¼ cup lime juice

1 cup fresh sour cherries, bundled in a *bouquet garni*

Garnish (optional)

lime slices

1. In a 4-quart saucepan, mix water and sugar together and bring to a boil, uncovered, over high heat. Stir periodically with a spoon.

2. When the water boils and the sugar dissolves, add the lime juice and cherries. Cook, uncovered, over medium/low heat for 20 minutes or until light, cherry-infused syrup has formed.

3. Set aside to cool. Remove cherry sachet and squeeze juices from sachet into saucepan. Store in a glass jar at room temperature until ready to use.

4. This syrup is not only delicious but also beautiful. Mix with water in a ratio of three parts water to one part syrup, along with some ice cubes to keep it chilled. Garnish with slices of lime.

Yield: 2 cups syrup

Tricks of the trade

To add flavor and color, sour cherries are added to this syrup while it simmers. I put cherries into a sachet and close the top. This bundle is called *bouquet garni* in French. If you do not have these ready-made sachets (much like coffee bags), you can use cheesecloth to make your own.

❧ YOGURT SODA ❧

Dooch

This refreshing beverage is traditionally consumed in Iran along with kebab. However, since we do not mix milk and meat, I love having it as a late snack or a mid-morning energizer. There is nothing like a glass of cold minty *dooch* in a hot summer day!

8 oz. fat-free yogurt

16 oz. carbonated water

1 teaspoon dried mint

1 teaspoon salt

¼ teaspoon pepper

sprig fresh mint for garnish (optional)

Combine all ingredients and stir until a smooth but free-flowing liquid is obtained. Serve very cold and garnish with a sprig of mint, if desired.

Yield: 2 cups

Tricks of the trade

Obviously, creamy Greek yogurt is preferable when making this recipe. I like to use non-fat, but it definitely tastes better with whole-fat yogurt. Feel free to experiment, adjusting the amount of carbonated water to the consistency of your choice. *Dooch* can easily be refrigerated, but make sure to mix it well before drinking it.

❧ CHICKPEA COOKIES ❧

Kuluche Nochkotchi

This delicious cookie is traditionally available at the kosher Persian bakeries only in the shape of a clover. I wanted to shape it differently to decorate the table at the *brit mila* of one of my boys, so I decided to make them myself in the shape of zoo animals. They were such a hit. I can't wait to make them in the shape of little hearts for a Persian-style *Sheva Brachot*!

2 cups chickpea flour

2 tablespoons all-purpose flour

1¼ cups confectioner's sugar

1 tablespoon cardamom

1½ sticks softened unsalted *parve* margarine

Garnish

ground or slivered pistachio nuts

1. Preheat oven to 350°F. Line a cookie sheet with parchment paper.

2. Combine first four ingredients in a mixing bowl.

3. In a small saucepan over low heat, or in a Pyrex® bowl in the microwave, melt the margarine.

4. Mix melted margarine into dry ingredients, making a crumbly dough that becomes compact when pressed together.

5. Press the dough together and flatten to a thickness of about 1 inch. Cut out shapes using a small (1-inch) clover cookie cutter or any other mini-cutter. Place 1 inch apart on the prepared baking sheet and garnish with ground pistachio nuts or a slivered pistachio inserted in the middle. Bake for 15 minutes; cool on racks.

Yield: approximately 70 1-inch cookies

Tricks of the trade

This dough is very crumbly because it is supposed to "melt" in your mouth once it is baked. These cookies need to be handled with care to avoid breaking them.

You can find chickpea flour at any Middle Eastern store; See resources on my website for online ordering.

✑ PERSIAN RICE COOKIES ✑

Kuluche Berenji

If you are looking for a handsome cookie, this is it! The white-and-black look is very tailored, and the fragrance of the rose water and cardamom are delectable. These "melt" in your mouth and are simply delicious along with *chai* (tea).

2 sticks unsalted *parve* margarine
(8 oz.)

1 cup sugar

1 egg

1 teaspoon rose water

½ teaspoon cardamom powder

3 cups rice flour

Garnish

poppy seeds

1. Preheat oven to 350°F. Line a cookie sheet with parchment paper.

2. Using a stand mixer fitted with a flat paddle attachment, cream margarine and sugar for a few minutes. Add egg, rose water, and cardamom powder and combine. Pour in the flour cup by cup, slowly mixing until a smooth dough is achieved.

3. Form balls 1 inch in diameter and place on prepared cookie sheet. Using the round side of a metal decorating tip, press down on each cookie to emboss it with an "Olympic logo" design. Sprinkle with poppy seeds.

4. Bake in the oven for 15 minutes.

Yield: 25 cookies

Tricks of the trade

Rice flour can be purchased at many Middle Eastern stores. If you do not have any close by, you can make your own flour by grinding rice grains in a food processor, or see my website to order online. These cookies should remain white; do not leave them in the oven too long or they will tan. Let them cool before removing from pan.

❧ PURIM COOKIES ❧

Hamantashen

This is a great recipe to make with kids. I love getting my kids all excited about the holidays, and getting messy over a batch of *hamantashen* is part of the fun! *Hamantashen* are cookies that are traditionally consumed during the holiday of Purim. *Hamantashen* cookies mimic the three-cornered hat that the villain, Haman (boo!) wore. *Hamantashen* actually means "*Haman's pocket*" in Yiddish…wait a minute! Yiddish? Yes, in fact, back in Iran there were no *hamantashen*! Very funny, considering that all the events that lead to Purim happened in Iran. Traditionally, Persian Jewish families in Iran made halvah for Purim. I love *halvah*, but I can't give up my *hamantashen* on Purim!

Another beautiful explanation for eating cookies with hidden fillings is because Queen Esther was a hidden Jew.

My friend Shifra Schwartz taught me this recipe.

3 eggs
1 cup sugar
¾ cup canola oil
⅓ cup apple juice *or* sweet wine
1 tablespoon vanilla extract
1 teaspoon almond extract
1 tablespoon baking powder
5 cups flour

Fillings (your choice)

strawberry *or* apricot preserves
chocolate chips *or* brownie mix, prepared according to package directions
prune butter

1. Preheat oven to 350°F. Line three cookie sheets with parchment paper.
2. Beat eggs and sugar until creamy. Add oil and combine. Add juice or wine and extracts. Add baking powder. Gradually add the flour until a dough with smooth consistency is achieved.

3. Flatten a portion of the dough ⅛-inch thick. Cut out 3-inch diameter circles and spoon ½ teaspoon preserves or any other filling onto the middle. Pinch at the corners with wet fingers, sealing very well. Place raw cookies about 1 inch apart onto prepared cookie sheets. Repeat until all the dough has been used.
4. Bake for 10 to 15 minutes until the bottom is golden. Cool on racks.

Yield: 50 cookies

Tricks of the trade

When I first made these cookies they looked more like a Mexican sombrero than the famous three-cornered hat. To keep the corners together, it is helpful to brush egg onto the edges of each dough circle. It is imperative you do not overfill these cookies; if you do, they will pop open—at which point they are totally useless and have to be tragically eaten by the chef (ahem, me!) before anyone dares to see them. Another great tip is to show as little of the filling as possible. Pinch them very well (getting all your aggression out) with moist fingertips and, to prevent the dough from drying out, keep the remaining dough inside a zipper-top plastic bag while you work on each batch.

❧ GOLDEN DOUGH SPHERES ❧
SOAKED IN ROSE WATER SYRUP
Bamieh

These little dough balls are really true to their name—they resemble a *bamieh*. *Bamieh* is Farsi for the vegetable we know as okra. You might think these do not resemble the okra you are used to seeing, elongated and green. But the miniature version of okra looks just like this dessert. It is impossible to eat just one of these little spheres of pleasure…Consider yourself warned!

Dough

1 cup water

1 stick unsalted *parve* margarine (4 oz.)

½ teaspoon salt

1 cup flour

5 eggs

Syrup

Refer to the syrup recipe in *Baklava* (page 309)

Additional

4 cups canola oil for frying

1. In a small nonstick saucepan, bring water, margarine, and sugar to a boil. Add the cup of flour, all at once, mixing rapidly. Reduce the heat to medium and keep on mixing until a ball of dough that detaches easily from the pot forms. Set aside and let cool for at least 10 minutes.

2. In the meantime, make the syrup according to the instructions on page 309. Pour prepared syrup into a large bowl.

3. Transfer cooled dough to a stand mixer fitted with a flat paddle attachment. Add the eggs, one by one, making sure each egg has completely incorporated into the dough before adding the next one.

4. Transfer the dough to a pastry bag fitted with a medium star pastry tip.

5. In a 4-quart saucepan, heat the oil until it reaches a temperature of 350°F. Drop in a 1-inch size strip of dough, squeezing the pastry bag and cutting the dough with kitchen scissors as it comes out of the tip. Fry until the dough is golden and puffed.

6. Scoop the *bamieh* out of the oil and place into a strainer to cool.

7. When balls have cooled, transfer them to the bowl of cold syrup. Soak the *bamieh* in the syrup for about 3 minutes.

Yield: about 100 pieces

Tricks of the trade

With anything that needs deep-frying, it is very important to bring the oil to a temperature of 350°F. If you do not have a frying thermometer, test the oil with a small piece of dough. If the ball of dough rises to the top when dropped in the oil, the oil is ready. If the oil is not at the right temperature, the food is more likely to absorb more oil than necessary. If you fry a lot of food, it might be smart to invest in a deep fryer because it makes reaching the right temperatures much easier.

If you do not have a pastry bag or a pastry tip, you can use a storage-size zipper-top bag, making an opening with scissors at one end.

❧ ALMOND MULBERRIES ❧

Toot

These almond paste treats are so simple yet so delicious. Persians love eating these along with *chai* (tea) instead of sugar cubes. You can make the dough yourself or simply buy ready-made almond paste (much easier!), which is available at many supermarkets. Just roll each *toot* in powdered sugar and then garnish with the pistachios. By the way, this is a great project to do with your kids!

With ready-made almond paste

1 (8 oz.) can ready-made almond paste

1 teaspoon rose water

½ teaspoon cardamom powder

If making from scratch

1½ to 2½ cups ground almonds

1 teaspoon ground cardamom

1 cup confectioners' sugar

2 tablespoons rose water

1 tablespoon water

1 cup sugar

Garnish

½ cup slivered pistachios *or* slivered almonds

food coloring, powdered sugar, and/or edible glitter (optional)

IF MAKING WITH READY-MADE ALMOND PASTE

1. Using your hands, mix the almond paste, rose water, and cardamom until a pliable dough forms.

2. Pinch off a marble-size piece of almond paste and shape it like a tear. Roll each "tear" into powdered sugar or garnish of your choice.

3. Insert a single slivered pistachio into the round side of the tear.

IF MAKING FROM SCRATCH

1. Mix all ingredients until you obtain a paste that doesn't stick to your hands and has the consistency of play dough.

2. Pinch off a marble-size piece of almond paste and shape it like a tear. Roll each "tear" into powdered sugar or garnish of your choice.

3. Insert a single slivered pistachio into the round side of the tear.

Yield: 20 pieces

Tricks of the trade

If the almond paste is too sticky, use powdered sugar instead of flour, ½-teaspoon at a time, to get the right consistency. You can also dye the almond paste with food coloring to achieve any color you would like. Serve on a platter; if not serving immediately, cover with plastic wrap to avoid dryness or store in an airtight container.

❧ CHOCOLATE TRUFFLES ❧

כדורי שוקולד

Kadurei Chocolate

My good friend Ronit Armin is not only Persian but also Israeli! Her home is a sanctuary to all things delicious. Every time she comes to me for Shabbat I try to politely suggest that she should bring this dessert—or else! My kids love making these chocolate truffles and, of course, they love eating them. They are so easy to make.

2 (4.2 oz.) packages *parve* vanilla tea biscuits

¾ cup sugar

½ cup cocoa powder

1 teaspoon vanilla extract

½ stick unsalted *parve* margarine

⅔ cup water

Fillings (optional)

raisins, candied cherries

Garnish

Cocoa powder, edible glitter, coconut shavings, powdered sugar, *and/or* colored sprinkles.

1. Grind the tea biscuits in a food processor fitted with a metal blade. Add remaining ingredients and process until moldable paste is formed. If paste is too soft, place in the refrigerator for 10 minutes until it becomes moldable.

2. Shape into 1-inch chocolate balls.

3. Optional: Insert a raisin or candied cherry into the middle.

4. Roll in desired garnish and place into small cupcake holders.

Yield: approximately 40 pieces

Tricks of the trade

Roll the truffles with clean, dry hands to prevent the dough from sticking. Each ball should be about 1 inch in diameter. The tip of your thumb is about 1 inch long. I often use mine as a guide when shaping these truffles so they are all the same size. Make sure to cover with plastic wrap to avoid drying. These are a great make-ahead dessert. I bet you won't be able to resist the temptation of eating one!

৵ PERSIAN HALVAH ৵

Persian halvah is not like the regular *halvah* you are used to. The word *halvah* refers to several dense and sweet desserts made with nuts or flour. In contrast to the more popular Israeli *halvah* made of sesame paste, in Iran, *halvah* is flour based with a hint of rose water. I actually think Persian *halvah* is much better! It has a soft, play-dough consistency that is very agreeable to the palate. The taste is heavenly and very exotic. Persian *halvah* is intertwined in many areas of the life of Persian Jews. *Halvah* is the food of choice after fasts and it is also one of the essential foods to be given away on Purim for *mishloach manot*. It is very easy to make and very easy to eat!

Syrup

1½ cups water

1 cup sugar

½ teaspoon saffron

1 teaspoon cardamom powder

¼ cup rose water

Dough

2 cups flour

1 cup canola oil

Garnish

slivered pistachios and/or almonds

1. To make the syrup, bring water and sugar to a boil in a 4-quart saucepan. When sugar has dissolved, turn off the heat; add saffron, cardamom, and rose water. Stir and set aside.

2. In another 4-quart saucepan, toast flour over high heat for no more than 3 minutes, stirring constantly with a wooden spoon to avoid burning. Watch carefully; as soon as the flour becomes light brown, reduce heat to medium and add oil. Cook for 1 minute, stirring constantly.

3. Add syrup and mix rapidly. Almost immediately bright yellow dough, similar to play dough, will form.

4. To serve, flatten dough into a shallow round platter and garnish with slivered pistachios and almonds, or cut into shapes and garnish.

Yield: 9 inch round *halvah*

Tricks of the trade

It is important to mix the dough very well. If too many flour lumps remain, process in the pot with an immersion hand blender until a thick paste is achieved. Since this dough is very pliable, my children enjoy helping me shape halvah with cookie cutters in a myriad of shapes and sizes. Look at the stars in the picture!

❧ SAFFRON ICE CREAM ❧

Bastani

This is my husband's favorite ice cream. When I learned how to make it, he could not have enough! You can make it *parve* to be served after a meat meal if you use *parve* vanilla ice cream. It is also delicious made with dairy ice cream…your choice! The whipped cream slabs are optional.

Ice cream

1 pint *parve* or dairy vanilla ice cream

¼ teaspoon saffron

3 tablespoons rose water

2 tablespoons slivered pistachios, divided

Garnish (optional)

½ cup *parve* or dairy whipping cream, not whipped

1. Remove ice cream from freezer and let it stand for 20 minutes or until it becomes easy to manipulate. If using cream garnish, pour ½ cup whipping cream (¼-inch thick) into flat plate and place it in the freezer until it hardens.

2. Mix saffron and rose water and fold into softened ice cream. Fold in the pistachios, reserving some for garnish.

3. Remove the whipping cream crust from the freezer and break into pieces. Fold some pieces into the ice cream and reserve a few for garnish.

4. Serve in small bowls and garnish with the remaining pistachios and frozen whipping cream.

Yield: 1 pint

Tricks of the trade

Saffron can be ground in a small mortar and pestle or using the back of a spoon against the wall of a cup.

This ice cream can also be made in an ice cream maker. Simply follow your appliance instructions for vanilla ice cream (dairy or *parve*) and add the remaining ingredients in the list below.

❧ SHIRAZI RICE NOODLE SORBET ❧

Faludeh

This is one of the most popular Persian desserts. It is certainly an interesting sorbet like nothing you have tasted before! My husband loves it, while I have to admit it took me some time to get used to it. The noodles in the sorbet give it an extra crunch. It is very easy to make and it makes everyone happy.

Sorbet

2 cups water

1½ cups sugar

¼ cup rose water

3 ounces rice noodles (rice sticks), broken into 2-inch pieces

Garnish (optional)

2 tablespoons sour cherries in heavy syrup

2 tablespoons slivered pistachios

2 tablespoons lime juice

1. In a 4-quart saucepan, bring water and sugar to a boil. When sugar dissolves, remove from heat. Add rose water; stir and set aside.

2. In a small saucepan, cook rice noodles according to package instructions. Drain and mix with sweetened rose water.

3. Pour into a metal bowl or a 9" square baking pan and freeze. Remove from freezer after 1½ hours and rake with a fork to fluff up the ice. Return to freezer for 2 more hours.

4. Remove from freezer about 15 minutes before serving so sorbet is easy to scoop.

5. Serve in individual serving bowls and garnish as you prefer.

Yield: 4 to 6 servings

Tricks of the trade

To find sour cherries in heavy syrup and rice sticks, see resources on my website. This sorbet can also be made with an ice cream/sorbet maker. Simply follow your appliance instructions using the recipe below. Add the noodles at the end so they don't fall apart.

❧ PERSIAN ROULADE ❧

This is by far the most popular dessert at my Shabbat table! It is amazing to see people's eyes when I bring it to the table—and also to witness their puzzled faces trying to figure out the unfamiliar flavor they can't decipher (rose water).

Versatility is what is great about this recipe! You can use the same cake recipe I provide you, but the fillings are endless. Since I usually serve this cake after a meat meal, I use *parve* (nondairy) whipping cream (such as Rich's Whip®). Other fun fillings are raspberry jam, Nutella® (if dairy), and even date butter. I also like to use rum or brandy mixed with a bit of water to moisten the cake if I do not have rose water handy. I promise, this will be a hit! Check out a video for this recipe at my blog, kosher-persianfoodblog.com.

Cake

4 eggs

1 cup sugar

1 teaspoon vanilla extract

1 teaspoon baking powder

1 cup flour

⅓ cup rose water (to moisten cake)

Cream

1 pint *parve* whipping cream, divided

1 cup powdered sugar

Garnish (optional)

powdered sugar

4 strawberries

parve whipping cream

chocolate shavings *or* melted chocolate chips (optional)

1. Preheat oven to 350°F. Line a 17"x12"x1" jellyroll sheet with parchment paper. Set aside.

2. Beat eggs in the bowl of a stand mixer for 1 minute or until fluffy. Add sugar and vanilla and continue beating for 3 minutes or until the mixture begins to turn pale yellow.

3. Gently and thoroughly fold in baking powder and flour with a flat spatula, making sure not to deflate the eggs. Spread batter evenly onto the prepared cookie sheet. Bake for 15 minutes or until center springs back when lightly pressed.

4. In the meantime, whip *parve* whipping cream until peaks form. Add sugar and combine. Set aside.

5. When cake is ready, hold the corners of the paper and remove from tray onto a flat surface. Peel cake off paper. Roll, 12-inch side in, along with the parchment paper. Set aside for a few minutes.

6. Unroll and use a pastry brush to moisten the top of the cake with rose water. Spread cream evenly on the cake, leaving some for garnish. Roll again.

7. Place on a platter, seam side down, and garnish with powdered sugar, melted chocolate, *parve* whipped cream, and strawberries, as desired. Refrigerate if not serving immediately.

Yield: 10 slices

Tricks of the trade

The eggs should be at room temperature so that you can whip them to maximum volume. The secret to making the parchment paper stay in the baking pan is to spray the pan with a little oil or water before lining it. Cut slits in the corners of the paper for a snug fit. This cake freezes beautifully—just wrap in parchment paper and then in foil. Also, it is important to use parchment paper and not wax paper; these are not the same product. Make sure not to overbake this cake or it will crack. You can drizzle some powdered sugar on the cake before rolling it so it doesn't stick to the parchment paper. For a cleaner look, you can cut off both ends of the cake... I'll bet you can't resist eating them!

❧ PERSIAN RICE PUDDING ❧

شله زرد

Sholezard

Here is another fantastic recipe from my friend Liora Youshaei. She is the queen of *sholezard*! I love when she comes over, because, even though I try to *tarof*, pretending I don't want her to bother, she always brings me this delicious dessert. It is so refreshing in the summer time to take cold *sholezard* and eat it in the backyard while the kids are at play...*Olam Haze*!

2 cups rice

14 cups water, divided

½ cup canola oil

3 cups sugar

1 teaspoon ground cardamom

½ teaspoon ground saffron

⅓ cup rose water

Garnish (optional)

ground cinnamon

slivered almonds

slivered pistachios

dried rose petals or hips

1. In a medium covered saucepan, bring 8 cups water and rice to a boil. Uncover, lower heat to medium/low, and cook for 20 minutes, stirring occasionally. Add 6 cups water and continue to simmer, uncovered, over low heat for 20 minutes, stirring occasionally.

2. Add oil and cook for 15 minutes. Add sugar and cook for 15 minutes. One by one, add cardamom, saffron, and rose water, stirring to make sure everything is well combined. Remove from heat. If the rice has not dissolved, process inside the pot with an immersion hand blender until a thick, pudding-like paste is achieved.

3. Transfer batter to a 9"x13" serving dish or individual ramekins. Once the batter has set, garnish with a sprinkling of ground cinnamon, dried rose hips, slivered almonds, and/or slivered pistachios.

Yield: 25 servings

Tricks of the trade

Many recipes will tell you to soak the rice when making *sholezard*, but there is no need with this recipe. This recipe looks gorgeous when made in individual ramekins... look at the picture!

❧ PERSIAN BAKLAVA ❧

Everyone seems to love the taste of *baklava* but fear the thought of making it. I dare you to make this recipe! It is actually so simple you will always wonder, "What was I afraid of?"

Did you know *baklava* is a Turkish word? However, many Middle Eastern countries not only claim it as their own but also use this name and have adapted this recipe to their tastes. Persians add rose water, saffron, and cardamom to their *baklava*, while others do not. No one really knows where it came from, but it is agreed that it was the food of royalty. *Phyllo* means "leaf" in Greek, because this dough is "as thin as a leaf." Phyllo is not to be confused with puff pastry; these are not substitutes for each other.

Baklava
1 (16-ounce) box frozen phyllo dough, defrosted

canola oil spray

Filling
2 cups chopped walnuts

1 cup chopped pistachios

½ cup sugar

½ cup rose water

1 tablespoon ground cardamom

Syrup
2 cups sugar

2 cups water

½ cup rose water

¼ teaspoon ground saffron

¼ teaspoon ground cardamom

Garnish
ground pistachio nuts

1. Preheat the oven to 350°F. Spray an oven-to-table 9"x13" baking pan with canola oil.

2. Combine all ingredients for nut filling.

3. Place 13 phyllo dough sheets in the bottom of the pan, draping them in one by one and spraying with oil between each sheet. Fold in the extra dough of each sheet, adjusting it to the shape of the baking pan; this will make no difference once the *baklava* is baked.

4. Press in the nut filling. Drape another 15 phyllo dough sheets on top of the nuts, one by one, spraying with oil between each sheet. Tuck in the extra dough from each sheet to adjust it to the shape of the baking pan. Using a sharp knife, cut the *baklava* carefully into 1½-inch diamonds or squares.

5. Bake for 45 minutes to 1 hour until the *baklava* looks golden.

6. In the meantime, make the syrup by bringing sugar and water to a boil over high heat in an uncovered 4-quart saucepan. When sugar dissolves, add the rose water, saffron, and cardamom. Cook, uncovered, over medium/low heat for 20 minutes or until light syrup has formed. Cool and store in a glass jar at room temperature until ready to use.

7. When the *baklava* is done and while it is still hot, brush with 1 cup of syrup, making sure to cover all surfaces and crevices. Garnish baklava with ground pistachios. To serve, cut along previous cut marks before removing from the pan.

Yield: approximately 35 pieces

Tricks of the trade

This recipe is a little healthier since I use cooking spray instead of brushing on oil or butter. Keep in mind you will have syrup left over, which should be stored in a glass jar, just like pancake syrup. This syrup will be good to use for months! You can use this syrup to make *Bamieh* (see page 293) or the next time you make *baklava*. It is almost impossible to stop sugar syrup from eventually crystallizing. This is because it is made of super-saturated sugar. However, if that were to happen, you can heat it in the microwave to dissolve most of the crystals that have formed.

To make my life easier, I often buy nuts already chopped and store them in the freezer to maintain their freshness.

ᔯ PERSIAN CREAM PUFFS ᔰ

Noon'e Chamei

This is probably the most beautiful dessert in this book...to my eyes, that is! These cream puffs are a completely French invention. They look so perfectly beautiful! My children love filling them with whipped cream—and eating them, of course. These are certainly hard to resist.

Dough

1 cup water

1 stick unsalted *parve* margarine (4 oz.)

½ teaspoon salt

1 cup flour

5 eggs

Cream Filling

1 pint (8 oz.) *parve* whipping cream, whipped

1 cup powdered sugar

Garnish (optional)

4 ounces semi-sweet melted chocolate chips combined with ⅛ teaspoon canola oil

powdered sugar

1. Preheat oven to 400°F. Line two cookie sheets with parchment paper.

2. In a small nonstick saucepan, bring water, margarine, and salt to a boil. When margarine melts, add flour all at once, stirring rapidly. Reduce heat to medium and continue to cook until a ball of dough that detaches easily from the pot forms. Set aside and let cool for 10 minutes.

3. In the meantime, make the cream filling by beating the *parve* whipping cream until it forms peaks. Add the powdered sugar and mix well. Store in a cool place until ready to use.

4. Transfer cooled dough to the bowl of a stand mixer fitted with a flat paddle attachment. Add eggs, one by one, making sure each egg has completely incorporated into the dough before adding the next.

5. Transfer dough to a pastry bag fitted with a large star pastry tip (Wilton 4B is perfect) or simply use an ice-cream scoop to form puffs. Form meringue-like mounds, 3" in diameter and 2" in height, directly on the prepared pans.

6. Bake for 20 minutes until golden brown; transfer puffs to a cooling rack.

7. When the puffs are completely cooled, cut in half, using a serrated knife, and fill the cavity with whipped cream.

8. Optional: Add ⅛ teaspoon of oil to chocolate chips and melt for 45 seconds in the microwave. Drizzle the chocolate on top of the puffs or simply sprinkle with powdered sugar.

Yield: about 20 cream puffs

Tricks of the trade

You have probably realized this is the same dough used to make *bamieh*, but in this case it is baked, not fried. (My arteries rejoice!) If you lack a pastry bag and pastry tip you can use a storage-size zipper-top bag and cut off one corner with scissors, or use an ice cream scoop to shape. Keep in mind: It is important that there be no cold drafts in your kitchen when you make these or they will deflate when taken out of the oven. Once cooked, these freeze beautifully.

❧ SLIVERED ALMOND BRITTLE ❧

Sohan'e Asali

My mother-in-law has fond memories of this dessert because it reminds her of *Pesach*. Her mother used to make these during Pesach because there were not many choices for desserts (during Pesach we do not consume *chametz*). This brittle is very easy to make and it is absolutely delicious!

¼ cup honey

¼ cup canola oil

¾ cup sugar

½ teaspoon crushed saffron threads

1 cup slivered almonds

Garnish (optional)

¼ cup crushed pistachios

1. Line two baking sheets with parchment paper. Set aside.

2. Pour honey, oil, and sugar into the middle of a small saucepan. The ingredients should form a pyramid; make sure they do not touch the sides of the pan. Turn the heat to high and bring to a boil, uncovered.

3. Reduce heat to medium and add saffron and almonds. Mix well. Simmer, uncovered, over medium heat for about 3 minutes or until a candy thermometer reads 285°F.

4. Remove from heat immediately and quickly spoon portions of the syrup (forming pools about 2 inches in diameter) onto prepared baking sheets. Sprinkle each portion with crushed pistachios. Allow to cool at room temperature for 20 minutes or until hardened.

Yield: 14 pieces

Tricks of the trade

Make sure to spray the spoon you use to make this recipe with canola oil to prevent the brittle from sticking to it. This makes cleaning up easier.

❧ PERSIAN DELIGHT ☙

Maskati

This incredible and easy dessert is so refreshing! It resembles Turkish Delight but it is softer in texture. It looks beautiful when served in individual ramekins or when cut into diamonds. If you have nice molds, use them in this recipe; it will mold just like jelly.

1 cup cornstarch

5 cups water

1½ cups sugar

3 tablespoons canola oil

1 tablespoon cardamom

3 tablespoons rose water

Garnish

slivered almonds

ground pistachio nuts

Tricks of the trade

When I styled Persian Delight for the picture on the facing page, I used a round cookie cutter. However, you can use any shape your mood calls for!

1. In a medium saucepan over medium/high heat, cook first five ingredients together, stirring constantly, until a uniform paste is formed (about 5 minutes).

2. Lower heat to medium/low and add rose water, stirring until the mixture looks like jelly (this happens very fast).

3. Pour into a 9"x13" disposable pan or an 8-cup mold and cool in the refrigerator. Once the mixture has set, cut into diamonds, if using a pan, and garnish with almonds and ground pistachio nuts. If using a mold, invert mold onto a serving platter and garnish as desired.

Yield: 20 pieces

❧ QUINCE IN HEAVY SYRUP ❧

Moraba'e Be

This jam-like concoction is absolutely divine! It is hard to believe the quince, which is a yellowish fruit, becomes burgundy in the cooking process. In fact, while the jam cools off, the burgundy color deepens. Make sure to add a few of the seeds of the quince in the saucepan before cooking. The cooked seeds will deepen the rosy color even more!

Interestingly, this is not the only use Persians have for these seeds. *Beh dune* (seeds of the quince) are also used by Persians to treat colds and coughs. The seeds are removed from the fruit and set aside to air dry. Then, mix 1 tablespoon of seeds in 1 cup of hot water and steep for a few minutes until the water gets very thick, like jelly. The first time my mother-in-law gave me this concoction was my on wedding day (what a day to have a cold) and it helped me tremendously.

This jam is delicious for breakfast along with cream cheese and bread. The syrup from this recipe is also delicious mixed with water and ice!

3 quinces, cored and cut into ¼-inch slices (do not peel)

6 quince seeds

2½ cups sugar

5 cups water

1 tablespoon cardamom

Garnish (optional)

1 tablespoon lime juice

1. In a 6-quart saucepan, bring the sliced quince, seeds, sugar, and water to a boil, uncovered, over high heat. Add cardamom; reduce heat to medium.

2. Simmer for about 1 hour and 45 minutes or until the quince has developed a light burgundy color and the sugar has become syrupy.

3. Garnish with lime juice if desired.

Yield: 4 cups

✦ WALNUT-STUFFED DATES ✦

Ranginak

My children love making *ranginak*. It is actually a great way to get them involved in the kitchen and strike up a good conversation. After all, I have to make sure my boys make excellent future husbands. What can I say? At least they will know how to make dessert!

½-pound box medjool dates (depending on the serving dish and quantity of people)

1 cup halved walnuts

Syrup

5 tablespoons *parve* margarine

5 tablespoons flour

1 tablespoon powdered sugar

Garnish

1 tablespoon cinnamon

toasted sesame seeds (optional)

1. Select a nice pie dish to set up the *ranginak*. Take each medjool date and make a small vertical incision with a knife on its side. Remove the pit.

2. Replace each pit with a walnut half and press the cavity shut with your fingers. Arrange the dates vertically one next to the other in the pie dish.

3. Make the syrup by melting the margarine in a small saucepan and stirring in the flour and powdered sugar. Cook until golden. The syrup's consistency should resemble that of cough syrup. Drizzle over the arranged dates, filling all the crevices; garnish with cinnamon and toasted sesame seeds, if desired.

Yield: 8 to 10 servings

Tricks of the trade

Make sure to check inside the dates when taking the pit out, because I have found insects. (As you may know, insects are not kosher.) This recipe can be used for Pesach if you skip the syrup. In fact, when I am lazy (which is pretty often) I drizzle the stuffed dates with *tahini* sauce, powdered sugar, and cinnamon powder instead of the syrup. The result is marvelous! The dates in this recipe can be arranged in many different ways. They also look very nice arranged like a round pyramid on top of a round platter with the syrup poured over it. Some people also add toasted sesame seeds as a garnish.

☙ JELLY OR CREAM DOUGHNUTS ☙

Sufganiot or Pirashkee

Sufgniot are jelly doughnuts traditionally eaten during the holiday of *Chanuka*. *Sufganiot* are golden dough on the outside with delicious jam filling inside. The reason these are eaten during *Chanuka* is because they are fried in oil, thereby commemorating the miracle of the oil and the menorah. In fact, it is taught that Adam and Eve received a *sufganiah* as they were leaving the Garden of Eden. The word *sufganiah* is a combination of three Hebrew words: *suf* (end) *gan* (garden) *iah* (G-d), which loosely means, "the end of the Garden of G-d." Some say that it was a message from G-d to teach us that even though life on earth might seem plain and bumpy on the outside, there is plenty of sweetness inside. We just have to "dig" deep enough to get to it!

Persians have a delicious dessert called *pirashkee* that is nothing less than a doughnut filled with custard. I provide you with the custard recipe here if you want to make this delicious version of a *sufganiah*.

Yeast mixture

½ cup warm water

2 envelopes active dried yeast (4½ teaspoons active dry yeast)

1 teaspoon sugar

Dough

1 stick unsalted *parve* margarine at room temperature (8 tablespoons)

¼ cup sugar

2 teaspoons salt

¼ cup water

2 large eggs

2 tablespoons brandy

4¼ cups flour, divided

4 cups canola oil, for frying

Filling (your choice)

strawberry jelly

raspberry jelly

chocolate spread

custard (*parve* or dairy) see next page

Garnish

powdered sugar

1. To make the yeast mixture: In a small bowl combine the warm water, active dry yeast, and sugar. Cover and set aside.

2. In a stand mixer fitted with a flat paddle attachment, combine margarine, sugar, salt, water, eggs, brandy, and 2 cups flour. Mix well. Add the yeast mixture and remaining 2¼ cups flour. Mix until uniform, pliable dough is formed.

3. Transfer dough to a piece of parchment paper (12"x17") and flatten with a rolling pin to 1-inch thickness. Cover with plastic wrap and set aside to rise for 1 hour.

4. In a 6-quart saucepan, heat the canola oil to fry the *sufganiot*. The oil is ready when a candy thermometer reads 350°F.

5. Using a 2-inch circular cookie cutter, cut circles of dough. Drop dough into the hot oil and fry each side until brown. Remove from the oil, using a slotted spoon, and place into a colander. Set aside to cool.

6. Once cooled, inject your choice of jelly into the *sufganiah* using a squeeze bottle or a pastry bag fitted with a long filling tip. Sprinkle generously with powdered sugar.

Yield: about 20 *sufganiot*

VANILLA PASTRY CREAM (DAIRY CUSTARD)

This recipe is to fill Persian *pirashkee*. My mother-in-law loves this! It was her idea to fill *sufganiot* with this delicious cream. In my country we also have a version of *pirashkee* called *bomba*, which in Spanish means *bomb*. I guess that refers to the fact that eating too many of these is equivalent to bombing your scale! This is my mother's recipe for *crema pastelera* (dairy custard). It is super-easy to make and absolutely delicious. You might just want to forget filling any doughnut and simply eat it all alone! You can make this cream low fat using low-fat condensed and regular milk. I measure the milk using the same can the condensed milk came in…one less thing to wash!

1 (14-oz) can condensed milk

1 cup milk

1 teaspoon vanilla extract

2 egg yolks

5 teaspoons corn starch

1. In a medium nonstick saucepan, combine all ingredients. Bring to a boil.

2. Cook for 1 minute, mixing constantly, until it starts to bubble and thicken.

3. Cool to room temperature before using.

Yield: 2 cups

Persian Holiday Tutorial

When I first learned how to be a Jew, I learned everything the Ashkenazi way. My rabbis made sure I became an "expert" in Ashkenazi *kashrut*, as well as all laws pertaining to *Halacha* (Jewish Law) and *brachot* (blessings). And then the unimaginable happened: my world (at least my gefilte fish and kugel world) shattered when I married a Sephardic Jew! Traditionally, a woman takes her husband's *minhagim* (customs). I literally had to start learning from scratch again because the customs and laws of Sephardim and Ashkenazim are so different.

I do have to admit, as I was slowly learning how to be a Sephardic Jew, I realized I was very fortunate! I loved being Ashkenazi (it lasted but a few months) but being Sephardic was so much easier! Who doesn't like an easier life? I will not start rubbing it in by listing the many leniencies in the Sephardic world… that would simply be cruel. However, I do have to admit that eating rice on Pesach (even after checking it three times) puts a smile on my face. In sum, I feel the change was *bashert* and I have embraced it–although I do have to admit to eating a whole log of gefilte fish once because I was missing it so much!

However, there is something very special about being a Sephardic Jew that has little to do with food or customs and makes me feel extremely proud. When I go to synagogue and I see people from all walks of life, I feel so good. I see some women who seem very religious and others who seem they are not. I see men with velvet *kippot* and I see men with the shabby folded *kippot* that were either sitting in a back pocket for too long or collecting dust in a little basket at the entrance of the synagogue. I see women who seem to be immersed in their prayers and women talking away. I see men who seem engrossed in introspection and men who seem to be taking a virtual trip far away. However, they all have one thing in common. The second the *Sefer Torah* is brought out, all of them stand up in unison and, with a love I cannot describe in words, give it the most unparalleled attention and respect. The women all gather toward the Torah and kiss it fervently, like a mother kissing her newborn. The men are all happy, faces shining, carrying the heavy load an encased Sephardic *Sefer Torah* can be. Beautiful embroidered shawls are draped over the Torah while the fortunate man who gets to read opens the precious case. I often take one more look around the room, and all I see are women and men, teary-eyed, completely connected and immersed in the moment, ready to listen to the very words Hashem spoke. It is an experience that I love witnessing over and over again, and I find it unique to the warmth and deeply-rooted traditions that are characteristic of Sephardic Jews. There is no question in my mind that *Gan Eden* looks and feels exactly the same: many different types of Jews, from all walks of life, sharing together a common and most important passion: their love for Torah.

It is an immense honor for me to have talked to many Rabbanim in the Persian Sephardic world about the different customs we practice during the holidays. It is with utmost love I share these *minhagim* with you and, if you are a Persian Jew, it is a gigantic honor to be able to document this precious information for our children and grandchildren.

It is taught: "More than the Jews have kept Shabbat, it is Shabbat that has kept the Jewish people." This could not be truer when it comes to Persian Jews. Persian Jews, like many Sephardic Jews, are what they call "traditional." From what I have observed, this means that their Jewish identity is so deeply rooted that they keep many *mitzvot* (commandments) extremely devotedly.

One of the first Shabbatot I celebrated in my life was at my in-laws' home. It was very beautiful to see how Momon (my mother-in-law) lit the candles. Then we sat at the table to make *Kiddush* and *Hamotzi*. That is when the cultural mishaps started! My father-in-law made *Kiddush* and started passing the *kiddush* cup around for people to take a sip. This was done in age order; that is, the older you were, the sooner you got to drink. Everyone was taking a sip from the same cup! I saw in amazement that no one even flinched at the fact that they were all sharing germs. When the cup arrived in front of me, I stared at it for a long time, noticing my mother-in-law's lipstick left on the rim. Purely because of peer pressure, I forced myself to surrender and drink from this cup. I will always remember how, even though my stomach turned upside down, there was a very nice feeling of unity and family. (I guess the alcohol in the wine killed all the germs, since no one became ill!)

But that is not all! I was still in shock when, all of a sudden, two store-bought challot (you can make your own! See recipe below) were set on the table. My father-in-law said a blessing and used his hands to rip off pieces of bread. All I could think about was, *Where have his hands been?* And then, in the moment I least expected it, a piece was bread was thrown to me! What was I supposed to do? Catch it? Throw it back at him? Eat it and pretend that nothing unusual had happened? Then, I realized this was the norm—all the guests had their bread thrown at them! All that I could think of was, *We are so different!*

However, never mind all the differences and funny anecdotes; there was something very unique and special about these people. I remember that, no matter where Sammy and I would end up later on Friday nights, it was always a priority to go to his parents' home for *Kiddush* and *Hamotzi*, because it was Shabbat and that is what all good Persian boys do on Friday night. I will never forget one Friday when Sam and I wanted to drive to Vegas and would be traveling late, unable to make it for Shabbat dinner. At the moment of our departure, his mother gave us a little "Shabbat dinner" picnic she had made, with candles, challah, a little bottle of grape juice for *Kiddush*, and, naturally, a three-course meal! Sam and I stopped on the way and had our very own Shabbat dinner! It was a magical moment that I will never forget. It was one of those moments that change a person forever. I was so touched by her gesture and I felt how important this was for her. As Sammy said *Kiddush* in the middle of nowhere, with the flame of the candles I had just lit shining and dancing in his eyes, I realized this was a *mitzvah* I wanted to keep for the rest of my life!

Today, I am a religious woman and know more about the Shabbat liturgies and traditions than many ordinary Jews. Wait a minute, I take that back; in the words of Sarah Yoheved Rigler, "There is no such a thing as an ordinary Jew!" Every Jew is special in a unique way. Today, more than ever, I enjoy the Shabbat to the max, and when I hear my husband saying *Kiddush* I tear up, because he doesn't have to stand close to my Shabbat candles for me to see the light of Torah dancing in his eyes. I consider myself the most fortunate person alive. To think all this joy started at a magical Shabbat evening under the stars on our way to Vegas!

I want to share with you many of the Persian customs used when celebrating Shabbat. These *minhagim* (customs) are what have kept the Persian Jews close to Torah through the ages. Having married a Persian Jew, I am now honored to keep these customs and pass them on to my children and grandchildren. I fervently pray that my children will also appreciate them and that the same light I see in my husband's eyes will dance in the eyes of the next generation!

Shabbat Dinner Menu סעודת ליל שבת

The menu possibilities for Persian Shabbat meals are almost endless. Feel free to play around and experiment. It is important to note that back in Iran people were accustomed to having a small pre-Shabbat meal. This small meal was designed to make the person look forward to the ultimate feast (and to keep them from starving)! The food of choice was often a dish called *shami* (or *tapalak*—in Shiraz) (see page 137), along with fried eggplant, zucchini, and lavash bread.

Traditionally, the Shabbat meal is the best meal of the week, featuring bread, appetizers, fish, meat, chicken, rice, side dishes, and dessert. This menu is mostly based on my mother-in-law's Shabbat menu and what I traditionally serve in my own home.

Appetizer

Water Challah, page 334

My Favorite Baked Salmon, page 81

Green Relish for Fish, page 81

Shirazi Salad, page 51

Eggplant Dip—*Babaganoush*, page 39

Chickpea Dip—*Chummus*, page 45

Fried Eggplants—*Chatzilim*, page 41

Variety of Olives and Pickled Vegetables

Entrees

Chicken in Tomato Sauce and Saffron, page 111

Persian Steamed White Rice—*Chelo*, page 186

Herb Stew with Dried Limes—*Chorosh Sabsi*, page 153

The Persian Matzah Ball—*Gondy*, page 113

Veal or Lamb Roast with Dates and Apricots, page 123

Potato Salad with Hard-boiled Eggs—*Salad'e Olivie*, page 55

Dessert

Persian *Roulade*, page 305

Fresh Fruit Platter

Persian Tea—*Chai*, page 265

If you ask any Jewish woman, Persian or not, what her afternoon is like right before Shabbat she will answer, "Chaos!" You can quote me on this: It doesn't matter how many dishes you have prepared before Shabbat; you will always feel a last-minute rush up to the moment of lighting your Shabbat candles. It might seem this is bad; however, the truth is that nothing that comes easy is ever appreciated. Therefore, the toil we all go through before Shabbat is like the storm before the calm. It only helps to enhance the peaceful feeling a woman experiences right after candle-lighting. Setting the table and preparing the hot dishes should all be tasks that have been accomplished before kindling the Shabbat lights.

It is customary for the husband to set up the candles for his wife. The candles can be made of wax; the use of wicks in olive oil is also popular (my choice). *Halacha* (Jewish Law) calls for the lighting of two candles. This is because in the Torah, the *mitzvah* of Shabbat is mentioned as "To remember Shabbat" and "To keep Shabbat." Therefore, a married woman lights two candles to commemorate these two phrases. Persian tradition maintains that a single girl should wait until she is married to light her own candles, because as long as she lives with her parents, her mother is the one to have the privilege. There are those who follow another beautiful tradition, to light one candle for each child in the home. This is derived from the fact that women, with their special wisdom and sensitivities, are the only beings that can touch the soul of another human being. Therefore, she is to light a candle for each of her children in order to ignite the light of Torah within their hearts. Once the candles are lit, a sudden and magnificent peace warms the heart…that is, until I hear my 2-year-old screech for *gondy* and rice!

What You Need for a Persian Shabbat Table

Your nicest china and tablecloth

Two candles (usually set on a side table)

Kiddush cup

Red *Kiddush* wine

Two challot

A challah cover (a napkin suffices)

A salt shaker

A prayer book with the blessings for Shabbat

An appetite!

When the men and other guests return from the synagogue after the evening prayers (*Arvit*), the meal begins. It is said that traditionally, two angels accompany the men from the synagogue (*kaniza*) to the home. First, the song of "*Shalom Alecheim—Welcome Unto You*" is sung by all guests, specifically welcoming the visiting angels and asking them to stay and share in the meal. Then the head of the family and guests sing "*Eishet Chayil—A Woman of Valor.*" This is a beautiful poem recited for the wife in a gesture of admiration and gratitude. Afterwards, the husband makes *Kiddush* over red wine, using a nice silver goblet; he either hands around the goblet for guests to take a sip in order of seniority or serves a few ounces in small cups for the guests (our preference to avoid sharing germs!). At this point, the children receive blessings from their parents and kiss their mother's hand in a show of appreciation for her hard work. In the beginning I felt really weird doing this, but after changing all those diapers I realized I ought to be walking around with a tiara!

After *Kiddush*, some Persians have the custom to make *brachot* over rose water, a quince or other fragrant fruit, and other foods that call for additional blessings. Since the normal Shabbat liturgy calls for fewer *brachot* than we say during the week, these blessings are recited in order to keep to the traditional quota of one hundred *brachot* each day. One should only have a very small piece of these foods to avoid having to make an after-blessing.

At this point, all the guests wash their hands before partaking of the bread. Hands are washed three times each, using a washing vessel, and the blessing of "*Al Netilat Yadayim—[Who commanded us] regarding the ritual washing of the hands*" is said. All return to their seats and stay quiet (which is very hard in a Persian household!) until the bread is eaten. The challot are uncovered and the husband says the blessing of "*Hamotzi lechem min ha'aretz—Who brings forth sustenance* (lit., *bread*) *from the earth.*" He then proceeds to rip off pieces of the challot and dip them in salt three times, commemorating the salt used for the sacrifices by the High Priest in the Temple. He either throws the challah to each guest as a sign that this bread is not the bread of mourners or places the pieces on a platter that is handed around the table for guests to help themselves.

Finally, the time to eat arrives! The many salads and fish are set on the table and all the guests help themselves. After the appetizers, the plates and utensils used with fish are removed to avoid what our sages call a "*sakana* (*dangerous situation*)," and the main dishes are brought to the table. Guests and family indulge in the flavors of fine food and wine while many share a thought based on the Torah portion of the week (*Devar Torah*). The guests also sing many Shabbat songs with Middle Eastern melodies. After the meal, the *Birkat Hamazon* (blessing after the meal) is said and then dessert and *chai* (tea) are brought to the table for new blessings. The conversation and delight of Shabbat go on and on until the guests retire and go home.

Shabbat Lunch Menu שבת יום סעודת

This meal in Persian homes tends to be less formal. While the table is still dressed to the *n*th degree, the meal itself consists of one hot dish and several cold dishes. Back in Iran, it was customary to have *Hale Bibi* in the winter and *Code* in the summer. Here is the menu my mother-in-law serves:

Appetizer
Challah, page 334

Fried Whitefish, page 85

Chickpea Dip, *Chummus*, page 45

Eggplant Dip, *Babaganoush*, page 39

Variety of Olives and Pickled Vegetables

Entrees
Lavash Bread, page 35

Halim, *Hale Bibi*, or *Code*, pages 169-173

Chatzilim, page 41

Fried Zucchini

Boiled Potatoes in their skin (served cold)

Hamim Eggs—Tochmomorgue Shabbati, page 177

Shami, page 137

Limes

Dessert
Chai, page 265, and Assorted Pastries

Each individual uses a fork to mash the potatoes, *Hamim* eggs, fried zucchini, and *chatzilim*, forming a thick paste. Lime juice, salt, and pepper are added to the mixture, making it soft in texture and savory in flavor. This paste is absolutely delicious and is eaten spread on challah or on small pieces of warm lavash bread, which is then rolled into bite-size wraps. These are the Persian pleasures of Shabbat!

❧ CHALLAH, WOMEN, AND JUDAISM ❧

Women are very fortunate to have an integral role in Jewish life. We have been blessed with a unique wisdom (called *bina* in Hebrew). This is the wisdom that enables us to have that "extra" sense and sensibility. It is also the wisdom that enables us to multitask! Just trust me on this—for a mother, multitasking is crucial!

Women have three major mitzvot to fulfill. The first is lighting the Shabbat candles, the second is *Taharat Hamishpacha* (family purity and the secret to a happy marriage), and the third is making challah. I have never known any woman who does not feel a huge sense of accomplishment after making her own bread. Yes, you can buy challah at the store; I am all for that when I cannot manage to make it myself. However, the *kedusha* (holiness) and *bracha* (blessing) that making it brings to the home and the family—not to mention the taste and yummy smell emanating from it—are enough to convince me to make it myself!

Back in Iran there was no bread one would call challah. Persian Jews used Persian breads such as lavash or barbari to make the blessing over bread. This is why I jokingly say that challah is the Ashkenazi gift to the world! For Persian Jews and most Sephardim, water challah is the only challah that requires the blessing of *Hamotzi*. While our Ashkenazi sisters use eggs in their dough, we try not to. This is because the eggs render the dough more like cake than actual bread. Although, if you are invited to an Ashkenazi home you can recite *Hamotzi* over their challah, in your own home it is preferable to say it on water challah. Water challah is also a better canvas for the many savory dips Sephardim serve at the table.

The following recipe can be made by hand or by using an electric mixer large enough to hold 15 cups of flour. You might be thinking, "That is so much dough!" Well, you can either freeze some of it for next week or give a few challot away...what a way to put a smile on someone's face! The reason I am giving you a recipe for 15 cups is so that you are able to make the *bracha* "*L'hafrish challah teru-ma...*—[*Who commanded us*] *to separate the challah* [*the portion consecrated for the Kohanim*]...." Also, it is customary to give *tzedaka* (charity)...a few coins in a *pushka* will do...I just love that Yiddish word! Then, proceed to wash your hands three times each, using a washing cup, previous to making this special dough. Trust me, if I can make this, you can too!!

❧ WATER CHALLAH ❧

Tricks of the trade

There is one gadget that I could not do without when making challah: my beloved Bosch mixer. It can handle huge amounts of dough and, while I agree that making challah by hand can be therapeutic, I find that keeping my sanity can be therapeutic too. I definitely recommend a mixer to busy moms or anyone in need of sanity. In terms of yeast, I like using dry active yeast because it is very easy to find and store. I keep it in the freezer to make it last longer.

Don't be fooled by the name! *Challah* is not the fluffy cloud, the magical and satisfying edible sponge we savor Shabbat day. *Challah* is actually the piece of dough we burn because we don't have a Temple or *Kohanim* to take their part of it. The challah we eat should simply be called bread...or perhaps absolutely delicious and enticing bread, that is!

Note: The *bracha* provided below is said in the Sephardic community. It differs slightly from the *bracha* said by Ashkenazim. If you are Ashkenazi, please check in your *Siddur* for the proper *bracha*.

The separated *challah* must be burned, but not while the challot are baking. Some people save their bits of *challah* to burn with the *chametz*; before Pesach; follow your local *minhag*.

For the yeast

3 tablespoons active dry yeast (do not let yeast scare you, it just bubbles...it doesn't bite!)

¼ cup sugar

1½ cups warm water (¾ cup boiling water mixed with ¾ cup cold water)

For the dough

1½ cups sugar

1 cup canola oil, plus additional for spraying on the dough

1 tablespoon salt

3 cups warm water, divided

1 (5–lb.) bag flour (approximately 15 to 15¼ cups flour)

For the glaze

1 egg, beaten

1 tablespoon oil

1. In a medium bowl, combine all the ingredients for the yeast mixture. Set aside.

2. In a large bowl or the bowl of a large mixer, place the sugar, oil, salt, 2 cups water, and 7 cups flour. Mix until a smooth paste forms.

3. Add the yeast mixture, which should be bubbling, to the dough. Then, add the remaining 1 cup water and 8 cups flour until a consistency like that of play dough is reached.

4. Pinch off a piece the size of a lime and say this *bracha*: "*Baruch Ata Ado-nay Elo-heinu Melech ha-olam, asher keedshanu be-mitzvotav vetzeevanu lehafrish challah teruma.*" This means: "Blessed are You, our G-d, King of the Universe, Who has sanctified us with His commandments and commanded us to separate *challah.*" Then lift up the piece and proclaim "*Hariv Zu'Challah*" which means: "This is *challah.*" Wrap the dough in a piece of foil; it must be burned , but not while the challot are baking! Keep in mind that the doors of heaven open up at this point and you can pray for anything your heart desires.

5. Spray the dough with canola oil and cover with plastic wrap.

6. Let dough rise 1 hour and then punch down. Then shape the challah. You can make braids or just big balls of dough. Several small balls of dough placed together in a round baking pan that has been sprayed with oil make a pretty "pull-apart" challah. Remember that challah grows; so don't make the balls too big. I shape 12 balls the size of limes and place them next to each other in a 9-inch baking pan.

7. Place the challah on baking sheets that have been covered with parchment paper or sprayed with oil. Mix the egg and the oil and paint challot with the glaze. Let it rise another 45 minutes to 1 hour.

8. Place into oven preheated to 350 °F for approximately 25 to 45 minutes, depending on the size. The challot should be golden brown and sound hollow when tapped on the bottom. Wait until the challot cool before putting into plastic bags. At this point you can use them, freeze them, or give them away. You can also wrap them in foil and warm them in the oven right before "*Hamotzi.*"

Tricks of the trade

This dough freezes really well. Since it is a lot of dough, you can use a large clean plastic bag sprayed with oil to store it and then freeze it. You can make this dough as early as 3 days in advance and keep it in the fridge (punching it down as it grows) until you are ready to bake.

If the yeast doesn't bubble after about 10 minutes, it's not going to get the dough to rise. Either the yeast is too old or the water was too hot! Try again with another 3 tablespoons of fresh yeast and lukewarm water (about 110°F).

❧

Seudah Shlishit — The Third Meal סעודה שלישית

It is said that a person is given two souls over Shabbat, so he/she should eat accordingly. Some bread, appetizers, and salad make this meal a pleasure! Also, a nice conversation over some yummy roasted nuts makes the Shabbat third meal a delight.

Havdala — Closing Shabbat הבדלה

The prayer that concludes the Shabbat is my kids' favorite! You will need a *Havdala* candle (or two regular candles held with their wicks together), a goblet, wine, myrtle (*hadassim*), mint (*nana*) or rose water, and a prayer book containing the rite of *Havdala*. This service concludes the Shabbat and begins a new week. Everyone wishes each other a "*Shavua Tov*," a good week. Some Persians have the custom of not saying that Shabbat has ended, but instead they say "*Shabbat beracha shod*," which is a euphemism that means "Shabbat was blessed," so as not to upset themselves at the conclusion of this holy and most beloved day.

⋟ ROSH HASHANA ⋞
The New Year Festival

THE PERSIAN ROSH HASHANA SEDER AND SYMBOLIC FOODS

The Jewish New Year is a grand celebration for Persians! Rosh Hashana is the day every single Jew is judged by G-d on a personal level. However, since on this day G-d judges us for transgressions committed against Him and not against other people, it is left to each person to call all those he might have wronged during the year and ask for *mechilah* (forgiveness). I admit this is very hard to do, but it leaves you feeling light as a feather!

Can you believe Persians have an actual Rosh Hashana Seder? Back in Iran you could have seen a lamb's head staring at you from the table, but today in America it is very hard to find. Therefore, a less gruesome item is used…a cooked tongue, of course! (Talk about getting rid of *Lashon Hara* [the evil tongue, i.e., gossip] for the rest of the year!) However, on a more serious note, Rosh Hashana is a special time to get closer to Hashem (G-d). It is said that in these times the King of Kings is more available than ever. No wonder the Rosh Hashana Seder is based on saying several *"Yehi Ratzons"* over symbolic foods. *"Yehi Ratzon"* means "May it be Your will"; we are asking Hashem to fulfill our desires through blessings. Many of the *"Yehi Ratzons"* are plays on words, so it is not very easy to translate them. Many prayer books contain the *Yehi Ratzons* and their translations, along with explanations of the puns. You can also download these blessings from my website (www.kosherpersianfood.com).

Here are the symbolic foods along with the *Yehi Ratzons* so you can celebrate Rosh Hashana à la Persian! This Seder is to be performed after *Kiddush* and before the blessing over the bread, so be sure to make the pertinent blessings on the different kinds of foods before eating them.

1. **Apple and honey** (The ever-popular Rosh Hashana staple…my kids' favorite!)

2. **Leeks** (Tear a piece apart with your hands. Some people have the custom of eating it as well.)

3. **Zucchini** (Simply fry it in a little oil and sprinkle with salt.)

4. **Black-eyed peas** (I use canned peas and simply add caramelized onions.)

5. **Lamb's head or tongue** (Persians love tongue…I can't even look at it. See recipe, page 147.)

6. **Beets** (I buy them canned, already cut up. Just add salt or make the beet salad, page 53.)

7. **Dates** (Make sure to check inside for bugs! I have even found worms in them!)

8. **Lung** (Lungs are hard to find in America. [Thank G-d!] Some

Persian Jews use popcorn for this *Yehi Ratzon*. We use fish, especially if Rosh Hashana falls on Friday night. Some people, in the absence of lungs, skip this blessing).

9. **Pomegranate arils** (One of the highlights of the evening for Persians!)

After these blessings have been recited, the meal continues as usual. Since I consider the symbolic foods a fine appetizer, I serve dinner right after the challah is portioned out and the *Yehi Ratzons* have been said. As a good omen to have a sweet new year, many Persian Jews indulge in sweet foods on Rosh Hashana instead of the classic sour dishes. So, make sure to skip the dried lemon when making Persian Chicken Soup (*Ab Goosht*) for Rosh Hashana.

Rosh Hashana Dinner Menu

Appetizer

Symbolic Foods

Entrees

Persian Chicken Soup with Dried Lemon and Cumin Seed — *Ab Goosht*, page 97 (Rosh Hashana version)

Persian Steamed White Rice — *Chelo*, page 186

Sweet Rice with Orange and Carrots — *Shirin Polo*, page 193

Lamb with Prunes Stew, page 143

Potato Salad with Hard-Boiled Eggs — *Sald'e Olivie*, page 55

Dessert

Persian Cram Puffs — *Noon'e Chamei*, page 311

Walnut-Stuffed Dates — *Ranginak*, page 319

❧ SUKKOT ❧

The Festival of Booths

Just reading the word "Sukkot" makes me happy! If anyone has ever been in a *sukka* they know what I am talking about. Yom Kippur has just passed and we have been forgiven by Hashem; we have triumphed! The time to celebrate is here and we celebrate big. Celebrating is even a commandment in this holiday. We build nothing less than a special hut, outside our home, to invite family and friends over to eat themselves silly on scrumptious food. These temporary dwellings are to commemorate the very *sukkot* that Hashem crafted for our ancestors in the desert. There were clouds of glory protecting us on all sides from the dangerous elements in the desert. Being in a *sukka* today not only reminds us of Hashem's generosity during those hard times, but also brings us back out into nature and forces us to put all our trust in the Ruler of the world, prompting us to be grateful for the warmth of our sturdy and stable homes.

The Persian Sukka and How We Shake the Lulav!

Many Persians are known for decorating their *sukkot* with beautiful Persian Rugs (making sure to roll them back home when rain starts to fall!). I have seen exquisite *sofres* (tablecloths) displayed on the walls of Persian *sukkot*. However, the most interesting and absolutely adorable decoration I have witnessed (besides children-made décor, of course) are cone-shaped cups hanging from the *schach* (ceiling of the *sukka*) filled with a delicious mixture of chickpea flour and sugar. It is customary to hang these treats for the kids to enjoy at the end of the holiday….as long as they have survived the squirrels! On page 249 you can find the recipe and the way I use this beautiful tradition.

Have you ever seen a Persian shaking a lulav? In case you might not know, a lulav (palm tree branch) is bundled with willow and myrtle. When I didn't know any better, I though it was some type of musical instrument! Along with the lulav, a beautiful and aromatic citron (etrog) is shaken as well. It is the most expensive citrus fruit one can buy. If you haven't seen a Persian shaking the lulav, get ready for a surprise! They point their lulavim and turn their bodies toward the direction to which they shake them. In general, Sephardic women do not say a blessing when shaking the lulav.

Sukkot Dinner Menu

Appetizer
Water Challah, page 334
Assorted Salads:
Chickpea Salad, page 63
Shirazi Salad, se page 51
Fennel Salad with Lime Juice, page 61

Entrees
Persian Steamed White Rice—*Chelo*, page 186
Quince Stew—*Choresht'e Be*, page 155
Stuffed Cornish Hens with Rose Petals, page 125
Rice with Lima Beans and Dill—*Baghala* Polo, page 195

Dessert
Chocolate Truffles—*Kadurei* Chocolate, page 297
Fresh Fruit Platter

↢ CHANUKA ↣
The Festival of Lights

Just saying the word Chanuka gives me the munchies for a steaming hot latke and a few presents, of course! Chanuka is a celebration of freedom. On Chanuka we commemorate many amazing miracles. At the time Chanuka was instituted, Jerusalem was in the hands of the Syrians, who lived the Greek way. Our tiny army was able to defeat them with the guidance of Yehuda Maccabee and we were able to take back the Temple that had been ruined. The Jews were able to find just enough oil to perform the rededication of the Temple (the Hebrew word for dedication is Chanuka), and that oil lasted eight days. The Jews were once again free to practice their religion, vanquish assimilation, and discredit Greek "wisdom." We light the Chanukiah (Chanuka menorah) to remember the rededication of the Temple.

Today, we celebrate Chanuka by doing the very things the Syrian Greeks forbade us to do! We learn Torah and rejoice by singing beautiful Jewish melodies. Some give the children money or little presents to reward them for all the mitzvot (commandments) they perform. We eat lots of delicious oily food to remember the miracle of finding the oil. And last, we light a chanukiah in our front windows. This way, everyone is to witness that we have remained and triumphed and our lives are devoted to Judaism more now than ever!

The lights in the chanukiah are set up from right to left (as you face the candelabra) but lit from left to right. That is, on the first night, the light is placed to the far right on the chanukiah; on the second day, we place the first light in that same spot, the far right, then add a candle to its left. But we light the second candle first. Persians (and most Sephardim) light only one chanukiah for the whole family.

Chanuka Menu

This time of year many friends and family members drop by to indulge in Chanuka celebrations. During the eight days, I probably fry hundreds of latkes and the dinners are very informal in nature. While latkes are not the traditional Chanuka food eaten in Iran, Persians have wonderful fried dishes that are easy enough to make at the last minute in case an extra handful of friends show up! Keep in mind that I have included *Sufganiot*, Israeli-style doughnuts, in this book. *Sufganiot* are not traditional Persian Jewish food, but if they are filled with vanilla pastry cream (see page 321) they become *Pirashkee*. Besides, how can anyone survive Chanuka without them?! Here is a list of foods that would make anyone's mouth salivate on Chanuka!

❧ PURIM ❧

The Festival of Lots

THE ULTIMATE PERSIAN HOLIDAY

The joys of Purim! What an amazing holiday! This holiday is especially significant for Persians because all the events that led to Purim took place in the city of Shushan in Iran. In fact, my mother-in-law still remembers going to visit the graves of Queen Esther and Mordechai. On my website, www.persiankosherfood.com, you can find everything you need to know about Purim along with tons of great pictures.

Esther in Farsi means *beautiful* (*as the morning star*), while Queen Esther's Hebrew name (Hadassa) means *myrtle*. When the myrtle leaves are crushed, they give a very sweet scent. Similarly, as Hadassa (Queen Esther) was being "crushed" in the palace by her evil husband King Achashverosh, this brought out the sweetness and the best in her. Queen Esther risked her life with unmatched courage and dignity for her people, becoming one of the most important heroines of the Jews. In her memory and to commemorate the three-day fast she endured, the day before Purim is a fast day known as "the Fast of Esther." In Iran, Persian Jews traditionally broke this fast with delicious Persian Halvah (page 299) which also became one of the staple foods to give away in *Mishloach Manot* bundles.

It is customary to listen to the *Megilla* two times on Purim: once at night and once in the morning. The best part of this, for my kids, is the tremendous noise made when the name of Haman (boo!) is chanted. In America we use all kinds of noisy objects, which are called *graggers*. Back in Iran they used to use firecrackers! These people really know how to party.

Nowadays, many people eat special Purim cookies called *Hamantashen*. *Hamantashen* are a delicious European invention and were not consumed at all in Iran. However, I would not feel it is Purim without them, so I provide you with the recipe on page 291.

❧

Purim Feast Menu

Appetizer

Water Challah, page 334

Salmon *Kebab*, page 83

Entrees

Chicken with Eggplant—*Joojeh Budemjune*, page 135

Persian Steamed White Rice—*Chelo*, page 186

Yellow Split Pea Stew—*Chorost'e Lape*, page 161

Tabouleh Salad, page 57

Beet Salad—*Salad'e Chogondar*, page 53

Dessert

Persian Halvah, page 299

Purim Cookies, *Hamantashen*, page 291

The Festival of Freedom

Pesach is a very special holiday for Persians because Persian Seders are completely extraordinary! There are special customs that take place throughout the Seder that will certainly keep you on your toes. For a complete list of customs, please refer to my website, www.kosherpersianfood.com. First, Persians use celery and white vinegar for the vegetable dipping. During the time the *Hagaddah* mentions the plagues, Persians cover the whole table with a tablecloth to prevent evil omens from entering the food. As the name of each plague is recited, the leader of the Seder is the only person to pour drops from his cup of wine into a bowl and then discard this wine as soon as possible. Shortly after, large scallions are given to all participants to whip each other during the song "*Dayenu* (It would have sufficed)." Hence, the dining room becomes a battlefield where all participants (in a joking manner) smack each other with smelly onions! Do I even have to mention that this is my children's favorite part?

Persians use romaine lettuce for bitter herbs (phew!) and the *charoset* (*Haleg*) is so absolutely delicious (see recipe in the next page) you are going to want to have it all year round. In fact, the Hillel sandwich (matzah, *charoset*, and romaine lettuce) is so delicious I truly feel another appetizer would be redundant. After the festive meal and the grace after meals, the *afikoman* is found. We eat a piece of it while wrapping our arm around our head to symbolize the route the Hebrews took from Egypt to Jerusalem. Singing, dancing, laughing, and a ton of camaraderie is constant at a Persian Seder, and even when the meal is over at late hours in the evening, the guests still want to stay to keep enjoying the magic!

Persians have a *minhag* (custom) of eating *kitniyot* (legumes) over Passover. Believe it or not, some Sephardim do not follow this custom. So I feel fortunate that Persians do! However, every privilege also comes with responsibilities. Rice and all legumes must be checked three times before the holiday. Persians can eat rice and some (not all) consume also corn, red beans, and black-eyed peas. Back in Iran, between the Seder and dinner, Persians used to eat one hard-boiled egg along with a dish made with little fried meatballs and a vegetable similar to mushrooms, called *akal*. Sadly, in America, this vegetable is not available and Persians consume only the hard-boiled egg.

The Persian Seder plate consists of vinegar (or salt water), boiled egg (*beitzah*), celery (*karpas*), romaine lettuce (bitter herbs), roasted lamb bone (*zoro'a*) and *Haleg* (*charoset*).

∾ PERSIAN CHAROSET ∾

Haleg

Persian *charoset* (*Haleg*) is fabulous! Traditionally, *charoset* symbolizes the mortar used by the Hebrews back in Egypt. This is my mother-in-law's *charoset* recipe.

1 (6-ounce) package ground walnuts (1½ cups)

1 (6-ounce) package ground almonds (1½ cups)

½ cup pistachio nut meats, ground

1 cup date paste

½ cup raisins, ground

½ cup grape juice

1 banana, peeled and ground

1 apple, peeled and ground

2 tablespoons charoset spice

Grind together all the ingredients that do not come already ground. Combine very well.

Pesach Menu

Since we host many Ashkenazi friends, I always serve mashed potatoes and *michel* (farfel stuffing) as well as rice and black-eyed peas for the Persians. Follow my blog at www.kosherpersianfoodblog.com for those recipes!

Appetizer

Hillel Sandwich, photo, page 346

Entrees

Veal Stew with Basil and Parsley, page 165

Rice with Cabbage and Black-eyed Peas—*Kalam Polo*, page 213

White Persian Rice, page 186

Persian Mussaka, page 127

Stuffed Artichoke Hearts, page 141

Cucumber Salad with Dill and Shallots, page 69

Dessert

Slivered Almond Brittle—*Sohan'e Asali*, page 313

Fresh Fruit Platter

Persian Tea—*Chai*, page 265

Shabezal: After-Pesach Dairy Party

Back in Iran there were no dairy products kosher for Passover. Therefore, every Jew was prohibited from consuming any dairy during the week of Pesach. Could you imagine how hard that must have been? Therefore, right after Pesach was over, Jews would have a "dairy" party and eat dairy again! It is funny that this party, contrary to the famous Moroccan *Mehmuna*, is concentrated on the consumption of dairy instead of *chametz*!

Tricks of the trade

I buy already ground walnuts and almonds to make my life easier. I also purchase date paste so I don't have to grind that either. These are easily available kosher-for-Passover at many kosher groceries. The rest of the ingredients I process together into a wet paste similar in texture to *chummus*. *Charoset* spice is made by *Sadaf* and you can get it online; or simply mix equal parts of cardamom, ginger, and cinnamon. Keep *haleg* refrigerated and if it gets too thick, thin it with grape juice or even sweet wine to give it a grown-up twist!

❧ SHAVUOT ❧

Celebrating the Giving of the Torah

Shavuot marks the anniversary of the giving of the holy Torah at Mount Sinai over 3,300 years ago. The Torah was given directly from Hashem to the Jewish nation. All the Jews present, about 2 to 3 million, heard the first few commandments directly from G-d. We received the written Torah and the Oral Torah together that day and cherish it to this day. The Torah not only changed the Jews into a nation but also ultimately changed the world into a place with morals and monotheism.

Shavuot is a very special day to me because on this holiday we learn how important and dignified it is to be a convert to Judaism. Over Shavuot we read the Book of Ruth. Ruth was the first convert to Judaism. She sacrificed a lot, but her reward was great. Ruth became the great-great-grandmother of King David, from whom Moshiach will ultimately originate. On Shavuot we learn the courage it takes to become part of the Jewish people and the tremendous responsibility this undertaking means. Just as she undertook all the commandments the day she converted, so did the Jews the day they received the Torah.

It is customary to stay awake all night on Shavuot while learning Torah. Many people read the whole Book of Psalms because it was Shavuot when King David (the author of the Book of Psalms) was born and when he died.

A tradition is brought down to eat dairy foods on the holiday of Shavuot. This is because the Jews, while waiting for the giving of the Torah, were unsure of the laws concerning milk and meat. Therefore, they ate uncooked dairy foods until they learned the laws and made their utensils kosher. However, the Talmud teaches, "There is no joy without meat and wine"; therefore, the sages say that on Shabbat and holidays, a festive meal should always include meat and wine. Persians take this very seriously and do not, for the most part, indulge in dairy as much as our Ashkenazi brothers do. Back in Iran, after midnight on Shavuot people used to drink milk while learning Torah, and some also ate a dairy soup called *Ash'e Mast* (page 245) in the morning.

❧

Shavuot Menu

Appetizer

Moroccan Salmon, page 87

Entrees

Persian Steamed White Rice—*Chelo*, page 186

Rice with Yellow Split Peas and Currant Raisins—*Polo Lape*, page 199

Okra and Tomato Stew—*Chorosht'e Bamieh*, page 159

Momonbosorgue's Delicious Stuffed Grape Leaves—*Dolmeh*, page 139

Hot Fava Beans—*Bagalah Garmak*, page 251

Persian Eggplant Omelet—*Kookoo Budemjune*, page 225

Dessert

Persian Halvah, page 299

Fresh Fruit Platter

∽ FAST DAYS ∽

Persian Customs Before and After Fasts

Fasting is very much a part of the Jewish religion. There are two main fast days (Yom Kippur and Tisha b'Av) on which we fast from sunset to the following day after three stars appear. There are also four minor fast days on which we fast from sunrise until three stars appear that night. These days are the Fast of Gedalia, the Fast of the Tenth of *Tevet*, the Fast of Esther, and the Fast of the Seventeenth of *Tamuz*. These fasts, except Yom Kippur, were established in light of the suffering the Jewish nation faced on those days. These fasts are to remind us to stop any negative behavior that might mirror our ancestors' in hopes that it will keep calamities from happening again.

But why should we fast? What is the purpose? After all, fasting is painful and difficult. Well, let me explain. Putting a child in a time-out or reprimanding that child for negative behavior can be difficult for the child and the parent as well. However, if you are a mother, you know that the purpose of a time-out (for the most part!) is to have the child isolated in a quiet place to think about his/her actions and rectify the negative behavior. If the rectification and the repentance are not there, the time-out is worthless. Similarly, Hashem is our Father and sometimes we know we need a time-out. However, while the time-out (in this case, fasting) is not easy, the real purpose is for rectification and repentance of our behavior. Fasting gives us that certain amount of physical pain needed to get in touch with our spiritual self and get back on track. At the end of a fast, we should focus on how much we learned about our potential in life and have a plan of action on how to achieve it.

The meals preceding Yom Kippur and Tisha b'Av, respectively, have certain requirements that apply to all Jews no matter their origin. Some Persian families choose to consume *Ab Goosht* (page 97) before the Yom Kippur fast as part of this required feast. It is also common to see families eating Fried Whitefish (page 85) and Rice with Lentils and Caramelized Onions — *Adas Polo* (page 207) before the fast of Tisha b'Av because these are foods for mourners. Also, during the Nine Days (the nine days preceding Tisha b'Av), when we are not permitted to consume meat, Persians eat a dish called *gheylak*, which is simply mashed potatoes topped with caramelized onions.

In my husband's family, people tend to break every fast with a warm cup of sweetened water with a drizzle of rose water. Some other families break their fasts with Persian Halvah (page 299), while others break their fasts with a mixture of chilled grated apples with a drizzle of rose water and sugar.

Non-leather Persian slippers to use on Yom Kippur

☙ THE LAWS OF TAROF ☙
AND OTHER PERSIAN PECULIARITIES I HAPPEN TO LOVE

*Tarof...*A PERSIAN INVENTION OR NOT?

Persians seem to think they have the copyright on *tarof*...but they actually don't! What Persians have on *tarof* that the rest of the world does not have is they have given it a name and they have mastered it to perfection! Let me explain. Everyone has *tarofed* in his or her life, at least once. You have *tarofed*, I promise! *Tarof* is the art of appearing dignified and respectful by means of restraint and self-control. You are probably thinking, "What? What is she talking about?" Let me illustrate: Have you ever prevented yourself from overeating at a dinner date so as not to appear to be a glutton, even though you really wanted to eat dessert and take the leftovers home? Right there, you just *tarofed*! Have you ever denied yourself the need to go to the ladies' room so as not to appear improper in front of your date? You just *tarofed*! Have you ever not accepted a ride, a drink, or anything that you really wanted or needed because you didn't want to come across as a loser, needy, or a nuisance? Yet again, you have *tarofed*! Let me show you the art of *tarof* the Persian way...after all, these people are the experts.

1. You do not accept anything from anyone, especially when it comes to physical necessities such as drink and food, unless the person has offered it three times (for men this also includes honors, like saying Kiddush, Hamotzi, or the blessing after meals at someone else's home).
2. You must not show that you are starving or thirsty or really need a place to rest until after that third offer. Remember: dignity and decorum by means of restraint and self-control!
3. After the third offer you should accept, reluctantly, and sometimes possibly blaming the person who offers for "making" you accept his/her offer!

There is one important note that must be made: Do not practice this method with non-Persians! It does not always work and you will have to starve, die of thirst, or go to a public bathroom. This works with Persians very well and they will think you spent ages in etiquette school mastering the art of being respectful and dignified. Trust me, it worked for me!

"Could I please have a knife?"

The first time I went to have dinner at Sammy's house I suffered from the "Lost in Translation" syndrome. You see, I come from a family where everything must be done the "proper" way. I even went to special after-school programs to learn about charm and etiquette. While growing up, I spent grueling hours learning all the different ways and methods of eating, drinking, walking in heels, and sitting like a lady. If I only had a picture of the many times I spent walking with a huge book balanced on my head to learn proper posture, I would have published it in this book for your enjoyment! But that is not how my Persian prince had been taught...not at all.

At our first dinner I was served *kebab*. Instantly, just like an expert piano maestro who knows the keys by heart, I reached to my right to find the knife–the missing knife! Instead I saw a spoon. I politely asked Sammy for a knife (at the same time wondering when the soup, which is supposed to come before the entrée, would appear), and he looked at me like I was speaking Chinese. Well, I do have to admit my English was not very good back then, but I think I could pronounce knife! He laughed and then I realized Persians (at least in my husband's family) simply don't use knives! My future father-in-law (who must have heard my request) turned to me and said, "You don't need a knife when meat is so tender and soft. Look–I cut with my fork!"

I have to admit that living among Persians one eventually has to surrender. When I am at my in-laws', I don't use a knife (please don't tell my mom). I have to admit it is great, and I feel like I am a cheating carnivore. I even eat with my hands sometimes! While eating at home, I do not set my husband's place with a knife; I set it with a spoon. However, to make me happy, I bought him a silver spoon!

"Reyna *joone* (dear), if you eat that you will be too *garmi* and get pimples!"
So, here comes one of my favorite Persian peculiarities: the laws of *garmi* and *sardi*! *Garmi* means hot in Farsi or, in technical terms, *alkaline*. *Sardi* means cold in Farsi, or acidic. When you hang out with Persians (especially people from Shiraz!) you will often hear them wondering, "Am I *garmi*? Are you feeling *sardi*?" I can almost hear my mother-in-law's words echoing in my head. "Reyna joone (dear), if you eat that, you will be too *garmi* and get pimples!" As if I didn't have enough trouble with my own conscience asking, "Reyna, are you *flashich* (meat) or *milchig* (dairy)?" (Yes, my conscience does speak to me in Yiddish sometimes!)

The point is that, according to Persians, too much *garmi* (alkaline) food, like peanuts, chocolate, and French fries, will cause a sore throat and pimples. Further, too much *sardi* (acidic) food, like watermelon, orange juice, and yogurt, will cause a stomachache. For over the years I had been laughing at this concept until something crazy happened. As I was researching very old Venezuelan recipes in a colonial cookbook that belongs to my mother, I came across a chapter about old Venezuelan colonial medical practices. Here they mentioned how the pH balance in the body is so important and how some foods are *calientes* (hot) and some are *frias* (cold). I was rooted to my seat! Do you mean that this *garmi* and *sardi* business is part of MY culture too?! Do you mean that this was practiced in my country as well?! I immediately called and apologized to my mother-in-law for driving her crazy about *garmi* and *sardi* all these years!

❧ GLOSSARY ❧

Note: The entries in the Glossary are English, Farsi, or Arabic unless otherwise indicated.

A"H—(Hebrew) aleha hashalom; lit., peace be on her; rest in peace.

ab gureh—sour grape juice

advieh—(also called baharat) a mixture of ground cloves, cardamom, ginger, cinnamon, and other spices (may substitute allspice)

aish—(Hebrew) lit., fire; an outreach organization

afikoman—(Hebrew) lit., that which comes after; dessert; the matzah eaten as the last part of the Pesach Seder

akal—vegetable similar to mushroom, found in Iran

Amerikayai—American

angear—figs

anise—(Spanish) fennel

arak—licorice-flavored liquor

Arvit—(Hebrew) evening prayers

arroz con pollo—(Spanish) a Latin dish made with chicken and rice

Ashkenazi—(Hebrew) literally, German; Jews of European origin

aveilim—(Hebrew) mourners

ba'alei Teshuva—(Hebrew) to return to Judasim

bach—garden

badam—almonds

bah, bah—(Farsi) exclamation meaning "delicious," "very good"

baharat—see advieh

balal—roasted corn on the cob

bashert—(Yiddish) 1. one's destined mate. 2. fated

basmati—(Sanskrit-Hindi) literally, the fragrant one; a type of long-grained rice

basunak—wedding songs

beh dune—quince seeds

beitzah—(Hebrew) egg

berenj—rice

bina—(Hebrew) wisdom; understanding

Birkat HaMazon—blessing after the meal

blech—(Yiddish) a sheet of metal placed over an open flame on the stove in order to warm food over indirect heat; an electric warming tray

borsch—(Russian) beet soup

boudoir biscuits—(French) biscuits that look like lady fingers

bracha (pl. brachot)—(Hebrew) a blessing

brit mila—(Hebrew) circumcision

budemjoon—eggplant

caliente—(Spanish) lit., hot

ceviche—(Spanish) marinated fish

cha—(Cantonese) tea

Chabad—(Hebrew) a specific Hasidic movement in Orthodox Judaism

chai sabs—Persian green tea

chai sefid—Persian white tea

chai—(Hebrew) life. (Farsi) tea

chaleh—aunty

challah—(pl. challot)—(Hebrew) rich bread, often braided, traditionally eaten on Shabbat

chametz—(Hebrew) leaven; leavened foods

champe—a type or rice used to made kateh; it is similar to American rice

Chanuka—(Hebrew) the Festival of Lights

charoset—(Hebrew) dip eaten during the Pesach Seder to symbolize the mortar used by Jewish slaves in Egypt to build cities before the Exodus

chattan—(Hebrew) a groom

chatzilim—(Hebrew) fried eggplant

cholent—Ashkenazi Shabbat stew

chummus—chickpea dip

couscous—pasta made of crushed and steamed semolina

crema pasterela—(Spanish) dairy custard cream

curcumine—root from which turmeric originates

darchin—cinnamon

dayenu—(Hebrew) lit., it is enough for us

Devar Torah—Torah portion of the week

duset daram—I love you; I care about you

echium amoenum—(Latin) borage plant flower

eshet chayil—(Hebrew) lit., a woman of valor; liturgical poem sung in honor of the wife before the Friday night festive meal

etrog—(Hebrew) citron

fava beans—broad beans

Farsi—the language of Persia

flashich—(Yiddish) meat; having eaten meat recently

frio (m.), *frias* (f.)—(Spanish) lit., cold

Gan Eden—(Hebrew) Garden of Eden

garmi—lit., hot or alkaline

gefilte fish—(Yiddish) chopped fish formed into loaves or balls and poached

Gemara—(Aramaic) literally, to study; volumes of the Talmud containing rabbinical commentaries and analysis of the Mishnah

gerdu—walnuts

ghaleb'e kookoo—special tool to shape kookoo

ghaliun—water-pipe

gheylak—mashed potatoes with onions

gishmak—(Yiddish) expression that means "fantastic"

golabi—pear

gole gabzaban—dried borage flowers

gragger—noisemaker used on Purim

gureh—green grapes

hadasim—(Hebrew) myrtle

hag—(Hebrew) holiday

hagaddah—(Hebrew) book that relates the story of the Exodus from Egypt

Halacha—(Hebrew) Jewish law

haleg—see charoset

hale Bibi—literally, aunt and grandmother; Shirazy cholent

hamantashen—(Yiddish) triangular cookies traditional served on Purim

Hamotzi—the blessing made before eating bread

Hashem—lit., the Name; a way to refer to G-d

havdala—(Hebrew) the ceremony to mark the end of Shabbat

hechsher—(Hebrew) kosher symbol or certification

HIH—his imperial highness

ibrik—long-handled copper jug used to make kahveh, Turkish coffee

joon—literally; life; it can be used as "dear" in English

kahveh—Turkish coffee

kalium—a water-pipe

kallah—(Hebrew) a bride

kand—sugar

kaniza—synagogue

karpas—(Hebrew) vegetable dipped in salt water during the Seder on Passover

kashk—whey

*kashru*t—(Hebrew) the laws of keeping kosher.

kateh—Persian sticky rice

kaveh chune—literally, Arabic for "coffee house"; Persian teahouse.

kedusha—holiness

kiddush—(Hebrew) lit., sanctification; (capitalized) prayer said over wine on Shabbat and holidays. (lower case) food served after Kiddush but before washing for bread

kippot—(sing. kippah) (Hebrew) head covering worn by Jewish males; yarmulke

kitniyot—(Hebrew) legumes, which can be eaten by Sephardic Jews during Pesach *koach*—(Hebrew) strength

kollel—(Hebrew) post-graduate school for married Torah scholars.

kosher—lit., fit for consumption

kugel—(Yiddish) a casserole or "pudding," usually made of potatoes, vegetables, or noodles

lashon hara—(Hebrew) evil speech

latke—(Yiddish) a fried pancake usually made of potatoes, vegetables, or cheese

lavash—a Middle Eastern bread, large and thin, paper-like, very flexible when first baked and crispy when toasted

lemon omani—dehydrated limes

levivot—(Hebrew) traditional Chanuka latkes

limoo—limes

lulav—(Hebrew) palm branch used on Sukkot

madbucha—Moroccan tomato and roasted pepper dip

matzah—(Hebrew) unleavened bread, eaten especially on Passover

ma'vdeh—a tool used to core eggplants and zucchinis, etc.

mechilah—(Hebrew) forgiveness

Megillat Esther—(Hebrew) the Book of Esther, read on Purim.

mehmuni—family parties

Mikvah—(Hebrew) bath used for ritual immersion

michel—(Yiddish) farfel stuffing

milchig—(Yiddish) dairy; having eaten dairy recently or not having eaten meat recently

minhag (pl. *minhagim*)—(Hebrew) customs

mishloach manot—(Hebrew) gifts of food traditionally given to friends as part of the Purim festival

mitzvah (pl. *mitzvot*)—(Hebrew) commandment; good deed

momom—mother

momonbosorgue—grandmother

moosir—shallots

Moshiach—(Hebrew) redeemer

nabat—rock candy

nana—mint

navi—(Hebrew) seer

neshama—(Hebrew) soul

nochkodchi—chickpeas

noglh—sugar-covered almonds

nooshejan—hearty appetite!

olam haze—(Hebrew) This World; the material world

paella—(Spanish) rice dish originating in Spain

panko—(Japanese) crispy breadcrumbs

parsha—(Hebrew) Torah portion of the week

parve—neither meat nor dairy; parve food may be eaten with either meat or dairy meals

Persepolis—an ancient Persian city

Pesach—(Hebrew) Passover

pishghaza—appetizers and side dishes

pita—(Aramaic) pocket bread

Purim—(Hebrew) holiday celebrating the hidden miracles delineated in the Book of Esther

pushka—(Yiddish) charity box

Rosh Hashana—(Hebrew) the New Year

sabsi—lit., green; fresh herbs

samovar—small teapot and kettle

sardi—lit., cold or acidic

sakana—(Hebrew) danger; a dangerous situation

schach—(Hebrew) roof of the sukka, usually made of bamboo or branches

seder—(Hebrew) a festival dinner, esp. on Passover

sefer—(Hebrew) book, esp. a book on a holy topic

Sephardic—(Hebrew) literally, from Spain; Jews of Spanish descent. Often refers to Jews from the Middle East, although the correct term in that case is Mizrahi

seitan—(Japanese) wheat "meat" used by vegetarians

seuda—(Hebrew) feast

seudah shlishit—(Hebrew) the third Shabbat meal, eaten during the late afternoon.

Shabbat (pl. *Shabbatot*)—(Hebrew) the Sabbath

shabezal—Persian dairy party celebrated after Pesach

Shalom alecheim—(Hebrew) traditional greeting literally meaning "peace be with you"

shambelileh—an herb

Shavuot—(Hebrew) holiday celebrating the giving of the Torah

sheshbesh—backgammon

sheva brachot—(Hebrew) festive meals eaten during the week after the wedding

Shiraz—a city in the south of Iran

shiva—(Hebrew) lit., seven; the seven-day mourning period observed after the death of a close relative

shlep—(Yiddish) to carry or drag a heavy load

shmear—(Yiddish) spread

sib—apple

siddur—(Hebrew) prayer book

simcha—(Hebrew) a joyous occasion

sofreh (pl. *sofres*)—a tablecloth decorated with golden embroidery and intricate designs

sukka (pl. sukkot)—(Hebrew) temporary dwelling built for the Jewish holiday of Sukkot

Sukkot—the Festival of Booths

tabouleh—bulgur

tadig—the crunchy, golden crust created by cooking rice Persian-style

taharat hamishpacha—(Hebrew) laws of family purity

Tamuz—(Babylonian) a month in the Jewish calendar

Tanach—the 24 Books of Scripture, including the Torah, the Prophets, and the Writings

tarof—polite refusal even though one really wants to accept

te—(Xiamen dialect; Spanish) tea

Tebet—(Babylonian) a month in the Jewish calendar

tehina—paste made of sesame seeds

Tisha b'Av—(Hebrew) the Ninth of Av, the anniversary of the Destruction of the Holy Temples

tochme afolagardan—sunflower seeds

tochme cadu—pumpkin seeds

tochme hendune—watermelon seeds

toot—mulberries

Torah—the Five Books of Moses

torshi—pickled vegetables

tudeli—stuffing

turmeric—yellow seasoning used in Persian cuisine; also known as curcuma

tzedaka—(Hebrew) charity

tzadeket—(Hebrew) literally, holy woman; a woman who follows Torah law and is gracious and loving

yehi raztons—(Hebrew) lit., May it be His [G-d's] will; declarations recited over traditional foods on Rosh Hashana

Yerushalmi kugel—(Hebrew-Yiddish) sweet and peppery noodle casserole

Yom Kippur—(Hebrew) the Day of Atonement

zaban—lit., tongue

Zaraza—a town located in Venezuela

zechut—lit., merit

zereshk—lit., sour; barberries

ziadune seeds—(nigella; wild fennel) seed, also known as onion seeds or cumin seeds

zoro'a—(Hebrew) roasted lamb shank; during the Pesach Seder it symbolizes G-d's mighty arm that delivered the Jews from Egypt

❧ CULINARY GLOSSARY ❧

al dente—cooked only until still firm to the bite

boil—cook in water that has reached a temperature of 212°F

bouquet garni—(French) a group of herbs tied together or enclosed in cheesecloth or a small cloth bag and placed into soup, etc., to infuse flavors.

broil—cook using direct heat, as in an oven

culinary—related to cooking

dredging—passing (food) through breadcrumbs, flour, etc., to coat.

drizzle—sprinkle lightly over

garnish—decorate

immersion hand blender—a slim blender that can be used directly in a container or pot

ISO—International Organization for Standardization

julienne—(adj. used to describe vegetables or other food) cut into thin strips. (verb) to cut foods into thin strips

marinate—to soak food in a marinade, a liquid, etc., designed to add flavor to a food

mortar and pestle—a cylinder and container used to crush spices, etc.

pickling—steeping in brine (salted water) or other liquid to preserve or flavor

process—put (food) through a food processor

relish—condiments used to enhance the flavors of food

roast—to bake, uncovered, in an oven

sauté—cooked or browned in a small amount of oil

sear—to cook quickly over high heat in order to seal in the juices (of meat, etc.)

shredded—cut or torn into small strips

simmer—to cook in liquid just below boiling point

skewer—a long thin pin of wood or metal used to hold food during cooking.

sliver—to cut into very thin strips

steeping—a technique used to draw the flavor from food into liquid; it requires soaking ingredients in water (usually hot) until the flavors from the ingredient are infused into the liquid

✑ BIBLIOGRAPHY ✑

Abolhassani, Mohsen. "Antibacterial effect of borage (echium amoenum) on Staphylococcus aureus." *Tehran: Brazilian Journal of Infectious Diseases*, Vol. 8. 2004.

Bard, Mitchell. "The Persians." *Jewish Virtual Library*. The American-Israel Cooperative Enterprise, 2010. Web. 17 May 2010. <http://www.jewishvirtuallibrary.org/jsource/History/Persians.html>.

Boskabady, Mohammad Hossein. "Effect of Nigella Sativa on Isolated Guinea Pig Trachea." *Archives of Iranian Medicine* (2002).

Central Bureau of Statistics. Chart. The State of Israel, 2008. Web. 17 May 2010. <http://www.cbs.gov.il/reader/?MIval=cw_usr_view_Folder&ID=141>.

Dangoor, Naim. "The Jews of Iraq: Congress Bulletin Montreal." *The Scribe* 1.74 (2001): 1-2. *The Scribe*. Web. 17 May 2010. <http://www.dangoor.com/74034.html>.

Davidson, Alan. *The Oxford Companion to Food*. n.d.

Dweck, Poopa, Michael Joseph Cohen, and Quentin Bacon. *Aromas of Aleppo: the Legendary Cuisine of Syrian Jews*. New York: Ecco, 2007. Print.

Gitlitz, David M., and Linda Kay Davidson. *A Drizzle of Honey: the Lives and Recipes of Spain's Secret Jews*. New York: St. Martin's, 1999. Print.

Glasse, Hannah. *The Complete Confectioner, or, Housekeeper's Guide to a Simple and Speedy Method of Understanding the Whole Art of Confectionary: The Various Ways of Preserving and Candying, Dry and Liquid, All Kinds of Fruit, Nuts, Flowers, Herbs, &C. ... The Different Ways of Clarifying Sugar ... Also The Art*. Printed by J.D. Dewick, 1800.

Haubold, Alexander. *Aqua Phoenix*. <www..aquaphoenix.com/misc/pomegranate>.

Jacobs, Joseph, and M. Seligsohn. "Shiraz." *Jewish Encyclopedia*. 2002. *JewishEncyclopedia.com*. Web. 17 May 2010. <http://www.jewishencyclopedia.com/view.jsp?artid=640&letter=S&search=Shiraz>.

Lalezar, Dr. Yunes H. "Rabbi (Harav) Or Sharga." *Iranjewish.com*. Teheran Jewish Committee (Iran), June 2006. Web. 17 May 2010. <http://www.iranjewish.com/Essay_E/Essay_e5_Orsharga.htm>.

Lim, S. K. *Origins of Chinese Tea and Wine*. Singapore: Asiapac Books Pte Ltd, 2004.

Mondal, T.K. *Tea*. Berlin: Springer, 2007.

Montagne, Prosper. *Larousse Gastronomique*. Larousse, n.d.

Philogos. "Chickpeas on Language." *Jewish Daily Forward* 2005.

Pliskin, Karen L. PhD. " Cross-Cultural Medicine A Decade Later." *The Western Journal Of Medicine* (1992): 395.

Price, Massoume. "A Brief History of Iranian Jews (Continued)." *Iranonline.com*. Manou & Associates Inc., 1996. Web. 17 May 2010. <http://www.iranonline.com/History/jews-history/2.html>.

Rasbridge, Charles Kemp and Lance. *Refugee and Immigrant Health*. Cambridge, 2004.

Roden, Claudia. *The Book of Jewish Food: an Odyssey from Samarkand to New York*. New York: Knopf, 1996. Print.

Sarshar, Houman. *Esther's Children: A Portrait of Iranian Jews*. Beverly Hills, Calif.: Center for Iranian Jewish Oral History, 2005. Print.

Tong, Liu. *Chinese Tea*. China Intercontinental Press, n.d.

UN. *International Coffee Organization*. 1963. 1963 <www.ico.org>.

USDA. *Nutrition Data*. 2003. 2009 <www.nutritiondata.com>.

Yarsheter, Ehsan. *Enciclopedia Iranica*. 1998. 2009 <www.iranica.com>.

INDEX

Note: Dishes are listed in Farsi and English in alphabetical order; dishes are also listed by English name under headings such as Appetizers, Desserts, etc.

Notes